fish

Always ready to go. Bondi fishing boats.

Coronation trout, Sumatra, Indonesia.

fish
pete evans

MURDOCH BOOKS

contents

a few words about fish ... 6

an A–Z of fish recipes

    abalone to crab ... 14

    cuttlefish to mangrove jack ... 46

    marron to pearl perch ... 80

    pipis to salmon ... 110

    salt cod to snapper ... 136

    sole to threadfin salmon ... 164

    tommy ruff to yabby ... 184

basic recipes ... 210

an A–Z of seafood ... 234

index ... 266

A cheeky little fella.

a few words about fish

Who would've thought that when Paul Hogan threw a prawn on the barbie all those years ago in a cunning campaign to lure tourists to our shores, he was perpetuating one of the greatest myths in world food: that Australia has a bountiful supply of seafood.

The simple fact is, we don't.

There are some 4000 known marine species living in the waters of our planet and, interestingly, about 3500 of them can be found in Australia's oceans, rivers and lakes. While our fishing grounds are the world's second largest by area (after those of the former republics of the USSR) and range across all five oceanic zones from tropical to arctic, we come in at around number eighty in production by volume. The New Zealand fishery's annual catch of just one fish (250,000 tonnes of hoki) is more than we produce in all our wild and aquaculture fisheries put together.

How can this be?

As the driest continent on the planet, the waterways that feed Australia's coastal zones are especially low in nutrients. This, in addition to nearly five years of chronic drought, means that our oceans are relatively barren of marine life. So, while we have an enormous fishing area and a prodigious range of species available, we just don't have the natural seafood resources you would assume.

Australians are now eating nearly 18 kg of seafood per person per annum. While this is way below the massive 213 kg per person the Japanese eat (and even well below the 142 kg of red meat and poultry we each consume annually), it is a dramatic increase from the 8.5 kg we ate only ten years ago. For a country that has so proudly survived on the sheep's back, it's interesting to note that we now consume almost twenty per cent more seafood than lamb — and that's despite Tom Cruise!

Seafood is becoming the hero protein of choice in Australia: so how are we supplying this rampant growth in demand, if our fisheries are small and relatively barren? The bottom line is: we aren't. Australia is a nett importer of seafood. We import nearly eighty per cent of the seafood we consume. Our exports are predominantly of high-value species (rock lobster, abalone, prawns and tuna), while we import the generally lower-value, skinless, boneless fish, calamari, octopus and farmed prawns.

The good news is that we have some of the most advanced commercial fisheries in the world. Australia's vast fishing grounds and limited resources demand that we take good care of our fisheries. The result is highly managed organisations that pretty much guarantee the quality and sustainability of Australian seafood. In fact, we have some of the most sustainable fisheries in the world: companies such as Spencer Gulf King Prawn and Southern Rock Lobster are not only standout examples of sustainable wild-catch fisheries, they are actually among the world's best.

So, Australian seafood ranks among the best in the world both ecologically and culinarily. Of course, it might sometimes be a bit more expensive than the imported frozen stuff sitting in the supermarket freezer, but let's remember that it's special and worth that little bit more.

And don't forget that you can always get out and catch your own. Recreational fishing is the number one sport in this country, with over four million recreational fishers wetting a line every weekend and holiday — that's a lot of fish to throw on the barbie.

Seafood sustainability — the next big thing?

Have you ever stopped to ask your fishmonger where your seafood came from or how it was fished? The everyday food choices we make have an enormous impact on the future of the fish in the waters covering over seventy-five per cent of our globe. Whether we are buying from a local fish market or supermarket, the future of seafood in Australia is dependent on us. There's simply no avoiding the debate on sustainable seafood.

Little more than two decades ago the orange roughy, more commonly known as the sea perch, was virtually unknown on Australian dinner tables. A few years ago it became one of the most popular and best-selling seafood items on menus across Australia, but it's also become one of the biggest controversies facing the commercial seafood industry. Regrettably, this fish's sudden rise to commercial success now threatens the species with extinction (which is why you won't find recipes for it here). Although international laws have been put in place to help maintain the species, scientists suggest that it may be commercially extinct within the next five years. Researchers are now just beginning an extensive study of this fish and its habitat.

And orange roughy is not the only species in danger of extinction. Off the New South Wales coast, gemfish were once so abundant that boats had difficulties navigating through the shoals. Today, the supply of gemfish is dwindling rapidly. With the demand for seafood in a boom phase since the early 1980s, the fates of the orange roughy and gemfish are not isolated.

At the other end of the spectrum, production of fish in association with fish farming is also posing a range of ecological, commercial and culinary questions. In particular, salmon, a fish widely enjoyed by the world's population, is being farmed at a rapid pace, but this allegedly eco-friendly practice is now being called into question. Salmon is not native to Australian waters and, as yet, we have no producers pursuing to farm salmon to globally recognised organic standards.

There is a growing band of chefs who advocate sustainable seafood as a solution to dangerously low and diminishing fish supplies. Sustainable seafood refers to fish and shellfish caught or farmed with consideration for the long-term viability of individual marine species and for the ocean's ecological balance. Here in Australia we have some of the world's most stringent controls on the commercial fishing industry. As a result, the chances of overfishing have been reduced to a minimum.

Aquaculture

According to the American seafood sustainability organisation, Chefs' Collaborative, in the next twenty years aquaculture will surpass capture fisheries in supplying the majority of the world's seafood. Aquaculture, or fish farming, is becoming more commonplace as a solution to problematic fish depletion. Today, over twenty per cent of our seafood and, in particular, half of the world's salmon supply, is farmed. Fish farming has an ecological impact all of its own, depending on the type of fish being farmed, how they are raised and where the farms are located.

Farmed fish such as salmon are raised in what's known as a net-pen. Envision cattle in a crowded feedlot: replace the cattle with salmon and then throw in some water. This equates to thousands upon thousands of fish thrown into an area of thirty cubic metres. Clearly, the issues relating to fish farming are not dissimilar to those faced by any intensive agriculture.

It is a tough decision to be proactive about seafood sustainability —how do you balance commercial, culinary and family needs, while maintaining this ecological balance?

If you decide that you are committed to sustainability, then you should become proactive: start paying attention to where, how and when your

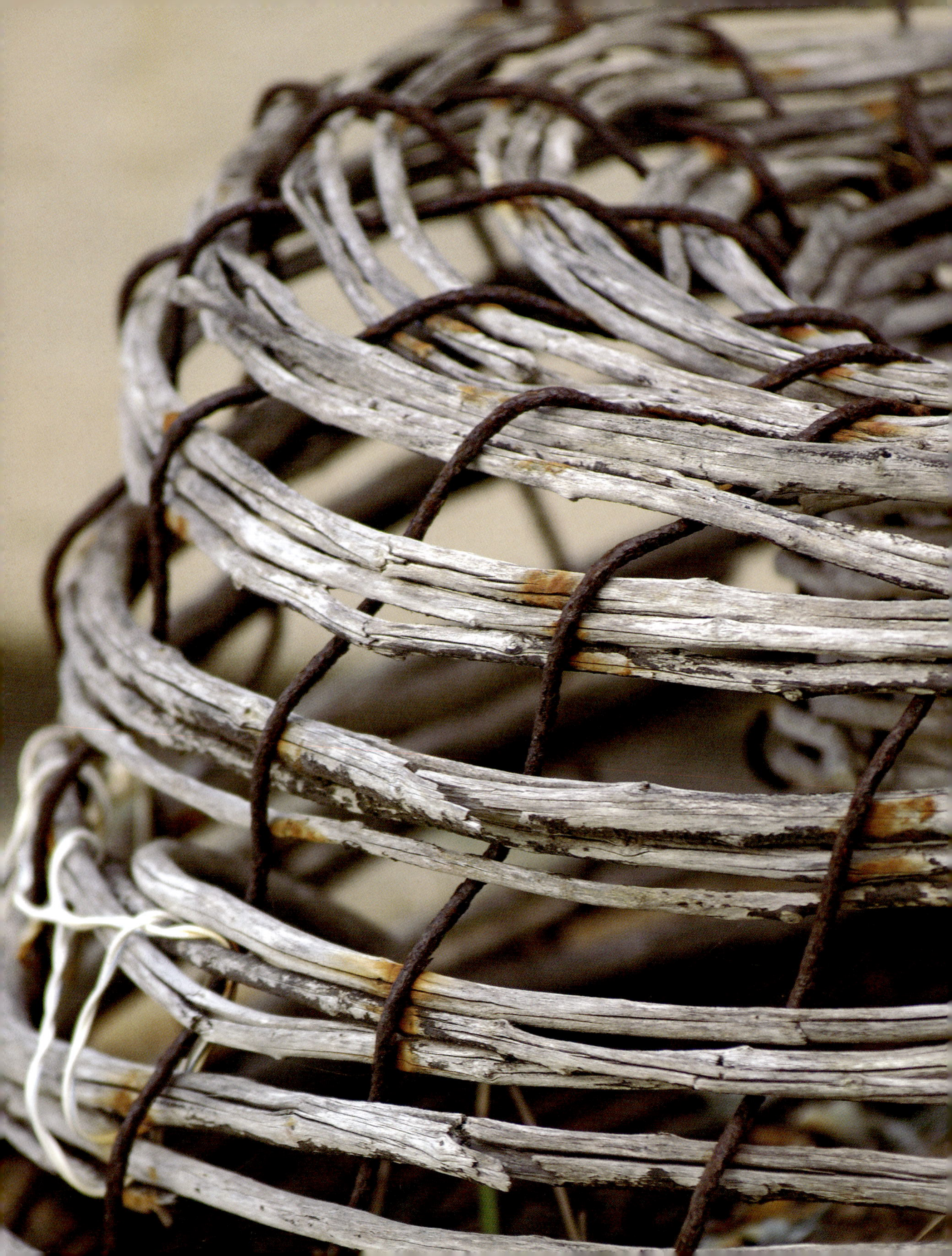

seafood was sourced by your supplier. The Australian Marine Conservation Society is a defender of consumers' right to know and supports reader-friendly labelling on menus, in fish shops and at wholesale markets, as well as general education for the public. Sustainability is a problem for every one of us. Let's look after the oceans for our children, and their children.

Don't worry, be happy: eat seafood

Our grandmothers knew seafood was good for us. Fish has long had a reputation as 'brain food'. A generation of young Australians were fortified with daily spoonfuls of cod liver oil. And it was over thirty years ago that doctors noticed the Eskimos of Greenland, with their predominant diet of fish, had very low levels of heart disease.

Now we're all getting the message that seafood is good for our health, but continuing discoveries by medical researchers around the world are demonstrating just *how* good it is. The National Heart Foundation recommends we eat fish at least twice a week for cardiovascular benefit, such as the lowering of blood cholesterol levels. The National Health and Medical Research Council advises eating one or two fish meals every week. And one of the world's most prestigious scientific bodies has gone further. An expert panel established by the American Academy for the Advancement of Science has recommended eating four to seven seafood meals every week. These sentiments have been echoed by health authorities around the world.

Medical researchers have found strong evidence of significant health benefits from seafood in relation to coronary heart disease, high blood pressure, irregular heartbeat, diabetes and rheumatoid arthritis. Also, promising early results have been reported in relation to bowel cancer, asthma and improved brain development. Researchers have reported benefits for memory loss, depression, pancreatic cancer, liver cancer and some other forms of cancer, and work in these areas is continuing.

Seafood is a high-nutrient, low-calorie food. It is high in protein but low in saturated fat. It is also a good source of some vitamins, particularly vitamin D, and of iodine. Fish provides a high ratio of protein to calories and, at a time when obesity is regarded as an epidemic in the developed world, reducing calories helps reduce the risk of dangerous weight gain. Seafood is an excellent 'diet' food for anyone watching their weight.

Along with the direct, positive benefits of consuming seafood, there is an indirect but equally important advantage: eating a meal of good, healthy seafood potentially displaces a meal of bad, unhealthy food that is high in saturated fat and loaded with calories.

Most importantly though, seafood is high in polyunsaturated fatty acids (PUFAs, such as the essential Omega 3), which are good for general health, especially heart health. Omega 3s are referred to as the 'good oils' and are probably best known for their role in reducing the risk of heart attack. They are also believed to help prevent stroke, diabetes, bowel cancer and rheumatoid arthritis, as well as reducing the symptoms of depression and other mood disorders.

These 'good oils' also play a very positive role in the health of infants, both before and after birth, for example in boosting brain development and eyesight. Because fish is so important in the diet of pregnant women to ensure adequate levels of Omega 3 and other nutrients in their babies, the Australian Government agency, Food Standards Australia New Zealand (FSANZ), recommends pregnant women eat fish two to three times a week. However, because some long-lived fish species concentrate naturally-occurring mercury in their flesh — and high levels of mercury can be harmful to babies — it is recommended that pregnant women (and children up to six years of age) should not eat shark (also called flake) or billfish (such as swordfish and marlin) more than once a fortnight and not eat orange roughy (sea perch) or catfish more than once a week.

The Australian Government's 'Recommended Dietary Intakes' of 2006 has for the first time included Omega 3 polyunsaturated fatty acids as essential nutrients. It is suggested that men consume an average of 610 mg and women 430 mg of long-chain (LC) Omega 3 polyunsaturated fatty acids each day. Seafood (in particular, oily fish such as tuna, salmon, mackerel and mullet) is by far the most abundant source of LC Omega 3 oils, with 100 g of the average fish containing 210 mg, oysters 150 mg, prawns 120 mg and lobster 105 mg (compared to just 22 mg in beef, 19 mg in chicken, 18 mg in lamb and virtually none in pork).

Seafood is also the prime source of iodine, an essential element actually deficient in the average diet in some parts of Australia. One serve of fish can provide 25 to 100 per cent of a woman's Recommended Dietary Intake of iodine. Fish is also the most abundant source of selenium, another essential element, and a rich source of the essential vitamins D and E, and fish such as tinned tuna and salmon with edible bones are a source of quality calcium.

Australia's Commonwealth Scientific and Industrial Research Organisation (CSIRO) advises that we include a variety of fish in our diets. By eating low-fat fish, you will be reducing the total fat in your diet, and by eating moderate to high-fat fish you will be consuming more Omega 3 fatty acids. Both modifications are beneficial. CSIRO gives examples of higher-fat fish as sardines, ocean trout, Atlantic salmon, tuna, herring and mackerel, and lower-fat fish as whiting, barramundi, trevally, flake (shark) and flounder. They advise that 'three to five fish meals per week should provide a useful amount of Omega 3'. The CSIRO experts also say it is better to replace some meals with fish, rather than add supplements (such as fish oil capsules) to your total diet.

The range of health benefits attributed to seafood is expanding, with new research regularly adding to the list. Australian scientists are now also testing fish oil as an antidepressant after overseas studies showed countries with high seafood consumption have lower rates of mood disorders. Sydney's Black Dog Institute has recruited people with mild to moderate depression to assess the benefits of fish oil supplements. Omega 3s are important for the permeability of cell membranes, allowing free flow of chemicals in and out of neurons in the brain. If people do not eat enough Omega 3-rich foods, it is thought these lower levels of Omega 3 in the brain may contribute to mood disorders. The Institute has said the suspicion is that dietary changes, if they are playing a part in mood disorders, may have been creeping up on us over the last three or four decades as we have been eating more processed foods. Seafood has frequently been described as a 'mood stabiliser'.

Of course, it is not just finned fish that provide beneficial doses of Omega 3 and other nutrients. These are also available in shellfish, such as oysters, mussels, scallops, prawns, crabs and rock lobsters. For example, to receive one gram of Omega 3, you could eat 75 g of swordfish, 455 g of snapper, 250 g of Spanish mackerel, 155 g of Atlantic salmon, 550 g of tiger prawns, 330 g of Sydney rock oysters or 300 g of blue mussels. One way to guarantee receiving all the health benefits of seafood is to eat a wide variety of different species several times a week.

Because significant health benefits are derived from the oil content of seafood, try not to 'overwhelm' its Omega 3 and other oils with cooking oil. Try steaming, microwaving, baking and grilling instead of always frying fish in oil. Deep-fried battered fish is a delicious meal (as an occasional indulgence rather than a regular event) but some researchers studying the benefits of Omega 3 believe that Omega 6 polyunsaturated fatty acids, found most commonly in vegetable oils, 'compete' with Omega 3 in our bodies. In fact, they blame the rapid rise in Omega 6 use over the last fifty years as a cause of increases in some health problems, including heart disease. So, rather than polyunsaturated vegetable oils, try to use a monounsaturated oil such as grapeseed or olive oil for cooking. Grapeseed has a high smoking point and also has the most neutral flavour of any of the oils, making it ideal for seafood cookery.

Great warehou in Micronesia.

Udo and me horsing around.

Beach fishing in Micronesia.

What a beauty.

Waiting for the big one.

abalone
bar cod barramundi blue-eye trevalla bouillabaisse bream bugs coral trout
crab

ABALONE schnitzels

Abalone is the most expensive ingredient to come out of our waters, and the one most people have never even tasted, let alone cooked. If you do get the chance to cook with this amazing seafood, I urge you to do as little to it as possible. I think the best way to treat it is with a simple crumb coating (I use Japanese breadcrumbs, known as 'panko'), a quick pan-fry and a squeeze of lemon. Job done.

You could also use SCALLOPS, PRAWNS or any firm white-fleshed FISH

200 g (7 oz) abalone meat
a sprinkle of hot chilli flakes
grated zest of 1 lemon
1 teaspoon chopped flat-leaf (Italian) parsley
60 g (2¼ oz/½ cup) plain flour
1 egg, lightly beaten with a splash of milk
30 g (1 oz/½ cup) Japanese breadcrumbs
grapeseed oil, for shallow-frying
lemon wedges, to serve

Put the abalone between two large pieces of plastic wrap or in a plastic bag and pound gently with a rolling pin or meat tenderiser (use the flat side, not the side with the notches). Beat the abalone until it is one paper-thin piece.

Cut the abalone into bite-sized pieces and put in a bowl with the chilli flakes, lemon zest, parsley and a pinch of sea salt. Toss to coat.

Put the flour in one bowl, the egg in another bowl and the breadcrumbs in a third bowl. Dip the abalone in the flour, then the egg, then the breadcrumbs, always shaking off the excess before dipping into the next bowl.

Heat the oil in a frying pan until it is quite hot but not smoking. Cook the abalone for about 1 minute on each side until golden. Drain on kitchen paper, season with sea salt and serve with a squeeze of lemon juice and maybe some aioli (page 212).

SERVES 8 AS CANAPES

black pepper-crusted **BAR COD** with lime and ginger

This is a beautiful recipe with only a few ingredients. The pepper is the main flavour and, although it might seem like a lot, it just works so well with this fish. And then the lime and ginger will really get your taste buds partying.

You could also use any deep-sea, firm white-fleshed FISH

2 tablespoons freshly ground black pepper
2 teaspoons ground sea salt
4 x 100 g (3½ oz) bar cod fillets, skin removed
olive oil, for frying
125 ml (4 fl oz/½ cup) veal glaze (available at good delis or butchers)
125 ml (4 fl oz/½ cup) chicken stock
20 lime segments, cut in half
1 tablespoon candied ginger, page 215
1 tablespoon candied lime, page 215

Preheat the oven to 160°C (315°F/Gas 2–3). Mix the pepper and salt together and use to coat the side of the fish where the skin was. Heat a little olive oil in an ovenproof non-stick frying pan over low heat and slowly cook the fish, pepper side down, until it is cooked halfway through. Turn the fish over and put the pan in the oven for a few more minutes, until the fish is cooked through. Leave to rest for 5 minutes before serving.

Meanwhile, mix the veal glaze and chicken stock in a pan over medium heat and cook until reduced by half. Add the lime segments and continue cooking until the sauce has thickened. Pour over the fish and top with candied ginger and lime.

SERVES 4 AS A STARTER

steamed BARRAMUNDI with lime coconut sauce

Aah, the mighty barramundi... Fishermen dream of heading north to tackle this magnificent fighting creature. I just dream of eating it. Large fish can sometimes become a touch dry so my favourite way to cook barra is either pan-roasting or steaming. It can stand up to some pretty strong flavours, so is a perfect fish for mixing with Asian ingredients.

You could also use JEWFISH, PEARL PERCH, CORAL TROUT, RED EMPEROR, SNAPPER or LOBSTER

LIME COCONUT SAUCE
2 teaspoons finely chopped fresh ginger
2 garlic cloves, chopped
1 green bird's eye chilli, finely chopped
grated zest of 1 lime
$1/2$ bunch coriander with roots and stalks, chopped
2 lemongrass stalks, white part only, finely chopped
2 kaffir lime leaves
440 ml (15$1/2$ fl oz) tin coconut cream
2 tablespoons palm sugar
1 tablespoon fish sauce
$1^{1}/2$ tablespoons lime juice

800 g (1 lb 12 oz) sweet potatoes, unpeeled
1 tablespoon finely chopped fresh ginger
1 tablespoon butter
4 x 160–180 g (6 oz) barramundi fillets with skin
2 tablespoons crispy shallots, page 221
1 lime, peeled, segmented

Preheat the oven to 180°C (350°F/Gas 4) and bake the whole sweet potatoes for 1$1/2$ hours, or until tender.

Meanwhile, to make the lime coconut sauce, heat a touch of oil in a pan and sauté the ginger, garlic, chilli, lime zest, coriander roots and stalks and lemongrass until just starting to colour (save the coriander tops to garnish). Tear one of the kaffir limes leaves, add to the pan with the coconut cream and simmer for 30 minutes. Stir in the palm sugar, fish sauce and lime juice. Purée and then pass through a fine strainer to remove any lumps.

Pound the ginger in a mortar and pestle, then add 125 ml (4 fl oz/$1/2$ cup) of water, then leave to infuse for 20 minutes to make ginger juice. Strain before using.

Peel the skin off the baked potatoes and purée the flesh with the ginger juice, butter and a bit of salt and white pepper.

Make a cut in the skin of the fish and then steam over fragrant, almost simmering water (you can throw in any Asian aromatics you might have around, such as lemongrass, kaffir lime, lemon, star anise) for 10 minutes or until the fish is just cooked through. You can tell when it's cooked because the cut in the skin will turn white.

Gently reheat the lime coconut sauce, then pour into the middle of the plate, place a mound of warm sweet potato purée on top and then cover with the barramundi.

Sprinkle some crispy shallots around the fish and top with a couple of lime segments. Julienne the remaining kaffir lime leaf and sprinkle the fish with a few slivers of lime leaf and the coriander leaves or some baby herbs.

SERVES 4

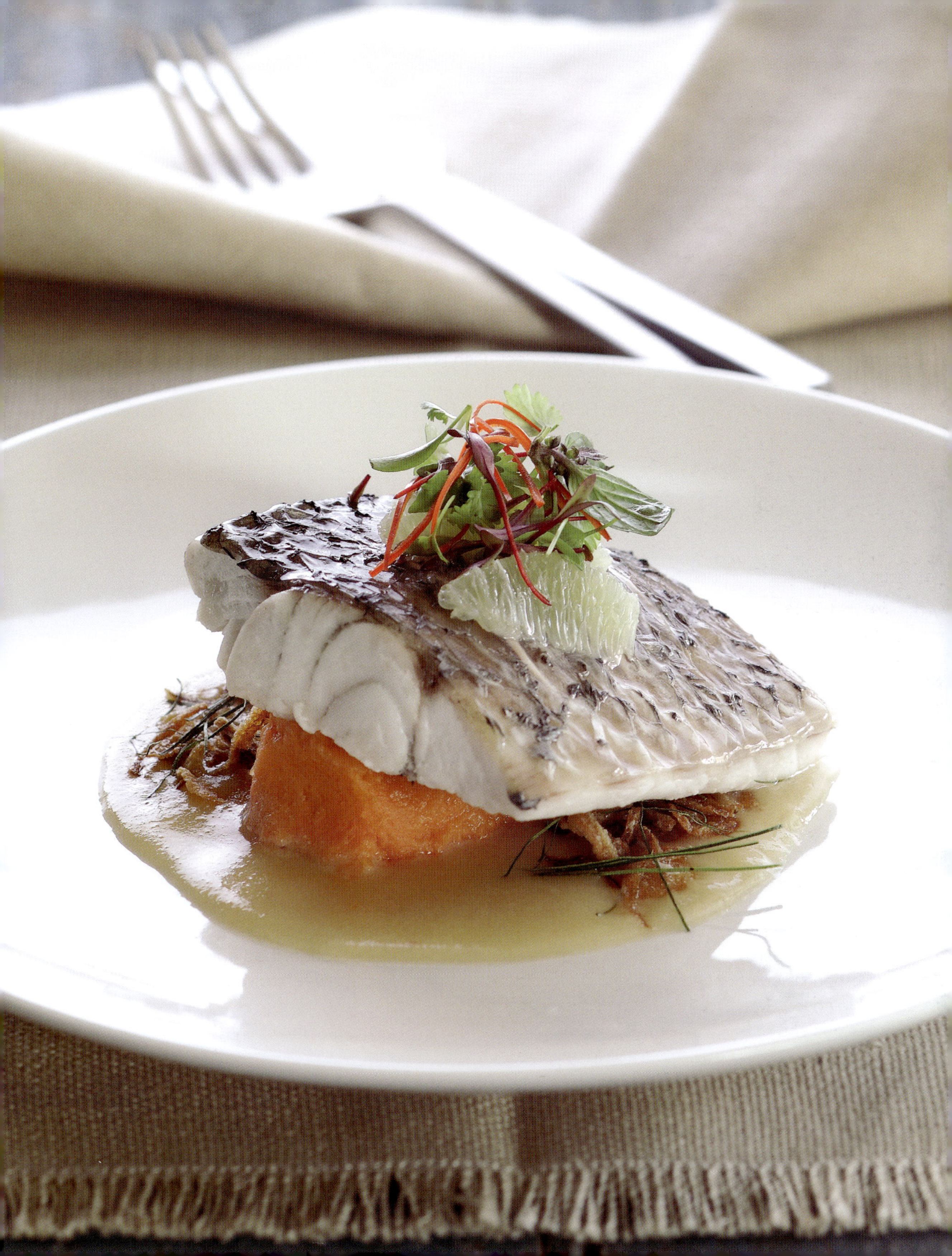

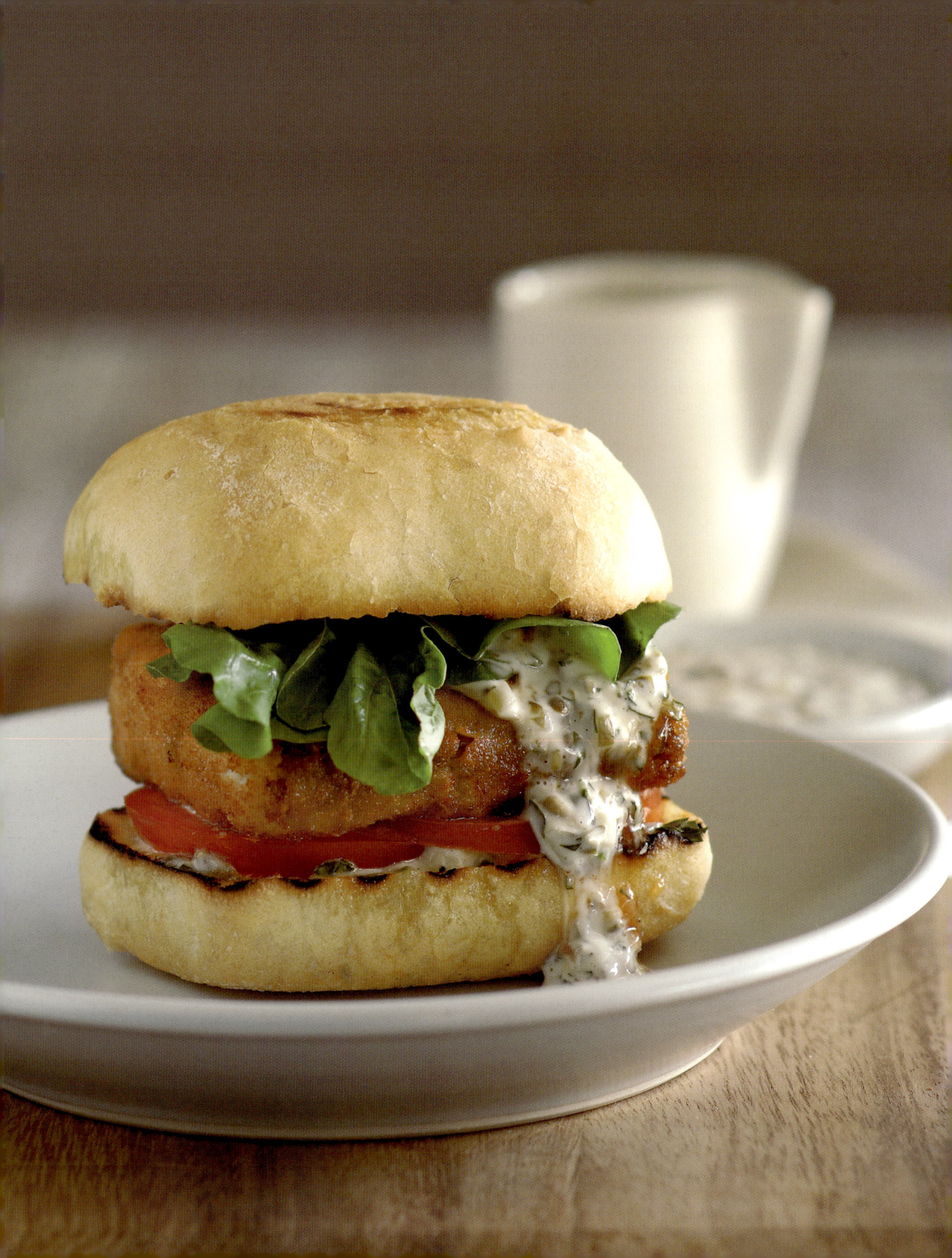

BARRA burgers from the top end

I love travelling and discovering what makes a town, state or country proud of its culinary heritage. Take, for instance, the scallop pie in Tasmania... never heard of it before I went to Tassie, but every bakery has its scallop pies and bloody delicious they are, too. (That recipe will have to be in the next book.) But I guess the other famous 'state' dish is the Northern Territory's barramundi burger. You don't realise until you visit the NT that it is their culinary treasure and they are, quite rightly, mighty proud of it. You can cook the barra any number of ways — grill, barbecue, smoke or fry. I like mine crumbed, with some tartare sauce and a bit of chilli jam. This makes a great lunch for the family.

You could also use any firm white-fleshed FISH fillet

4 x 100 g (3½ oz) barramundi fillets, skin removed
60 g (2¼ oz/½ cup) flour
1 egg, lightly beaten with a splash of milk
50 g (1¾ oz/½ cup) dry breadcrumbs
4 tablespoons olive oil
4 hamburger buns (these need to be very fresh and soft)
good-quality butter
4 tablespoons tartare sauce, page 231 or ready-made
1 tablespoon chilli jam, page 218 or ready-made
2 vine-ripened tomatoes, thinly sliced
a large handful of rocket leaves, dressed with lemon juice and olive oil

Season the barramundi with sea salt and toss lightly in the flour, then the egg and then the breadcrumbs.

Heat the olive oil in a frying pan until hot but not smoking and cook the barra fillets until cooked through and golden. Sprinkle with sea salt.

Meanwhile, halve and butter the buns and then toast them lightly under a hot grill. Fill each bun with a barra fillet, tartare sauce, chilli jam, sliced tomato and rocket leaves. Enjoy with a cold beer.

SERVES 4

BARRAMUNDI with porcini risotto

I've been making risotto for the last fifteen years, and I thought I knew how to make a pretty good version. That was until I met a guy whose family has been growing arborio rice in Italy for the last 400 years. He taught me how his family cooks risotto and I'll let you in on his little secret: there is no standing at the stove constantly watching and stirring and adding stock ladle by ladle. He says that is a fallacy. The real way to do it is to heat up a bit more liquid than rice, fry the base aromatics, add your rice and then stir in the hot liquid. Then you pop a lid on the pan, turn the heat to low and walk away for about a quarter of an hour. When you come back, the rice should be perfect. With this method you will be cooking risotto at least once a week. By the way, his surname is Ferron, so if you ever see that name on a bag of rice, you'll know it's regarded as one of the best in the world.

You could also use any firm white-fleshed FISH

olive oil, for cooking
2 teaspoons minced garlic
2 teaspoons minced French shallot
120 g (4 1/4 oz) arborio rice
185 ml (6 fl oz/3/4 cup) hot chicken or fish stock
2 teaspoons truffle paste (available at good delis)
120 g (4 1/4 oz) porcini (or other) mushrooms, diced
2 teaspoons grated parmesan cheese
2 teaspoons chopped flat-leaf (Italian) parsley or basil
4 x 100 g (3 1/2 oz) barramundi fillets
4 x 25 g (1 oz) pieces foie gras (optional)
125 ml (4 fl oz/1/2 cup) beurre rouge, page 214

To make the risotto, heat a little of the olive oil in a saucepan and gently fry the garlic and shallot until softened. Add the rice and cook for a minute, stirring well to coat all the grains. Then add the stock, truffle paste and porcinis and stir gently. Put the lid on the pan, turn the heat to its lowest setting and leave for 12–15 minutes, or until the rice is cooked. Stir in the parmesan and parsley.

Meanwhile, preheat the oven to 180°C (350°F/Gas 4). Fry the barramundi, skin side down, in a touch of oil in an ovenproof non-stick frying pan. Once the skin is golden, flip the fish over and place the pan in the oven for about 5 minutes, or until the fish is cooked through. Place a piece of foie gras on top of each fillet and return to the oven for 30 seconds to soften.

Spoon a little beurre rouge around each plate and place the risotto in the middle. Top with the fish. I like to serve this with some watercress leaves dressed simply with lemon juice.

SERVES 4

BLUE-EYE TREVALLA with baccala sauce on soft polenta

Pure comfort food doesn't get much better than this. I love the way the baccala (salt cod) gives a wonderful depth of flavour to the sauce. That said, you can leave it out and still end up with a delicious sauce that works wonders with the blue-eye and creamy soft polenta.

You could also use any firm white-fleshed FISH or any of the oil-rich species such as SARDINES or HERRINGS

625 ml (22 fl oz/2½ cups) fish stock
75 g (2½ oz/½ cup) polenta
3 tablespoons butter
4 x 160–180 g (6 oz) blue-eye trevalla fillets, with skin on, bones removed
1 quantity baccala sauce, page 212, warmed
extra virgin olive oil and grated zest of 1 lemon, to serve

Bring the stock to a simmer in a saucepan and add the polenta slowly, stirring constantly with a wooden spoon until it starts to thicken. Season with salt and pepper and cook, stirring, for about 20 minutes over low heat. Stir in 1 tablespoon of the butter.

Meanwhile, preheat the oven to 160°C (315°F/Gas 2–3). Heat a touch of oil in an ovenproof non-stick frying pan and cook the fish, skin side down, until crisp and golden. Turn the fish over, add the rest of the butter to the pan and put in the oven for 3–4 minutes, or until the fish is cooked through. Let the fish rest for a couple of minutes before serving.

Spoon warm polenta into each bowl, arrange the fish on the polenta and pour the baccala sauce over the top. Drizzle with some oil and sprinkle with lemon zest to serve.

SERVES 4

BOUILLABAISSE

Bouillabaisse is a seafood stew from the Provence region of southern France. Local fishermen would traditionally make this soup in cauldrons along the beach, using up any of their fresh catch that hadn't been sold at market. Bouillabaisse typically includes rockfish, shellfish, mussels and crabs and is flavoured with fresh herbs, saffron and orange zest. But, like many traditional dishes, the ingredients change according to the fresh seafood of that particular region.

Bouillabaisse is one of the best seafood recipes I have ever come across, and I thoroughly enjoy cooking it. I would serve this as a complete meal: it is so satisfying and anything served before or after would frankly pale in comparison. Rock cod is the base of this dish, so, if you haven't caught them yourself, please pick the freshest you can find at the fish market. This is a real fisherman and fisherwoman's meal.

You could also use RED MULLET

FOR THE BASE
3 small whole rock fish (such as rock cod or ocean perch), cut into large pieces
6 garlic cloves, sliced
½ leek, sliced
3 bay leaves
6 tomatoes, roughly chopped
3 pinches of saffron
1 carrot, sliced
1 celery stalk, sliced
about 150 g (5½ oz/1 cup) chopped fennel
1½ tablespoons fennel seeds

To make the soup base, put the pieces of fish in a large bowl and add the garlic, leek, bay leaves, tomatoes, saffron, carrot, celery, fennel and fennel seeds, oil, Pernod, pepper, orange zest and parsley stalks. Mix together well, cover and leave in the fridge to marinate overnight or for up to 2 days.

Heat a touch of oil in a large pan, add the contents of the bowl and sauté for a few minutes. Add the tomato paste and cook for 2 minutes. Add the fish stock, bring to the boil and simmer for 1 to 1½ hours.

Allow the soup to cool a little, then blend and pass through a strainer. Add salt to taste. You should now have a very rich and flavoursome soup base.

Pour the soup base into a clean pan, add the celery, leek and onion and bring to the boil. Reduce the heat to a simmer, and add your seafood (shellfish first, then prawns and finally fish) and cook for about 2 minutes.

3 tablespoons extra virgin olive oil
125 ml (4 fl oz/$^1/_2$ cup) Pernod
cracked black pepper
grated zest of 2 oranges
stalks from 1 bunch flat-leaf (Italian) parsley

FOR THE SOUP
2 tablespoons tomato paste
2 litres (70 fl oz/8 cups) fish stock
1 celery stalk, thinly sliced
1 leek, thinly sliced
1 small onion, sliced as thinly as possible
650 g (1 lb 7 oz) mixed seafood (mussels, prawns, chopped fish, thinly sliced squid, scallops, oysters or halved scampi)
4 tablespoons grated gruyère cheese
4 slices sourdough or crusty bread, toasted
chervil or parsley sprigs, to garnish

Meanwhile, spread the grated gruyère over the slices of toast and grill until melted. Depending on what seafood you are using in your soup, spoon some thinly sliced squid, a scallop and possibly an oyster or half scampi into a heated bowl. Pour the soup over the top and float the cheese toast on top. Garnish with chervil or parsley and serve with cracked pepper.

Bouillabaisse is traditionally served with a rouille — a French mayonnaise made from a base of cooked potatoes, saffron, capsicum, garlic and onion. You can find this in some good delis. You could also serve bouillabaisse with mayonnaise with a little saffron stirred through.

SERVES 4

pan-fried BREAM with potatoes and tamarind sauce

Bream is the fish that most people catch when they first wet a line. Everyone I speak to says it was one of the first fish they pulled in when they were a kid down by the river or lake. Unfortunately, the bream is often seen as the ugly brother to the snapper — which is strange, as I believe it's a tremendous eating fish.

You could also use SNAPPER, MANGROVE JACK, MULLOWAY or JEWFISH

4 tablespoons grapeseed oil
2 tablespoons butter
4 x 160–180 g (6 oz) pieces bream fillet, with skin on
2 pontiac potatoes, boiled, cooled and each thickly sliced into 4 pieces
125 ml (4 fl oz/½ cup) tamarind sauce, page 231
4 tablespoons diced, deseeded cucumber
4 tablespoons plain yoghurt
chilli powder, to garnish

Divide the oil and butter evenly between two pans and season both the fish and potatoes with some salt and pepper. Cook the fish, skin side down, in one pan until golden on one side, then flip over and cook until just done. Meanwhile, cook the potatoes in the other pan until golden on both sides.

Spoon tamarind sauce into the middle of each plate and scatter some diced cucumber over the sauce. Arrange the potato on top of it, then the fish, skin side up. Add a dollop of yoghurt and a sprinkling of chilli powder.

Great with steamed bok choy and an Asian beer.

SERVES 4

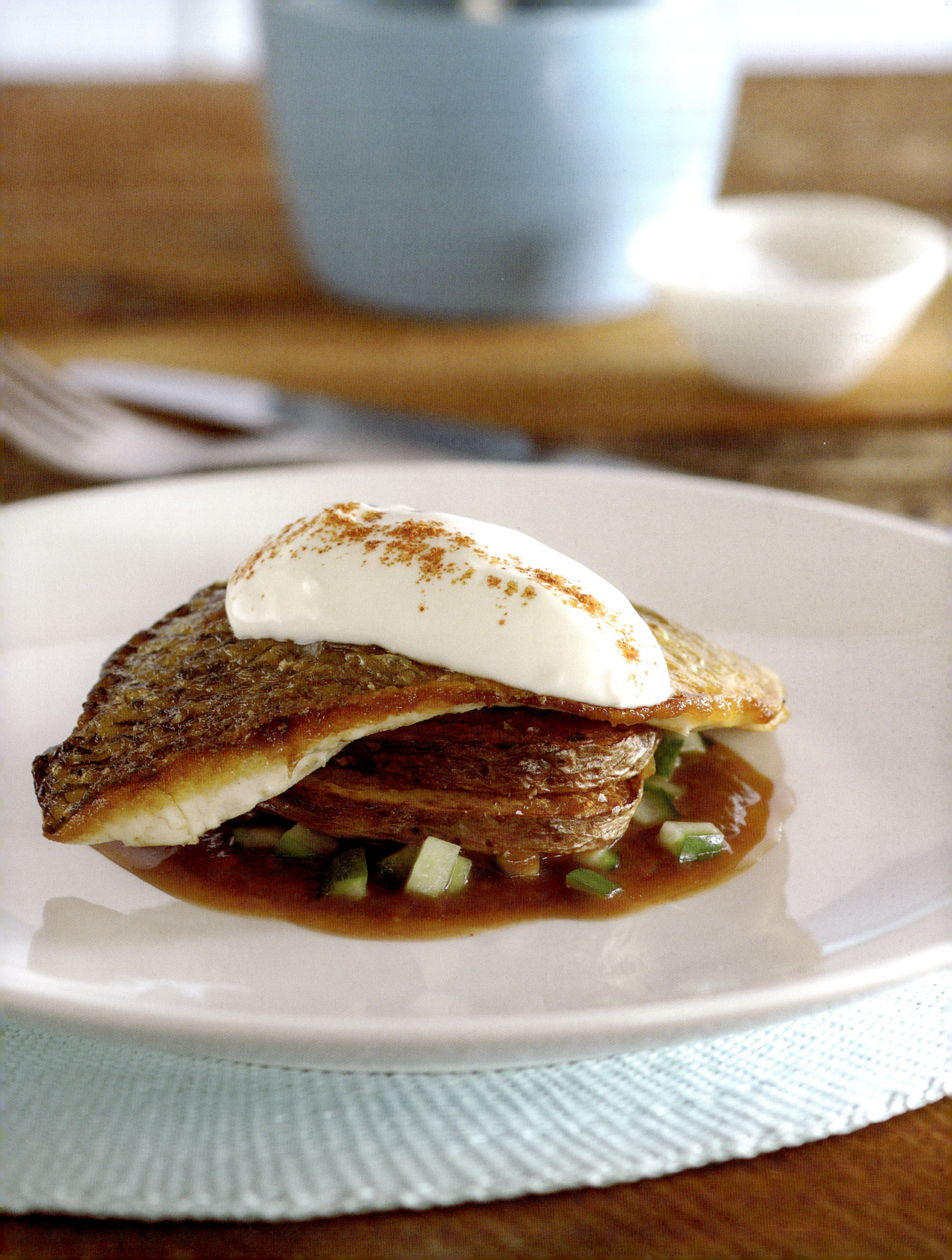

BUG meat fu yung with chinese sausage

I am fascinated by Chinese cooking. Take this recipe, for instance... how on earth did they come up with the idea of gently frying seafood in egg white until golden and then serving with a hot broth? The end result is such a textural masterpiece that it makes my mind boggle. When I cook this I like to add some Chinese sausage (lop cheong), which isn't necessarily authentic but makes the dish even more addictive.

You could also use LOBSTER, PRAWNS, MARRON, SCALLOPS or any firm white-fleshed FISH

350 g (12 oz) bug meat (either Moreton Bay or Balmain bugs — you will need about 1.2 kg/ 2 lb 10 oz unpeeled bugs)
3 tablespoons shaoxing rice wine
1 bird's eye chilli, finely chopped
1 tablespoon grated fresh ginger
4 egg whites
pinch of cream of tartar
grapeseed oil, for deep-frying
150 ml (5 fl oz) chicken stock
1 teaspoon sesame oil
2 teaspoons light soy sauce
1 teaspoon cornflour
50 g ($1^3/4$ oz) Chinese sausage (lop cheong), sliced
2 spring onions, white part only, sliced
2 spring onions, green part only, sliced
lemon wedges, to serve

Cut the bug tails in half and mix gently with 1 tablespoon of the shaoxing wine, the chilli, half the ginger and a pinch of sea salt.

Whisk the egg whites with the cream of tartar until you have stiff peaks, then gently fold in the bug meat so that it is coated.

Heat the oil in a deep-fat fryer or wok to 185°C (365°F) — check with a thermometer or drop a cube of bread into the oil: it should brown in about 10 seconds. Deep-fry the bug meat in batches until lightly golden and then lift out and drain on kitchen paper. If the meat starts to stick to the bottom of the wok, lift it off carefully with a long-handled spoon.

Mix together the chicken stock, remaining shaoxing wine, sesame oil, soy sauce, white pepper and some sea salt. Mix the cornflour with 2 tablespoons of cold water and stir in as well.

Heat a few tablespoons of the oil in a wok and then add the Chinese sausage, white spring onions and remaining ginger. Cook for about 30 seconds, then add the stock mixture and stir until thickened. Add the cooked bug meat and carefully toss together.

Pour onto a serving plate and garnish with the green spring onions and a squeeze of lemon juice.

SERVES 4 AS A STARTER

BUG tails with cucumber and roasted peanut salad

The first time I heard of bugs, I was seventeen and just starting my apprenticeship. I thought: 'You have to be joking; I'm not eating an insect', until it was pointed out to me that they are a cross between a prawn and a lobster. They can call them whatever they like, just as long as I have a good supply of them in the summertime.

You could also use PRAWNS, LOBSTER or ATLANTIC SALMON

- ¼ Lebanese cucumber, cut in half lengthways, deseeded and thinly sliced
- 3 tablespoons Thai salad dressing, page 232
- 2 tablespoons julienned fresh ginger
- peanut oil, for frying
- 6 quail eggs
- 1 tablespoon fish sauce
- 1 chilli, finely chopped
- 1 teaspoon finely sliced coriander leaves
- 8 Balmain bug tails, peeled and deveined
- a handful of roasted peanuts
- 125 ml (4 fl oz/½ cup) tamarind sauce, page 231
- a handful of perfect rose petals
- 1 tablespoon salmon roe

Put the cucumber in a bowl, heat up the Thai salad dressing and pour it over the cucumber. Leave for 30 minutes, then drain.

Fry the ginger in a little peanut oil until golden, then remove from the pan or wok and set aside.

Cook the quail eggs in boiling water with a splash of vinegar for 2½ minutes, then hold under cold water until cool and remove the shells. Heat the peanut oil in a deep-fat fryer or wok to 185°C (365°F) — check with a thermometer or drop a cube of bread into the oil: it should brown in about 10 seconds. Fry the eggs until golden and crispy. Mix the eggs with the fish sauce, chilli and coriander leaves and cut in half lengthways.

Heat a touch of peanut oil in a hot pan and fry the bug tails, turning once, until golden on both sides.

Place a small amount of cucumber in the centre of each plate, scatter with a few peanuts and then arrange the bug tails on top. Drizzle some tamarind sauce over each plate, arrange a few rose petals around the plate and place the quail eggs on the petals. Garnish with the fried ginger and the salmon roe.

SERVES 4 AS A STARTER

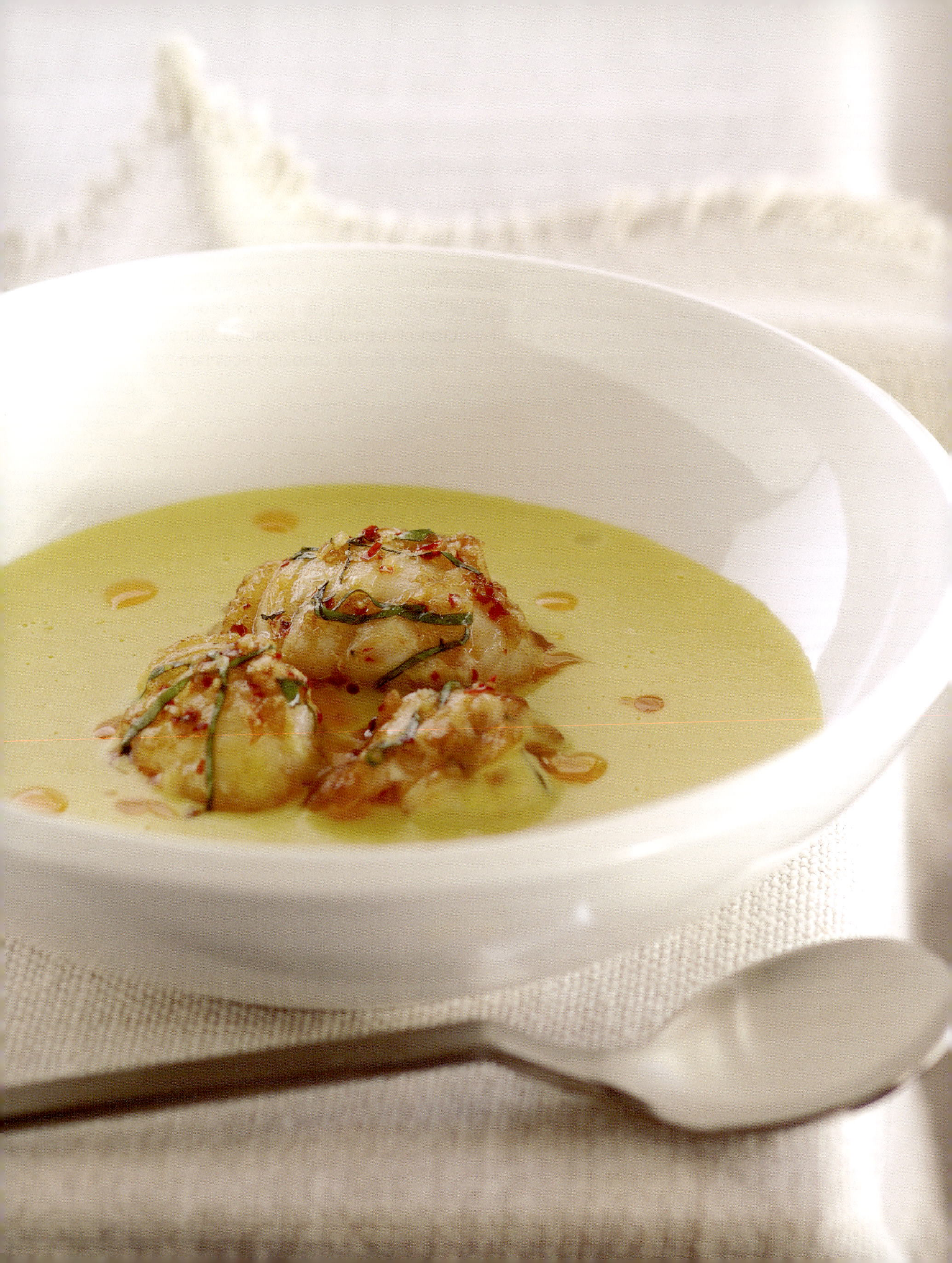

BUG tails with sweetcorn broth

I have been making a version of this soup in my restaurants and at home for over ten years now — I think it has to be my favourite soup of all time. You can team it with pretty much any shellfish but my best-loved is the combination of beautiful roasted Moreton Bay bugs with sweetcorn. Serve with some warm crusty bread for an amazing starter.

You could also use MUSSELS, LOBSTER, CRAB, SCAMPI or YABBIES

1 tablespoon butter
3 French shallots, sliced
2 garlic cloves, sliced
400 g (14 oz/2 cups) corn kernels, cut from the cob
1 litre (35 fl oz/4 cups) chicken stock
150 ml (5 fl oz) cream
8 Moreton Bay bug tails, peeled and deveined
4 basil leaves, finely sliced
2 teaspoons chilli oil, page 219

Heat the butter in a pan and gently cook the shallots and garlic until softened but not coloured. Add the corn and cook for another couple of minutes, then add the stock. Bring to the boil, reduce the heat and simmer for 20 minutes. Add the cream and cook for 2 more minutes, then remove from the heat and blend until smooth. Pass through a sieve and season with salt.

Season the bug tails lightly and heat a touch of oil in a frying pan. Fry the bugs for 1 minute on each side, or until golden outside and a little opaque inside.

Pour the soup into bowls and top with the bug tails, sliced basil and chilli oil.

SERVES 4 AS A STARTER

deep-fried CORAL TROUT salad with japanese dressing

One of the best ways to eat any reef fish is deep-fried. I know we should be eating less fried food but, as my Dad always taught me, everything is alright in moderation. This recipe is full of fresh salad ingredients that will make you feel good anyway.

You could also use any firm white-fleshed FISH, SCALLOPS, OYSTERS, PRAWNS or BUGS

90 g (3 oz/½ cup) rice flour
90 g (3 oz/½ cup) potato starch or tapioca flour
4 x 160 g (5¾ oz) coral trout fillets, cut into 5 cm (2 inch) pieces
vegetable oil, for deep-frying
2 handfuls of baby rocket
2 handfuls of baby mizuna leaves
2 handfuls of frisé lettuce leaves
a handful of mint leaves
a handful of coriander leaves
1 banana chilli, julienned
3 tablespoons julienned leek
4 tablespoons salmon roe
1 quantity Japanese salad dressing, page 224
2 tablespoons crispy garlic chips, page 220
4 tablespoons toasted almond flakes

Mix together the rice flour and potato starch and use to dust the pieces of coral trout.

Heat the oil to 185°C (365°F) in a deep-fat fryer or large wok — either measure this with a thermometer or drop a cube of bread into the oil: it should brown in about 10 seconds. Deep-fry the coral trout until golden and crisp. Drain on kitchen paper.

Mix together the greens, herbs, chilli, leek and salmon roe and dress with the Japanese salad dressing. Toss the fish through the salad and pile onto four plates. Sprinkle with the crispy garlic chips and the almonds.

SERVES 4

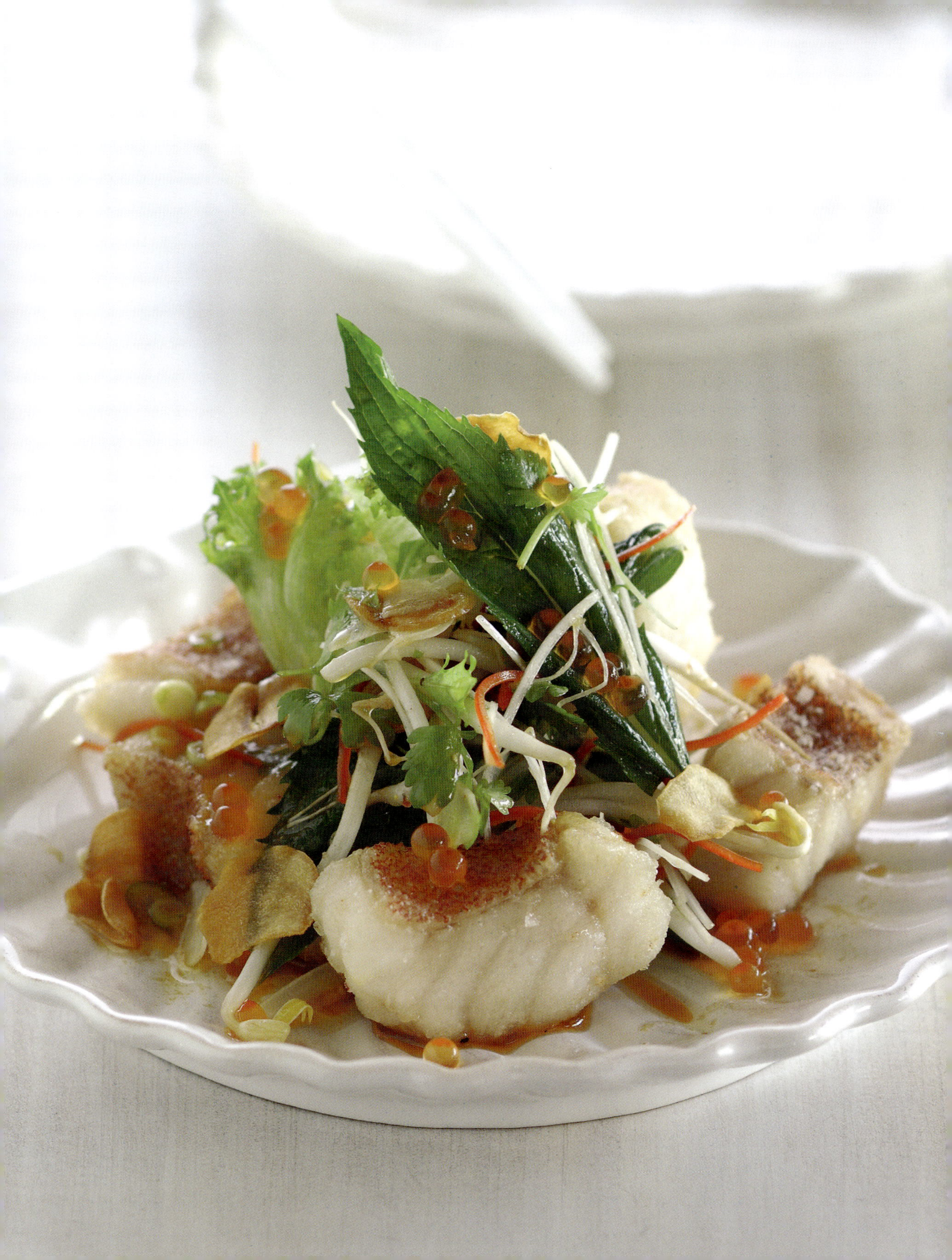

pan-fried CORAL TROUT with mud crab ravioli and beurre rouge

The classic sauce, created to perfectly complement seafood, is *beurre blanc* (white butter). This very simple sauce is made from a wine, vinegar and shallot reduction into which cubes of cold butter are whisked until the sauce is thick and smooth. You don't see it around as much these days, as cooks are always looking for healthier ways to prepare food. I tend to agree that rich butter-based sauces are a thing of the past, but sometimes I crave the taste and extravagance that only a dish of that style can provide. My sauce here trades white wine for red, to give equally impressive results.

You could also use RED EMPEROR, JOHN DORY, KINGFISH, SNAPPER, BLUE-EYE, MAHI MAHI, BARRAMUNDI or LOBSTER

flour, for dusting
8 gow gee wrappers or fresh pasta sheets cut into 5 cm (2 inch) circles
100 g (3½ oz) cooked mud crab meat or other crab meat
4 tarragon leaves
grated zest of ½ lemon and juice of 1 lemon
4 x 160 g (5¾ oz) pieces coral trout fillet, with skin
1 tablespoon olive oil
500 g (1 lb 2 oz) cavolo nero
1 quantity crispy leek, page 221
200 ml (7 fl oz) beurre rouge, page 214

To make the ravioli, sprinkle your bench top with a touch of flour and lay half the gow gee wrappers or pasta circles on the bench (the flour will prevent sticking). Brush the edges of the wrappers or pasta with water, spoon a little crab meat into the centre, top with a tarragon leaf and some lemon zest and sea salt, then lay another wrapper or pasta circle over the top and press the edges together to seal.

Season the coral trout with sea salt on both sides. Heat the oil in a pan and cook the fish, skin side down, until golden. Turn over and fry until just cooked through. (If the fish is particularly thick, you can finish the cooking in a 160°C/315°F/Gas 2–3 oven for a few minutes.) Let the fish rest for 5 minutes on a plate.

Add the cavolo nero to the fish pan and sauté until it has wilted. Squeeze the lemon juice over the cavolo nero, mix with a little salt and pepper and drain off the excess moisture.

Heat a large pan of salted water until boiling. Lower the ravioli gently into the pan and cook for 1 minute before lifting out with a slotted spoon.

Arrange cavolo nero in the centre of each plate, place the coral trout on top, then the ravioli and the crispy leek. Pour a little beurre rouge around the plate (not too much or it will overpower the fish).

SERVES 4

blue swimmer **CRAB** linguine

My first restaurant in Sydney was called Hugo's and this was our signature dish. We sold Hugo's after ten years and probably close to 75,000 servings of blue swimmer crab linguine. I still love cooking it to this day. Simon Fawcett, my first head chef, came up with the dish and Hugo's wouldn't have been the same without it. So, Simon, the diners of Sydney and I owe you a huge thank you.

You could also use any CRAB meat, PRAWNS, MUSSELS, PIPIS, VONGOLE or BUGS

4 tablespoons butter
8 garlic cloves, sliced
6 French shallots, sliced
2 bird's eye chillies, finely chopped
1 bunch coriander, including roots, chopped
100 ml (3½ fl oz) fish sauce
1 litre (35 fl oz/4 cups) vegetable or fish stock
24 cherry tomatoes, halved
500 g (1 lb 2 oz) linguine
320 g (11¼ oz) cooked blue swimmer crab meat
4 coriander sprigs
lime wedges, to serve

Heat a little of the butter in a large pan and sauté the garlic, shallots, chillies and chopped coriander root until golden. Add the fish sauce and cook for about 30 seconds to release the flavour. Add the stock and tomatoes, bring to a simmer and cook until you have a sauce that has reduced and thickened enough to coat the pasta. You don't need to add any salt; the fish sauce is the salt element in this dish.

Cook the linguine in a large pan of boiling salted water for 8–10 minutes or until al dente. Drain and toss with the sauce.

Add the crab meat and the rest of the chopped coriander and serve garnished with coriander sprigs and a squeeze of lime.

SERVES 4

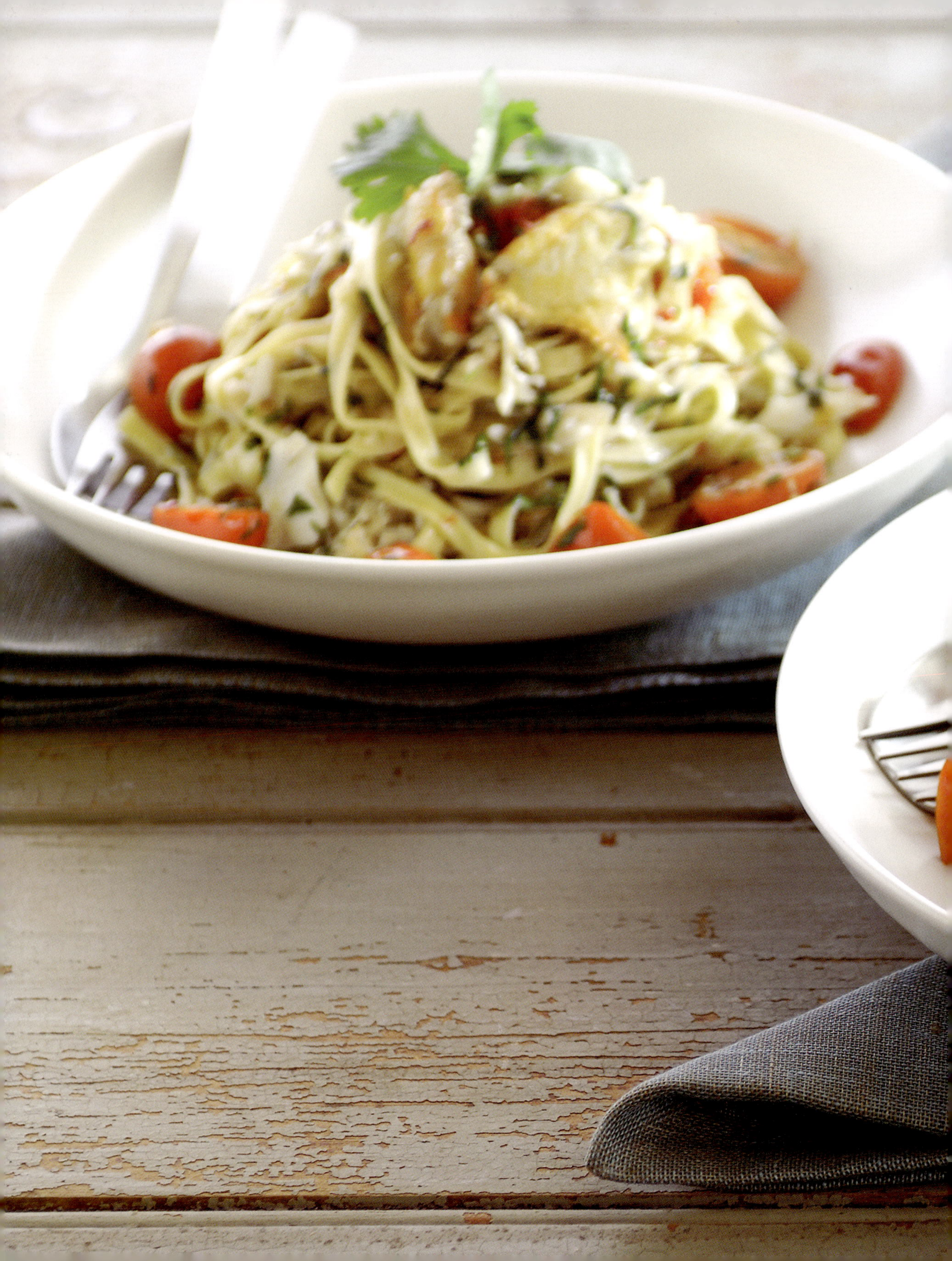

blue swimmer crab linguine

mud CRAB and chinese roast pork in rice paper rolls

This is a great recipe for getting the kids involved. They love to get their hands dirty and it's good to show them how much fun food can be. But these also work well for a grown-up party... chop everything beforehand, put all the fillings out in separate bowls and ask your guests to help themselves.

You could also use PRAWNS, YABBIES, SMOKED TROUT or SMOKED EEL

8 sheets rice paper
1 tablespoon chilli jam, page 218
1 cup vermicelli rice noodles, cooked following the packet instructions
100 g (3½ oz) Chinese barbecued pork (available in Chinatown)
100 g (3½ oz) mud crab meat
8 Thai basil leaves
8 coriander leaves
4 Vietnamese mint leaves
4 mint leaves
3 tablespoons finely julienned carrot
3 tablespoons finely julienned cucumber
3 tablespoons bean sprouts or snow pea shoots
1 tablespoon chopped roasted cashews or peanuts
1 quantity chilli caramel dipping sauce, page 217

Soak the rice paper sheets in very hot water for 10 seconds to soften them, then lay them out on a clean tea towel. Arrange a small amount of each filling ingredient in the centre of each rice paper sheet. Roll up to make spring rolls and serve with the chilli caramel dipping sauce.

SERVES 4 AS A STARTER

deep-fried blue swimmer CRAB with lemon aioli

There is a little seaside restaurant in Bondi called Sean's Panaroma. Sean is the King Midas of the restaurant world... everything he touches turns to gold, including blue swimmer crab. His cooking secret is to do as little as possible to the best ingredients he can find. This recipe is one of my favourites from his restaurant.

You could also use SQUID, PRAWNS, WHITEBAIT, FLOUNDER or SOLE

4 live blue swimmer crabs
125 g (4 1/2 oz/1 cup) plain flour
oil, for deep-frying (I use peanut, vegetable or grapeseed)
a large handful of flat-leaf (Italian) parsley leaves
4 tablespoons aioli, page 212
juice of 1 lemon

Put the crabs in the freezer for about an hour until they are unconscious. Remove the top shell by lifting the flap on the underside. Remove the gills (the spongy grey fingers) and any muck by rinsing very lightly and quickly under running water.

Using a cleaver, cut each crab into four pieces and, using the back of the cleaver or knife, gently crack open the claws. Lightly dust the crab with flour.

Heat the oil to 185°C (365°F) in a deep-fat fryer or large wok — either measure this with a thermometer or drop a cube of bread into the oil: it should brown in about 10 seconds. Deep-fry the crab in batches until crisp. Deep-fry the parsley leaves as well until crispy (take care, as they will splash). Toss the crab with the parsley leaves and some sea salt and cracked white pepper. Mix the aioli with the lemon juice and serve with the crab.

SERVES 4

chilli salt soft-shell CRAB with young coconut caramel and green papaya salad

Soft-shell crab has only been on Australian and New Zealand menus for the last five years or so, however, in the US and Japan it is not only common but also extremely popular. The crabs are caught just after they've molted their hard shells. Generally they are cooked whole, or chopped in half and the coral removed, so that you eat the whole crab: legs, top shell, everything. Once you wrap your head around the idea, you will find yourself hunting them down at your Asian grocers or ordering soft-shell crab at restaurants every time.

Queensland is starting to harvest its own soft-shell crab and hopefully within a few years we should have a constant farmed source of these beautiful culinary treasures. Until then, you will probably have to buy the frozen Asian imports from the fish market or ask your fishmonger to order some in. They are relatively cheap and make quite an impression at dinner parties.

You could also use PRAWNS, SQUID, BUGS, FLOUNDER or WHITING

GREEN PAPAYA SALAD
2 large handfuls of julienned green papaya
1 large handful of julienned daikon
2 kaffir lime leaves, julienned
2 tablespoons thinly sliced red Asian shallots
2 tablespoons roasted peanuts, crushed
1 small handful of coriander leaves
12 mint leaves
12 Vietnamese mint leaves
12 Thai basil leaves
nam jim dressing, to taste, page 225

To make the green papaya salad, gently mix together the papaya, daikon, kaffir lime leaves, shallots, peanuts and herbs and dress with the nam jim dressing (just enough to moisten the salad without smothering it).

To make the young coconut caramel, put the coconut juice, fish sauce and lime juice in a small pan and place over heat until reduced by three-quarters. Put the palm sugar in a cold pan, place over low heat and stir until melted and almost caramel. Add the coconut juice mixture to the palm sugar (be careful: it will spit) and cook until reduced to a syrup.

Scrape the flesh out of the coconut and cut into julienne strips. Add enough to the syrup to give a good ratio of coconut to dressing.

Chop the crabs in half and remove any mustard (the yellow part) from the head and body by holding them under gently running cold water. (The mustard can taste bitter if left in.)

COCONUT CARAMEL
1 whole young coconut
1 1/2 tablespoons fish sauce
1 1/2 tablespoons lime juice
60 g (2 1/4 oz) palm sugar, grated

4 soft-shell crabs
vegetable oil, for deep-frying
90 g (3 1/4 oz/ 1/2 cup) rice flour or tempura flour
1 tablespoon chilli salt spice, page 219
2–3 tablespoons grapeseed oil
2 banana chillies, finely chopped
1 tablespoon finely chopped garlic
1 tablespoon chopped coriander
4 betel leaves

Heat the vegetable oil to 185°C (365°F) in a deep-fat fryer or large wok — either measure this with a thermometer or drop a cube of bread into the oil: it should brown in about 10 seconds. Mix the rice flour with the chilli salt spice. Lightly dust the crab in the spiced flour and deep-fry in batches until golden and crispy. Drain on kitchen paper.

Heat the grapeseed oil in a wok and add the chopped chilli and garlic. Cook until golden, then add the chopped coriander and deep-fried crab and cook for 30 seconds. Season with sea salt.

Lay a betel leaf on each plate and stack the crab on top. Arrange the salad on the other side of the plate and spoon some of the coconut caramel beside it.

SERVES 4 AS A STARTER

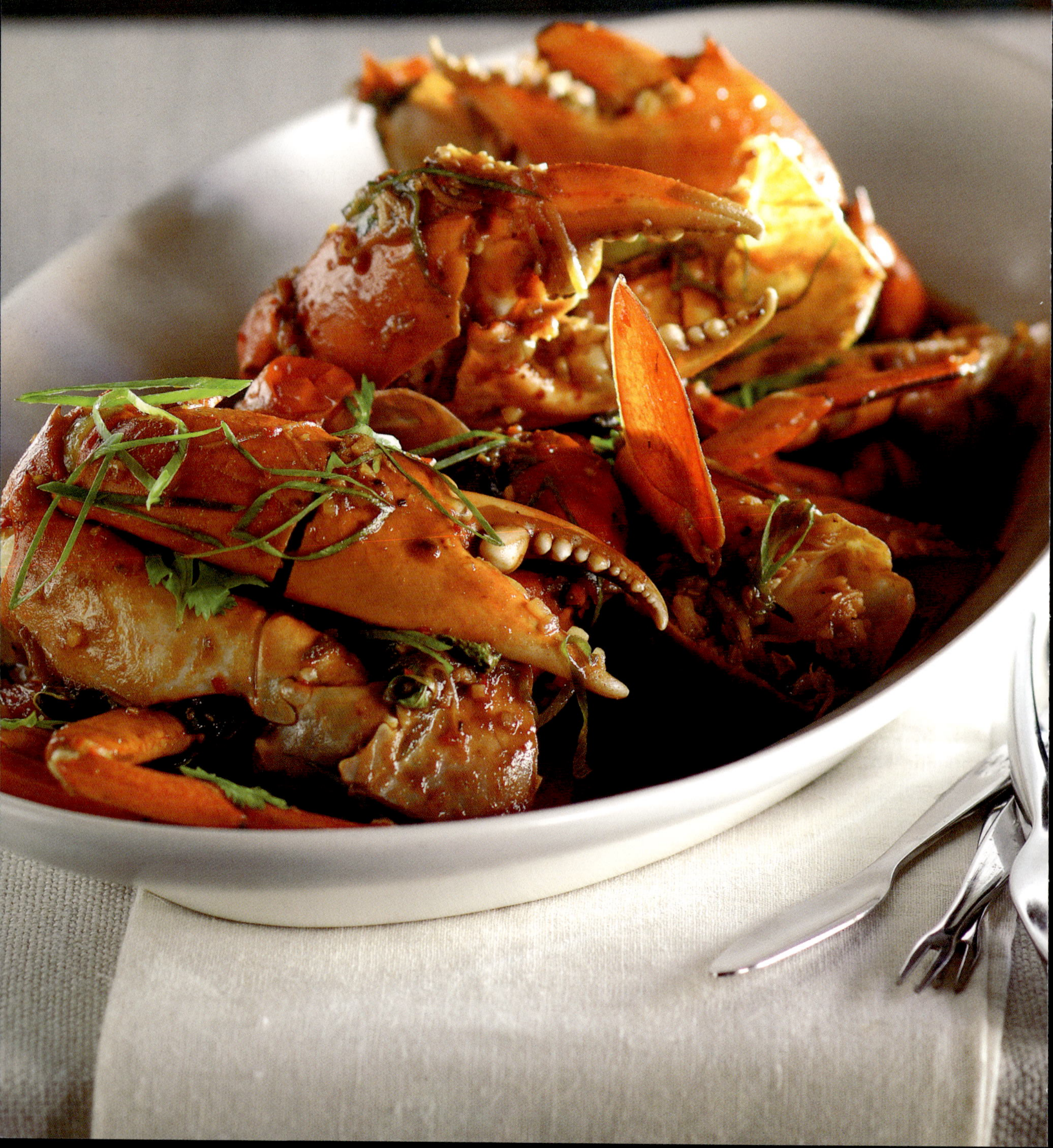

chilli mud CRAB

To catch and cook your own mud crab is one of life's great pleasures. This is my version of chilli crab or Singapore crab. It may not be truly authentic, but it tastes so good that I don't really care!

You could also use any CRAB, PRAWNS, LOBSTER, MARRON, BUGS, MUSSELS, PIPIS or VONGOLE

4 live mud crabs
125 ml (4 fl oz/1/2 cup) oil
8 garlic cloves, chopped
4 banana chillies, chopped
4 tablespoons julienned fresh ginger
2 tablespoons chopped coriander root
250 ml (9 fl oz/1 cup) tomato sauce (ketchup)
125 ml (4 fl oz/1/2 cup) sweet chilli sauce (I like to use linghams chilli sauce)
375 ml (13 fl oz/1 1/2 cups) chicken stock or water
125 ml (4 fl oz/1/2 cup) hoisin sauce
2 tablespoons fish sauce
1–2 tablespoons sugar
2 teaspoons sea salt
a handful of chopped spring onion, green part only
a handful of mixed mint, Vietnamese mint and coriander leaves
30 cherry tomatoes, cut in half

Put the mud crabs in the freezer for about an hour until they are unconscious. Remove the top shell by lifting the flap on the underside. Remove the gills (the spongy grey fingers) and any muck by rinsing very lightly and quickly under running water.

Using a cleaver, cut the crabs in half lengthways, then cut into three on each side. Crack the claws with the back of a knife or cleaver so they open a bit to let the sauce in.

Heat the oil in a large wok and cook the garlic, chilli, ginger and coriander root until fragrant. Add the crabs and toss for about 1 minute until they change colour. Add the tomato sauce, chilli sauce, stock, hoisin sauce, fish sauce, sugar and salt, stir well and bring to the boil. Cover and leave to simmer for about 10 minutes. Add the spring onions, herbs and cherry tomatoes. Serve with steamed jasmine rice, crab crackers, crab pickers, finger bowls and bibs.

SERVES 4

hot and sour soup with **CRAB** meat and tofu

Hot and sour is a Chinese term for dishes flavoured with chilli, white pepper, sesame oil, garlic, ginger and vinegar. This soup is so nourishing and full of flavour on a cold night that you'll want seconds, and thirds. The white pepper creates a beautiful and unique flavour.

You could also use any sort of CRAB meat (spanner, blue swimmer, mud or king crab)

75 g (2¾ oz) cooked pork loin or Chinese roast pork
200 g (7 oz) crab meat
2 tablespoons finely sliced bamboo shoots
1 tablespoon cornflour
1 litre (35 fl oz/4 cups) chicken stock
8 shiitake mushrooms, stalks removed, finely sliced
4 wood-ear mushrooms, julienned
100 g (3½ oz) silken tofu, diced
1 tablespoon shaoxing rice wine
2 tablespoons light soy sauce
2 tablespoons Chinese black vinegar
25 g (1 oz) vermicelli rice noodles
2 eggs, lightly beaten
2 teaspoons white pepper
2 tablespoons finely chopped spring onion
chopped coriander leaves
1 teaspoon each of sesame oil and chilli oil, page 219

Shred the pork finely and mix with the crab, bamboo shoots and 1 teaspoon of the cornflour in a bowl.

Bring the stock to the boil in a large saucepan. Stir in the pork mixture, then both types of mushrooms, the tofu, rice wine, soy sauce, vinegar and some sea salt. Meanwhile, soak the noodles in hot water for 5 minutes, then drain, rinse in cold water and spoon into four bowls.

Mix the rest of the cornflour with enough cold water to make a paste, add to the soup and simmer until thickened.

In a steady stream, add the beaten egg to the pan and whisk with a fork to break it up. Cook for 1 minute.

Sprinkle the white pepper into the noodle bowls, pour the soup over the top and garnish with spring onions, chopped coriander, sesame oil and chilli oil.

SERVES 4

linguine with mud CRAB aglio e olio

Aglio e olio is known as the 'college meal' in Italy, as pasta with garlic and oil is basically one of the cheapest dinners a student can cook. That said, I believe it is also one of the best recipes in the world. However, my version isn't entirely Italian — I am also taking a bit of inspiration from the Thai food mantra here: hot, salty, sour and sweet. If you can balance those flavours, then you are considered a good cook. I am using the heat from the chilli, the salt from the anchovies, the sour from the lemon zest and the sweetness from the mud crab. I know the Italian college kids probably don't use mud crab, but it is too good an indulgence to pass up.

You could also use any sort of CRAB meat (spanner, blue swimmer or king crab), PRAWNS, SCALLOPS, MARRON or SQUID

- 500 g (1 lb 2 oz) fresh linguine
- 125 ml (4 fl oz/½ cup) olive oil
- 12 garlic cloves, finely chopped
- 2 banana chillies, finely chopped
- 4 tablespoons chopped flat-leaf (Italian) parsley
- 3 anchovies and a bit of the anchovy oil
- 320 g (11¼ oz) cooked mud crab meat
- 2 teaspoons grated lemon zest

Cook your pasta in boiling salted water until al dente. Meanwhile, heat the oil in a large frying pan with the garlic and chilli until they start to turn golden. Throw in the parsley and cook for 10 seconds to release the flavour. Add the anchovies and their oil and cook for a further minute, breaking up the anchovies as they cook.

Drain the hot pasta, add to the pan and toss. Add the crab meat, toss well and sprinkle with the grated lemon zest just before serving.

SERVES 4

What I live for... surfing and fishing safaris.

Astrid with a great snapper.
Noosa, QLD.

My favourite style of cooking.
Udo, Brandon and me, Port Douglas, QLD.

Fish, anyone?

The mighty marlin.

cuttlefish
white fish & whole fish flathead flounder garfish kingfish lobster mackerel mahi mahi mangrove jack

CUTTLEFISH in squid ink with risotto

If you are buying or catching fresh cuttlefish or squid then I believe you should try to use the whole creature, including its ink, at least once in your life. The best recipes for using the ink are risotto or pasta — they will turn the most wonderful deep black imaginable. I was taught this recipe by my friend John Lanzafame, who creates seriously good Italian food.

You could also use SQUID or OCTOPUS

2 tablespoons onion confit, page 226
2 tablespoons garlic confit, crushed, page 222
1 tablespoon chilli confit, page 217
600 g (1 lb 5 oz) cleaned cuttlefish, cut into 2 cm ($^3/_4$ inch) strips
2 quantities Italian tomato sauce, page 223
250 ml (9 fl oz/1 cup) fish stock
2 tablespoons chopped flat-leaf (Italian) parsley
4 tablespoons squid ink
300 g (10$^1/_2$ oz/1$^1/_2$ cups) arborio rice
100 ml (3$^1/_2$ fl oz) white wine
400 ml (14 fl oz) hot fish stock, extra
1 tablespoon butter
4 tablespoons crispy shallots, page 221
grated zest of 1 lemon

Cook half the onion, garlic and chilli confits in a saucepan until fragrant. Add the cuttlefish and stir for 1 minute, then add the tomato sauce, fish stock and parsley and simmer for 30 minutes over very low heat. Add the squid ink and simmer for a further 30 minutes until the cuttlefish is tender (add more stock if necessary). Season to taste and keep on one side.

Fry the remaining onion, garlic and chilli confits in a large heavy-based pan until fragrant. Add the rice and cook for a minute, stirring well to coat all the grains. Add the wine and stir for about 2 minutes until it has almost evaporated. Add the extra hot stock and stir well. Put the lid on the pan, turn the heat to its lowest setting and leave for 12–15 minutes, or until the rice is cooked. Stir in the butter and season with sea salt and cracked black pepper.

Spoon the risotto onto plates, arrange the squid ink cuttlefish in the centre of the rice and finish with crispy shallots and lemon zest.

SERVES 4

old-school FISH cakes

My brother-in-law, Udo, and I caught an Australian sea salmon last year and, as we were pulling the tinny into Bondi, we saw Heath Ledger having a barbie on the lawn next to ours. Udo went over, introduced himself and gave Heath the salmon. I said, 'Why are you giving him the worst fish of our catch?' and he laughed that Heath had been living in America for a while and he had to wean him back slowly onto the good stuff. No wonder Heath's packed his bags and moved back overseas — it wasn't the paparazzi; it was Udo and his bloody salmon.

You could also use any firm white-fleshed FISH or CRAB meat

200 g (7 oz) salmon or firm white fish, skin and bones removed, soaked in milk overnight
200 g (7 oz) salt cod mash, page 229, or plain mash
2 teaspoons chopped parsley
2 teaspoons chopped chives
2 teaspoons chopped chervil
2 teaspoons chopped tarragon
1 teaspoon finely chopped preserved lemon
1 teaspoon chilli confit, page 217
flour, for dusting
2 eggs, lightly beaten with 2 tablespoons milk
80 g (2^3/$_4$ oz/1 cup) fresh breadcrumbs
olive oil, for shallow-frying
wild rocket, seeded mustard mayonnaise (page 224), lemon wedges, to serve

Finely chop the fish and gently mix with the salt cod mash, the herbs, preserved lemon and chilli and season with salt and pepper. Squeeze small handfuls of the mixture into small flat patties.

Put the flour in a flat bowl, the egg mix in another bowl and the breadcrumbs in a third bowl. Dust the fish cakes in flour, dip in the egg mix and coat in breadcrumbs. Heat the oil in a large heavy-based frying pan and shallow-fry the cakes until golden on each side, then lift out and drain on kitchen paper. Serve with rocket leaves, seeded mustard mayonnaise and lemon wedges.

SERVES 4 AS A STARTER

mexican **FISH** tortillas with guacamole

I was born in Melbourne, raised in Queensland and now live in Sydney and one thing that really annoys me is the way each place has something negative to say about the other. Unfortunately, I tend to take offence at every insult, as I consider myself as belonging to three states. I guess the oddest thing I've been called is a Mexican (as in, from south of the border). So, this recipe is a tribute to anyone from south of any border. It is the perfect dish for when you have a lot of people round and want to have a bit of fun with the food.

You could also use any firm white-fleshed FISH

8 x 60 g (2¼ oz) pieces warehou fillet
8 flour tortillas
8 tablespoons sour cream or crème fraiche
4 tablespoons tomato salsa sauce (from the supermarket)
2 handfuls of shredded purple cabbage or any type of lettuce

GUACAMOLE
1 avocado, finely diced
2 tomatoes, finely diced
1 bird's eye chilli, chopped
juice of 1 lime, plus 2 limes, cut into quarters to serve
1-2 tablespoons finely diced red onion
1 garlic clove, finely chopped
2 tablespoons chopped coriander
1 tablespoon extra virgin olive oil

Season the fish with salt and pepper, brush with a touch of oil and cook in a frying pan or on your barbecue for a few minutes on each side until cooked through.

Clean the pan or barbecue and place the tortillas on until they heat up (you want to lightly toast, not burn, them).

To make the guacamole, mix the avocado, tomato, chilli, lime juice, onion, garlic, coriander and olive oil together.

Fill the tortillas with the fish pieces, guacamole, sour cream, tomato salsa and purple cabbage and squeeze a bit of lime juice over the top.

SERVES 4

steamed whole FISH with shaoxing wine and soy

So many times in cooking, a food is really defined by the sauce with which it is served. The sauce is intended to enliven the palate and enhance the flavours of the food; it should absolutely never be overpowering. This recipe defines how a simple flavoursome sauce can really be a fish's best friend. I like to use coral trout or morwong for this dish.

You could also use SCALLOPS, PRAWNS, LOBSTER, BUGS, OYSTERS, SCAMPI, PIPIS, MARRON, CRAB or any firm white-fleshed FISH

2 whole fish (about 800 g/ 1 lb 12 oz each), scaled and gutted
125 ml (4 fl oz/½ cup) shaoxing rice wine
125 ml (4 fl oz/½ cup) light soy sauce
6 spring onions, julienned, keep the white and green parts separate (keep the green part in cold water in the fridge)
250–500 ml (9–17 fl oz/ 1–2 cups) peanut oil
4 garlic cloves, finely sliced
2 banana chilies, finely sliced
3 tablespoons julienned fresh ginger
4 tablespoons chilli sauce
a handful of coriander leaves
8 lime wedges

Make three incisions through the skin into the flesh on both sides of each fish and then put the fish on a plate in a steamer. Mix together the rice wine and soy sauce and pour over the fish. Sprinkle the white julienned spring onion over the fish, cover and cook until the flesh is cooked through but still moist. Take the fish out of the steamer and serve it on the plate you cooked it on.

Meanwhile, heat the peanut oil in a saucepan and cook the garlic, banana chillies and ginger over medium–high heat until golden and crispy. Remove and drain on kitchen paper.

Drizzle the chilli sauce over the fish, top with the coriander and green spring onions, scatter with the crispy garlic, chilli and ginger and serve with lime wedges, steamed rice, Asian greens and a cold Asian beer.

SERVES 4

steamed whole fish with shaoxing wine and soy

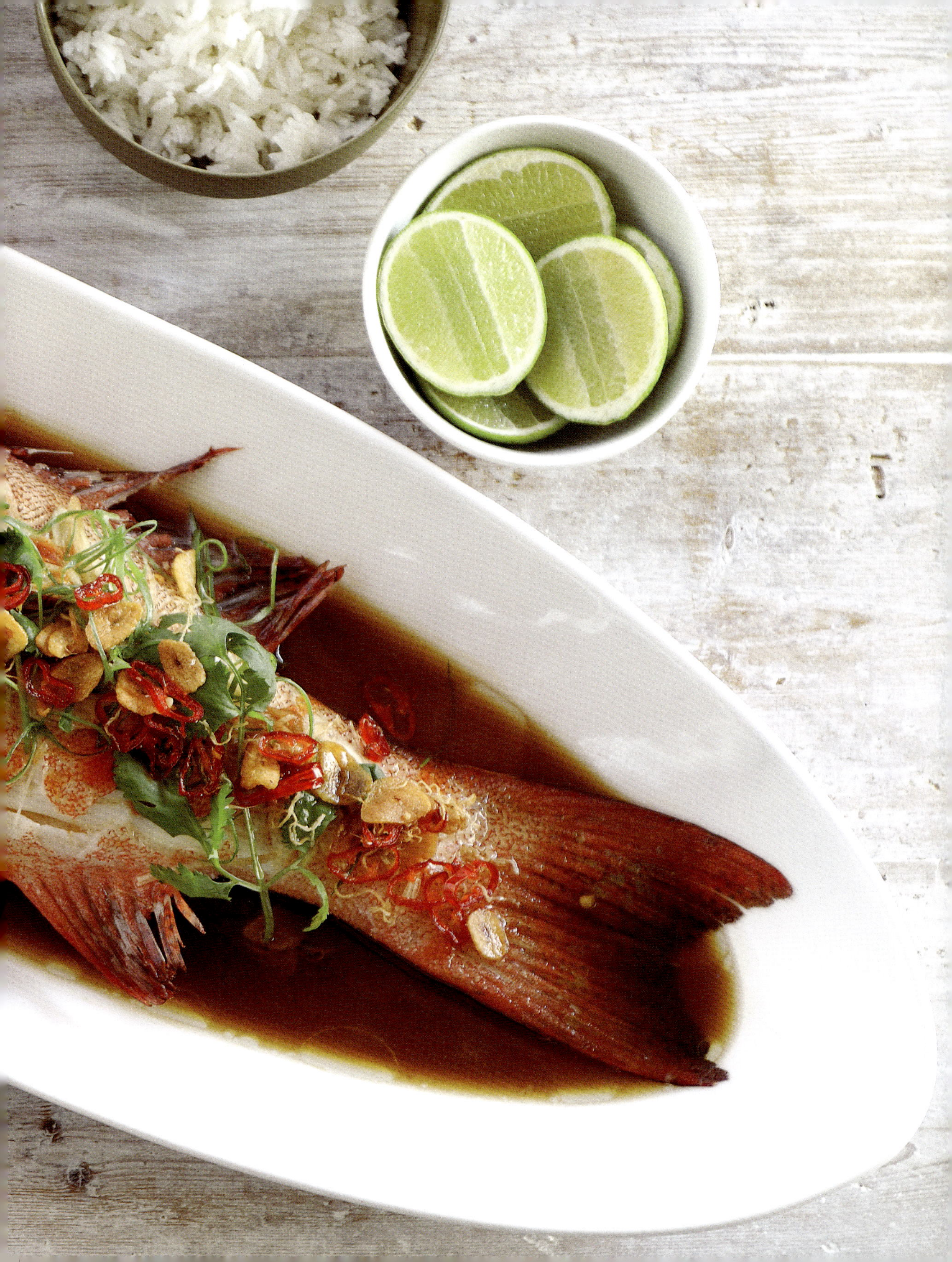

FISH laksa

What does 'laksa' mean? Loosely translated it means 'many', probably because there are so many bloody ingredients that go into making a good laksa. This wonderful spicy noodle soup originates from South East Asia where there are many different variations — made with or without coconut milk, depending on what country you're eating in. This is the favourite staff meal we cook in the restaurant (using off-cuts of fish so that nothing gets wasted). You really can use just about any firm white fish for this, but I particularly like using the jewfish because it is quite meaty and can easily stand up to the strong Asian flavours.

You could also use PRAWNS, BUGS, MUSSELS or any firm white-fleshed FISH

LAKSA PASTE
10 dried chillies (or 3 fresh bird's eye chillies)
1 teaspoon coriander seeds
1 teaspoon fennel seeds
seeds of 4 cardamom pods
1 teaspoon cumin seeds
4 cloves
1 red onion, roughly chopped
a pinch of sea salt
2 tablespoons chopped fresh ginger
1 tablespoon chopped galangal
4 garlic cloves
1 teaspoon chopped fresh turmeric (or $1/2$ teaspoon ground turmeric)
1 lemongrass stalk (the bottom third of the stalk only), chopped
6 candlenuts (or macadamia nuts)
10 Vietnamese mint leaves

Soak the dried chillies in hot water for 20 minutes, then drain. Finely grind the coriander seeds, fennel seeds, cardamom seeds and cloves with a mortar and pestle or spice grinder, then transfer to a blender with the chillies. Add the rest of the ingredients for the laksa paste and blend until smooth.

This will make about a cupful of paste, which is enough to make two batches of laksa. Any paste that you are not using immediately can be stored in a sterilised screw-top jar — one that has been either washed and dried at high temperature in a dishwasher, or washed by hand and then dried in a warm oven. Put the paste in the jar and then pour a little oil into the jar to cover the surface of the laksa paste.

This will keep in the fridge for up to a month. Alternatively, you can put the paste in an airtight container and freeze for 6 months or so.

Put the noodles in a bowl, pour hot water from the kettle over them and leave for 3 minutes before draining off the water. Alternatively, cook the noodles according to the packet instructions. Rinse the noodles in cold water and set aside.

Fry the laksa paste for 1 minute in a large saucepan until it becomes fragrant. Add the palm sugar and stir over the heat until dissolved. Add the fish sauce and fry for 5 seconds to release the flavour, then add the coconut milk and bring to the boil. Boil gently for 5 minutes, then add the stock, bring back to the boil and simmer for 10 minutes. Season with the lime juice.

½ teaspoon shrimp paste (available at Asian grocery stores)
1 bunch of coriander, including the roots and stems
½ teaspoon ground cinnamon

300 g (10½ oz) packet glass noodles (or other noodles if you prefer them)
125 ml (4 fl oz/½ cup) laksa paste, above
2 teaspoons grated palm sugar
1½ tablespoons fish sauce
750 ml (26 fl oz/3 cups) coconut milk
750 ml (26 fl oz/3 cups) chicken stock
1 tablespoon lime juice
240 g (9 oz) black jewfish or mulloway fillet, cut into bite-sized cubes
160 g (5¾ oz) bean sprouts
½ Lebanese cucumber, deseeded and julienned
1 kaffir lime leaf, very finely shredded
8 Vietnamese mint leaves
16 coriander leaves
2 bird's eye chillies, thinly sliced
1 quantity crispy shallots, page 221

Turn the heat off and add the fish cubes to the soup. Leave for a few minutes for the fish to poach (it will continue to cook in the bowls).

Spoon about a cupful of noodles into each bowl and top with the bean sprouts, cucumber and then fish. Pour the soup over the top and garnish with kaffir lime, Vietnamese mint and coriander leaves, chilli and crispy shallots.

SERVES 4

ho mok pla (steamed **FISH** curry)

Udo, my brother-in-law, and I were hunting the elusive jungle perch in Far North Queensland and I had this recipe in mind after a recent trip to Thailand. However, after talking to the locals about the fragility of the jungle perch population, we couldn't bring ourselves to eat the one that we'd amazingly managed to catch. Luckily we ran into some aboriginal men who had speared a blue-tail mullet and offered to share (it was a bloody big fish). So I substituted the mullet for the perch (a little like substituting a kombi van for a Ferrari). The end result was nothing short of a culinary masterpiece and I love the way there is a bit of alchemy left in the world.

You could also use any firm white-fleshed FISH, CRAB, PRAWNS, SCALLOP, LOBSTER or BUGS

200 g (7 oz) blue-tailed mullet fillet, skin and bones removed
2 eggs
3 tablespoons coconut milk
1 tablespoon fish sauce
1 tablespoon grated palm sugar, melted
1–2 teaspoons red curry paste
1 tablespoon finely sliced kaffir lime leaf
1 chilli, finely chopped
juice of 1 lime
8 banana leaf crosses, cut from 25 cm (12 inch) squares
10 Thai basil or coriander leaves

Finely dice the fish and place in a chilled bowl. Mix together the eggs, coconut milk, fish sauce, palm sugar, curry paste, kaffir lime leaf, chilli and lime juice and then stir through the diced fish.

Lay a banana leaf cross on your bench top, shiny side down, and fold three arms of the cross together to make a pouch. Spoon the fish mixture into the pouches, with a few leaves of Thai basil. Fold the last arm over to make a parcel and secure with short bamboo skewers.

Put the parcels in a steamer over simmering water and steam for about 5 minutes or until the fish is cooked through (open a parcel to check — it should look like a just-set custard). Cut open the parcels and serve with lime wedges and crispy shallots.

SERVES 4 AS A STARTER

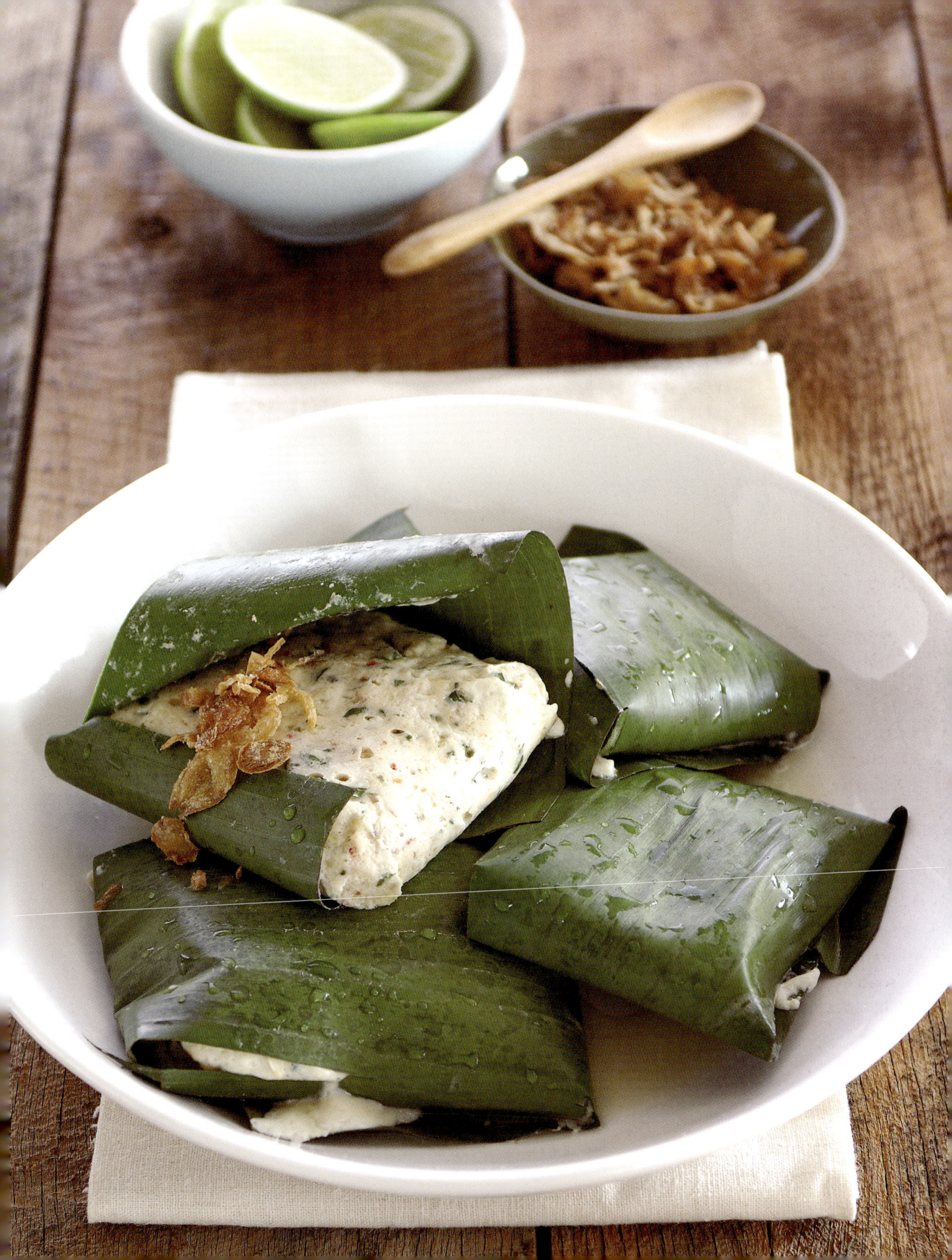

barbecued whole FISH with green mango relish

My partner, Astrid, is a wonderful cook, even if her repertoire only holds about four recipes. That said, she has honed those four dishes to nothing short of perfection. This is her recipe for a green mango relish that was taught to her over a decade ago by a Thai lady in Far North Queensland. It works really well with fried fish, too.

You could also use any whole FISH or fillets, or just about any of the CRUSTACEANS

2 whole small red emperors, scaled and gutted
1 tablespoon extra virgin olive oil
herbs and aromatics for stuffing (such as parsley, coriander, Thai basil, lemon slices, peppercorns, garlic, ginger, kaffir lime)

GREEN MANGO RELISH
1½ tablespoons grated palm sugar or caster sugar
1½ tablespoons fish sauce
1 green mango, peeled and finely grated
1½ tablespoons lime juice
2 red Asian shallots, finely diced (or 1 tablespoon finely diced red onion)
1 bird's eye chilli, finely chopped
1 tablespoon chopped coriander leaves
1 kaffir lime leaf, julienned

Preheat your barbecue. Rub the fish with olive oil and fill the stomach cavity with your choice of herbs and aromatics.

Put the fish on the barbecue and cook for 10 minutes on one side, then turn over and barbecue until cooked through. Alternatively, cook on a roasting tray in the oven at 180°C (350°F/Gas 4).

To make the relish, melt the palm sugar in a saucepan and add the fish sauce, then mix with the green mango, lime juice, Asian shallots, chilli, coriander and kaffir lime. Serve with the fish.

SERVES 4

baked FISH with organic lemon jam

I love the idea of cooking a fish whole and just serving it with a couple of condiments — that way, people can appreciate the full, unadulterated flavour of the fish or add a touch of something to spice it up if they like. This lemon jam recipe is a wonderful addition to the table for a whole barbecued fish — you use the whole lemon, skin and all, so make sure you use organic or thin-skinned fruit without wax on them.

Any whole FISH or fillets work a treat with this lemon jam

2 medium-sized mangrove jack, or other whole fish suitable for baking or barbecuing
olive oil, for coating
herbs and aromatics for stuffing (such as parsley, coriander, Thai basil, lemon slices, peppercorns, garlic, ginger, kaffir lime)

ORGANIC LEMON JAM
1 organic lemon, thoroughly scrubbed, roughly chopped, pips removed
1 teaspoon sea salt
2 tablespoons sugar
2 tablespoons extra virgin olive oil
1 tablespoon oregano or basil leaves

Rub the fish with olive oil and fill the stomach cavity with your choice of herbs and aromatics. Preheat your oven to 160°C (315°F/Gas 2–3) and cook the fish until it is cooked through (or put it on a piece of foil rubbed with butter, fold up into a parcel and bake on the barbie for about 10 minutes on each side).

To make the jam, put the lemon, salt, sugar and some cracked pepper in a food processor and purée, drizzling in the olive oil as you mix. Add the herbs and continue blending for 20 seconds. Taste and adjust the seasoning before serving with the fish.

SERVES 4

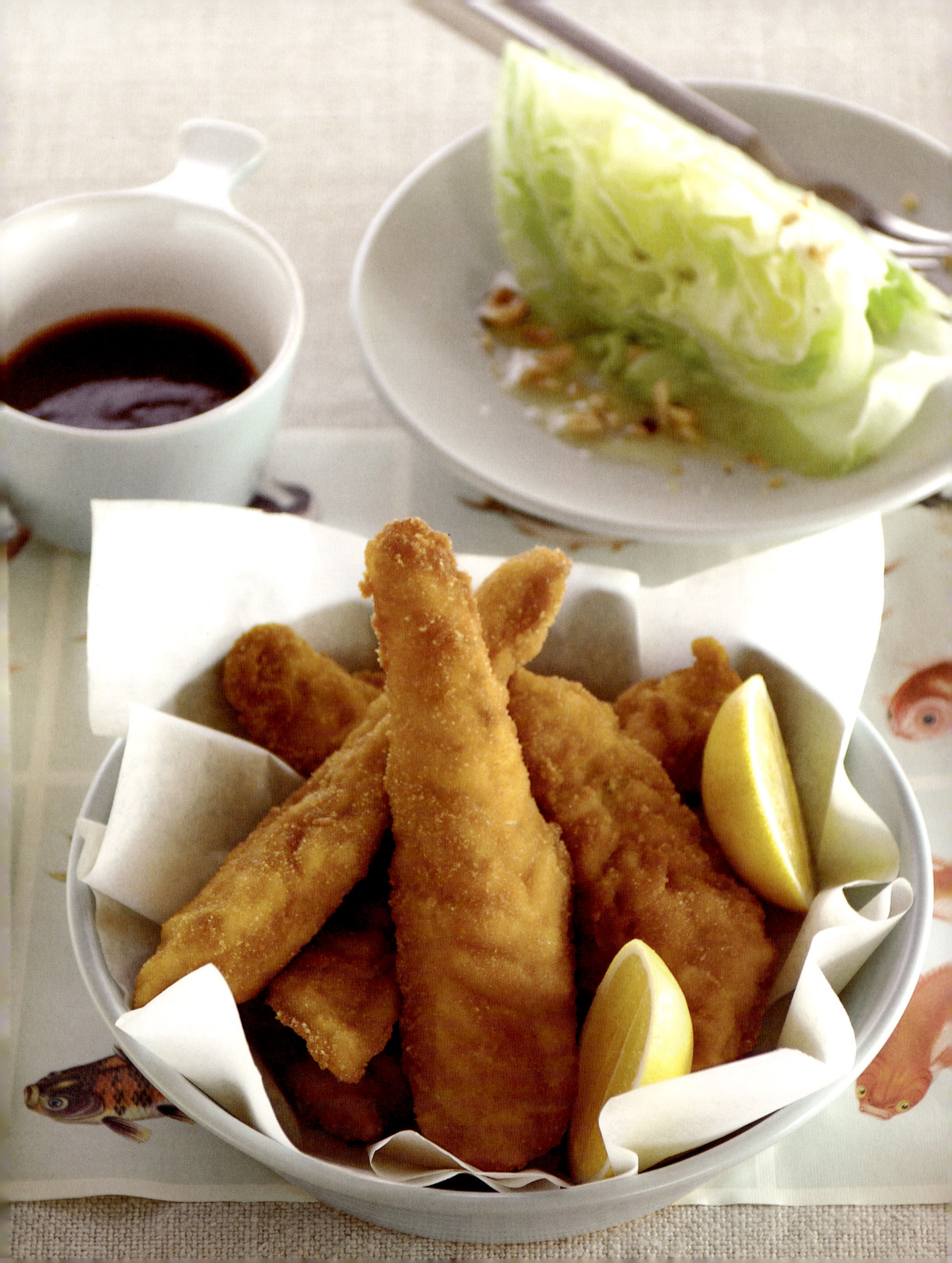

crumbed FLATHEAD with chilli sauce and iceberg lettuce

Of all the fish in the ocean, flathead would have to be one of the most primitive looking. I get the feeling that, just like sharks, they might have been cruising the world's waters for millions of years — maybe that's why they taste so bloody good. This fish would have to be in my Top Five and I love to prepare it the simplest of ways... crumbed. There is a secret that I have learnt along the way: that the best way to crumb a fish, especially flathead, is with the world's favourite brand of cornflakes.

You could also use any firm white-fleshed FISH or CRUSTACEAN

1 tablespoon roasted crushed hazelnuts
4 tablespoons extra virgin olive oil
1 tablespoon white wine vinegar
1 iceberg lettuce, cut into 8 wedges
60 g (2 oz/½ cup) plain flour
2 eggs, lightly beaten
50 g (1¾ oz/1 cup) Kellogg's cornflakes crumbs
about 700 g (1 lb 9 oz) flathead fillets, skin and bones removed
125 ml (4 fl oz/½ cup) grapeseed oil
lemon wedges and chilli sauce (I like linghams), to serve

Whisk together the hazelnuts, olive oil and vinegar to make a dressing and dress the lettuce.

Put the flour in one shallow bowl, the egg in another and the cornflake crumbs in a third. Lightly season the fish with some sea salt, then dust lightly with flour and coat in the egg and then the cornflake crumbs, patting the crumbs on firmly.

Heat the oil in a frying pan and fry the fish for 30–45 seconds until golden and crispy, then turn over and cook for a further 30 seconds until crispy on that side.

Drain on kitchen paper and serve with lemon wedges, chilli sauce and the dressed iceberg lettuce.

SERVES 4

tetsuya's warm **FLATHEAD** carpaccio with black bean dressing

I have had the good fortune in my life to meet some of my idols face to face, and the highlight so far was when Tetsuya Wakuda agreed to be a part of my fishing show. We had a wonderful day fishing off Udo's Chinese junk for flathead and snapper and then headed off to Tetsuya's restaurant with our catch. He prepared the most amazing dish I have ever tried in my life and I'm very honoured that he's agreed to share it here. Thanks, Tets.

You could also use KINGFISH, JEWFISH or SNAPPER

- 4 tablespoons dried wakame seaweed
- 200 g (7 oz) flathead fillet
- lots of ground white pepper
- 4 tablespoons finely julienned fresh ginger
- 4 tablespoons grapeseed oil
- 1 bunch of coriander, with roots and stalks
- 2½ tablespoons soy sauce
- 3 tablespoons mirin
- 100 ml (3½ fl oz) chicken stock
- 2 teaspoons chopped salted fermented black beans
- ½ garlic clove, minced
- 1 teaspoon chopped chilli
- 1 small rasher bacon
- 2 spring onions, white part only, finely sliced
- grated zest of 1 orange
- 4 spring onions, green part only, finely sliced
- 2 tablespoons snipped chives

Preheat the oven to 150°C (300°F/Gas 2). Soak the wakame seaweed in water for 10 minutes to soften it, then drain.

Make sure you remove all the skin from the flathead. Starting at the tail, slice the flathead paper-thin on an angle. Lay the fish out, slightly overlapping, on a platter or individual plates. Season with lots of freshly ground white pepper and the ginger. Drizzle with the grapeseed oil to coat the fish lightly.

Put the plate in the oven for 2–3 minutes, or until the plate is hot and the fish is just starting to cook slightly (but still rare to raw).

Prepare the coriander: finely chop the roots and measure out 1 teaspoonful. Finely chop the stalks and measure out 1 teaspoonful. Keep the leaves whole — you will need a small handful.

To make the dressing, heat the soy, mirin and chicken stock until simmering. Add the black beans, garlic, chilli and coriander root. Cut the bacon into julienne strips (you need about 2 tablespoons) and add to the pan. Remove from the heat and add the coriander stalks.

Drizzle some warm dressing over the fish and then top with the seaweed, white spring onion and orange zest. Spoon some more dressing over these and then finish with the green spring onions, coriander leaves and chives.

SERVES 4 AS A STARTER

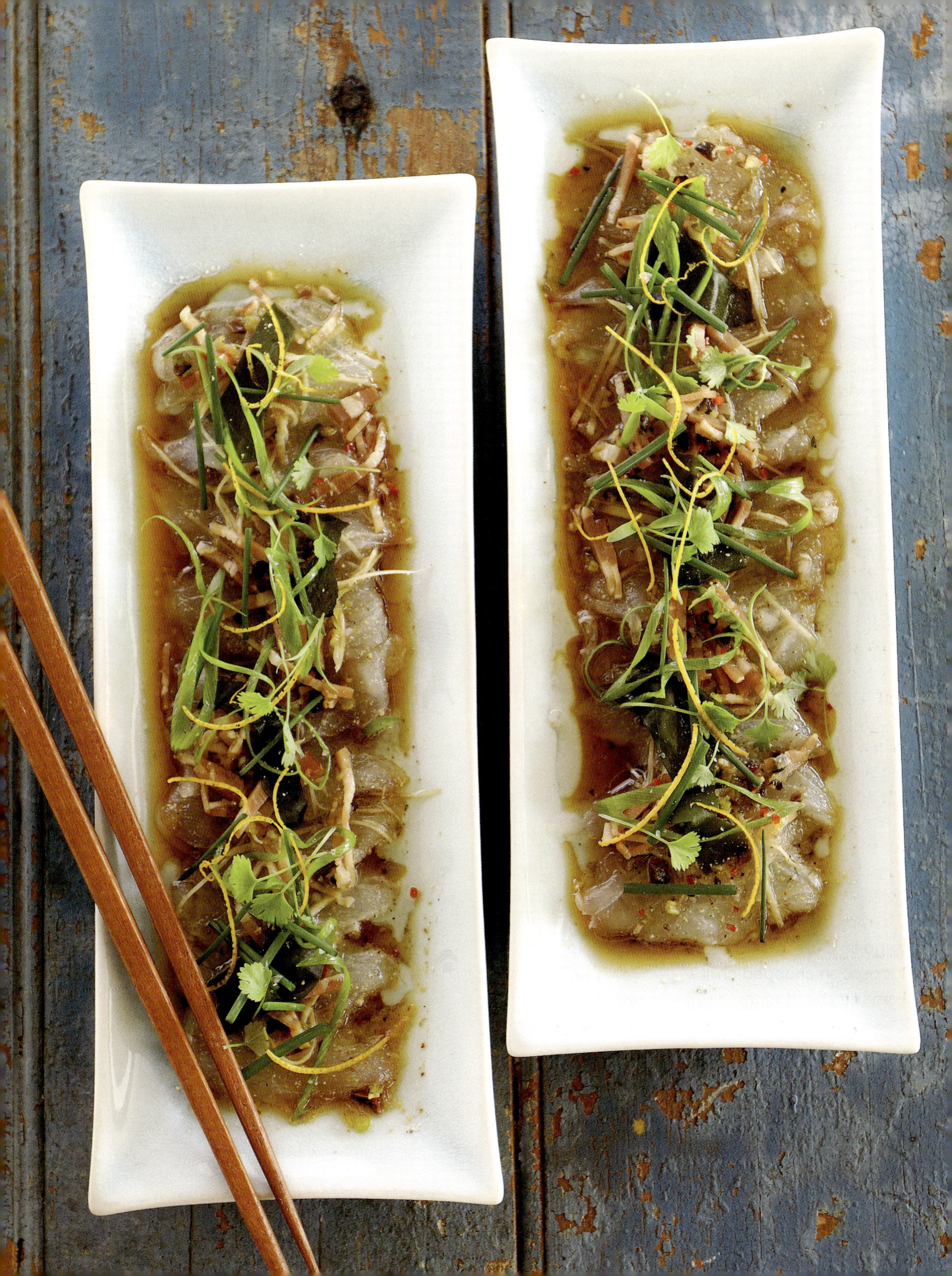

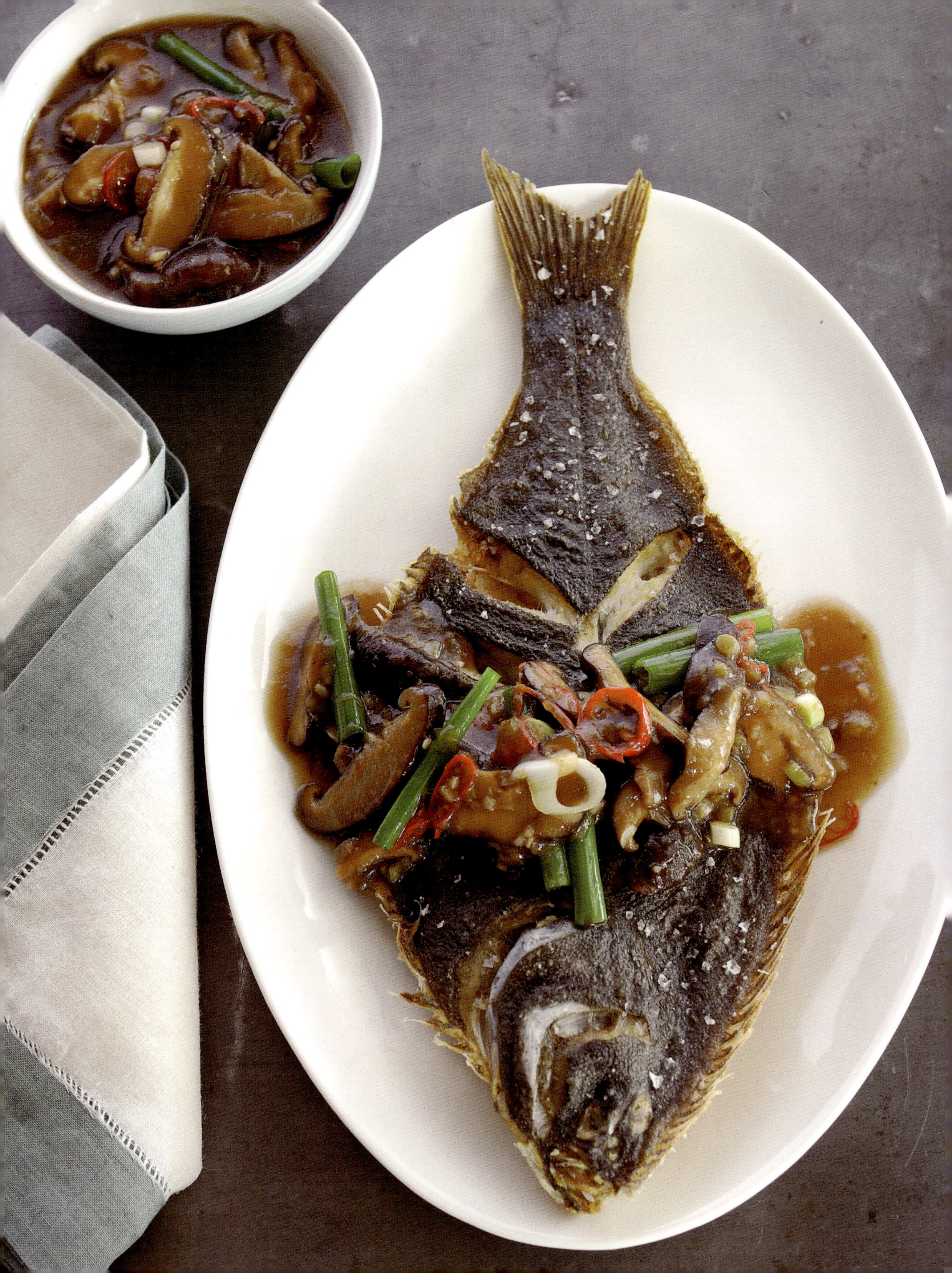

deep-fried FLOUNDER with chinese shiitake mushroom sauce

I have been very blessed to be around great cooks all my life, from my mum, brother and sister, to all the people I've worked with over the last two decades who have shaped the way I cook today. The person who has been the greatest influence over the last few years would have to be Poldy, my mother-in-law. She is the best cook I have come across, with a true passion for food. She produces two or three steaming hot dishes every night without fail, plus rice and vegies. I think she may be the best Chinese cook in Australia — which is not bad, considering she emigrated from Austria close to fifty years ago.

You could also use SOLE, SNAPPER, CORAL TROUT or RED EMPEROR

12 dried Chinese shiitake mushrooms

oil, for deep-frying (I use peanut, vegetable or grapeseed)

4 whole flounder, scored on both sides

plain flour, for dusting

4 garlic cloves, finely minced

1 tablespoon grated fresh ginger

1–2 bird's eye chillies, finely chopped

4 spring onions, white part only, finely sliced

125 ml (4 fl oz/^{1}/$_2$ cup) oyster sauce

2 tablespoons cornflour

6 spring onions, green part only, finely sliced (kept in iced water)

lemon wedges (you decide)

Soak the shiitake mushrooms in a couple of cupfuls of hot water for about 10 minutes, then drain (saving the water). Discard the stalks and slice the mushrooms.

Heat the oil for deep-frying in a large wok or deep-fat fryer to 185°C (365°F) — either measure this with a thermometer or drop a cube of bread into the oil: it should brown in about 10 seconds. Season the fish with sea salt and dust lightly with flour. Pop the fish carefully into the hot oil and cook for 5 minutes, or until the flesh is cooked through and the skin is crispy and golden. Lift out and drain on kitchen paper, then put on a plate.

Meanwhile, heat a wok with a touch of oil and cook the garlic, ginger and chilli until fragrant. Add the white spring onion and cook for 30 seconds more. Add the mushrooms, oyster sauce and about 250 ml (9 fl oz/1 cup) of the mushroom soaking water. Mix the cornflour with 125 ml (4 fl oz/^{1}/$_2$ cup) of water, stir in to the sauce and cook for about 2 minutes. If the sauce seems too thick after 2 minutes, stir in some more mushroom water (or tap water) until you like the consistency.

Pour the sauce over the top of the fish and finish with the green spring onions. You could serve with some lemon wedges as well, if you like a bit of acidity.

SERVES 4

salt and pepper FLOUNDER

I get so excited when I visit South Australia — I think Adelaide might just be my favourite city to eat in (well, for their Chinese food anyway). Their Chinatown, in Gouger Street, is alive with energy and beautiful wafting aromas that make you want to visit every restaurant. My favourite spot would have to be Yin Chow and the highlight for me is their salt and pepper flounder. This is the way this fish is meant to be eaten — again and again.

You could also use any firm white whole FISH or fillets, SQUID, PRAWNS or OYSTERS

1 quantity Szechuan spice mix, page 230
60 g (2 oz/$1/2$ cup) plain flour
4 whole flounder, scaled and gutted
vegetable oil, for deep-frying
2 tablespoons finely chopped garlic
2 tablespoons finely chopped banana chilli
6 spring onions, green part only, finely sliced
lemon wedges, to serve

Mix half the Szechuan spice mix with the flour. Score the fish with three incisions into each fillet (there are two fillets on each side of the fish), then dust with the spiced flour. Heat the oil in a deep-fat fryer or large wok to 185°C (365°C) — either measure this with a thermometer or drop a cube of bread into the oil: it should brown in about 10 seconds. Deep-fry the fish for about 5 minutes or until the flesh is white and the skin golden and crispy. Drain on kitchen paper.

Deep-fry the garlic and chilli until golden and crispy. Remove with a slotted spoon and drain on kitchen paper.

Arrange the fish on plates and sprinkle with more spice mix, the garlic and chilli and the spring onions. Serve with lemon wedges.

SERVES 4

pan-fried GARFISH with sea urchin butter

One of the highlights of writing a book is coming up with new recipes. This is one of my favourite dishes in the book — it really shows off two fantastic and under-rated seafoods with a minimum of fuss.

You could also use PRAWNS, LOBSTER, SCAMPI, BUGS or WHITING

14 sea urchin roe
120 g (4 oz) unsalted butter, softened
grated zest of 1 lemon
8 butterflied whole garfish, heads and bones removed
3 tablespoons white wine
1 tablespoon lemon juice

To make the sea urchin butter, finely dice the sea urchin roe and fold through the butter. Fold in the lemon zest, some sea salt and cracked white pepper and then wrap in plastic wrap and refrigerate if you're not using it immediately.

Heat the sea urchin butter in a large frying pan until it starts to foam. Add the garfish, skin side down, and cook for 15 seconds. Turn over and cook for another 15 seconds, then lift out onto a serving plate. Add the wine and lemon juice to the pan to deglaze. Season to taste and pour over the fish. Serve with a crisp garden salad.

SERVES 4

salad of fennel-crusted KINGFISH with grapefruit and mint

I have written earlier about aquaculture in Australia and won't dwell on it here, but the eating qualities of the farmed Hiramasa kingfish are astonishing. The fat content in these reared fish is about twenty per cent, which makes them perfect for sushi or eating raw or rare. You can buy the lemon-infused olive oil from a deli or good supermarket. The spice mix of fennel seed, black peppercorns and sea salt rubbed on the fish makes it very addictive and will have you wanting more... and more and more.

You could also use TUNA, SALMON, PRAWNS or SCALLOPS

4 x 80 g (2¾ oz) kingfish fillets, skin and bones removed
2 tablespoons fennel seed and pepper spice mix, page 222
1 tablespoon olive oil
2 handfuls of finely sliced fennel
16 pink grapefruit segments
16 mint leaves
juice of 1 lemon
3–4 tablespoons lemon-infused olive oil
4 anchovies, finely diced
1 long red chilli, finely sliced
2–3 handfuls of watercress leaves

Roll the kingfish fillets in the spice mix. Heat the olive oil in a frying pan and cook the kingfish for about 30 seconds on each side, until it is sealed evenly but still rare in the middle. Take the fish out of the pan and let it rest for a few minutes.

Mix together the rest of the ingredients to make the salad and spoon onto plates. Slice the kingfish and arrange on top of the salad.

SERVES 4 AS A STARTER

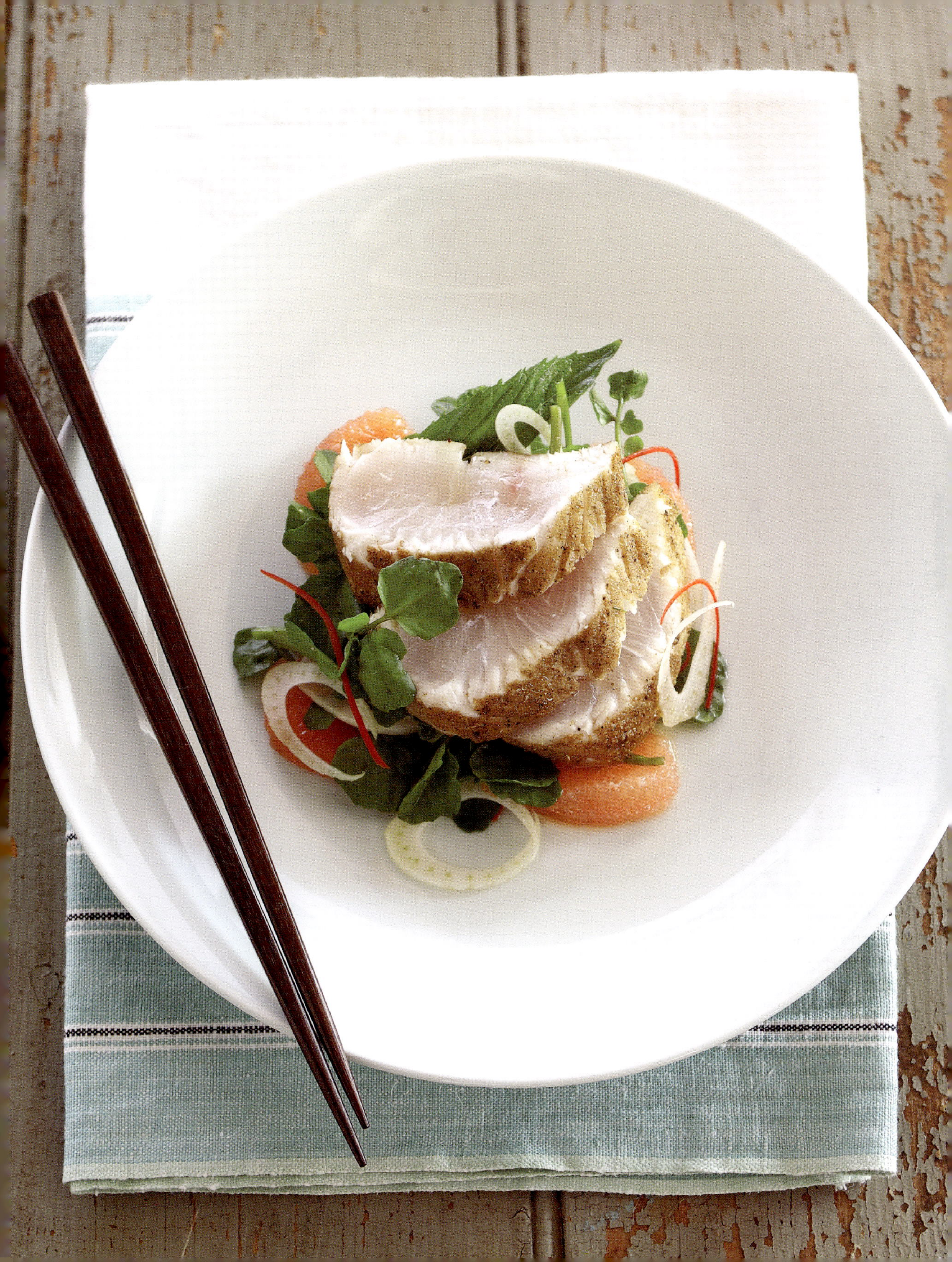

KINGFISH sashimi with pineapple, crispy shallots and nam jim

When I'm designing a dish, I always look for a few main points: flavour and taste, smell, eye appeal, texture and seasonality. So, I start with a blank canvas (or plate, in this instance) and start building with those features in mind. This simple recipe gets a big tick in every column.

You could also use OCEAN TROUT, TUNA, SALMON, SPANISH MACKEREL, CORAL TROUT, JEWFISH, PRAWNS, SCALLOPS or OYSTERS

240 g (9 oz) sashimi-grade kingfish fillet, skin and bones removed
2 tablespoons nam jim dressing, page 225
2 Thai basil leaves, julienned
2 tablespoons finely diced ripe pineapple
2 tablespoons crispy shallots, page 221

Slice the kingfish fillet thinly and evenly and arrange on four plates. Dress with the nam jim and then scatter with basil, pineapple and crispy shallots.

SERVES 4

stir-fried rock **LOBSTER** with chilli jam

Chilli jam works fantastically well with a lot of seafood, whether it's cooked into a dish, as in this recipe, served on the side, or even spread over the top of a fish after barbecuing. It adds an element of richness and heat that really gets the taste buds working. For this dish I like to cut the rock lobster into medallions and stir-fry it with the shell on — I find it gives the dish a real depth of flavour.

You could also use CRAB, BUGS, PRAWNS, any reef FISH or MUSSELS

2 x 800 g (1 lb 12 oz) live rock lobsters
4 tablespoons grapeseed oil
4 banana chillies, cut down the middle lengthways, seeds removed
4 garlic cloves, finely sliced
2 tablespoons julienned fresh ginger
4 tablespoons chilli jam, page 218
100 ml ($3^1/2$ fl oz) chicken stock
2 tablespoons oyster sauce
2 tablespoons fish sauce
1 tablespoon sugar
a handful of coriander leaves
a handful of Thai basil leaves
8 Vietnamese mint leaves
2 kaffir lime leaves, julienned
juice of 2 limes

Put the lobsters in the freezer for a couple of hours until they're unconscious. Put each lobster on a chopping board with the head towards you. Place a sharp knife between the eyes and cut through the head. Remove the head and reserve any mustard to add to the sauce if you like. Use a cleaver or heavy-duty kitchen knife to cut the lobsters into 2.5 cm (1 inch) thick medallions, leaving the shell on.

Heat the oil in your wok and fry the chillies, garlic and ginger until fragrant. Add the lobster and toss well, then add the chilli jam, stock, oyster sauce, fish sauce and sugar and any mustard from the head.

Cook for 4–5 minutes (adding more stock if necessary), then add the herbs, kaffir lime leaves and lime juice and serve immediately with steamed rice.

SERVES 4

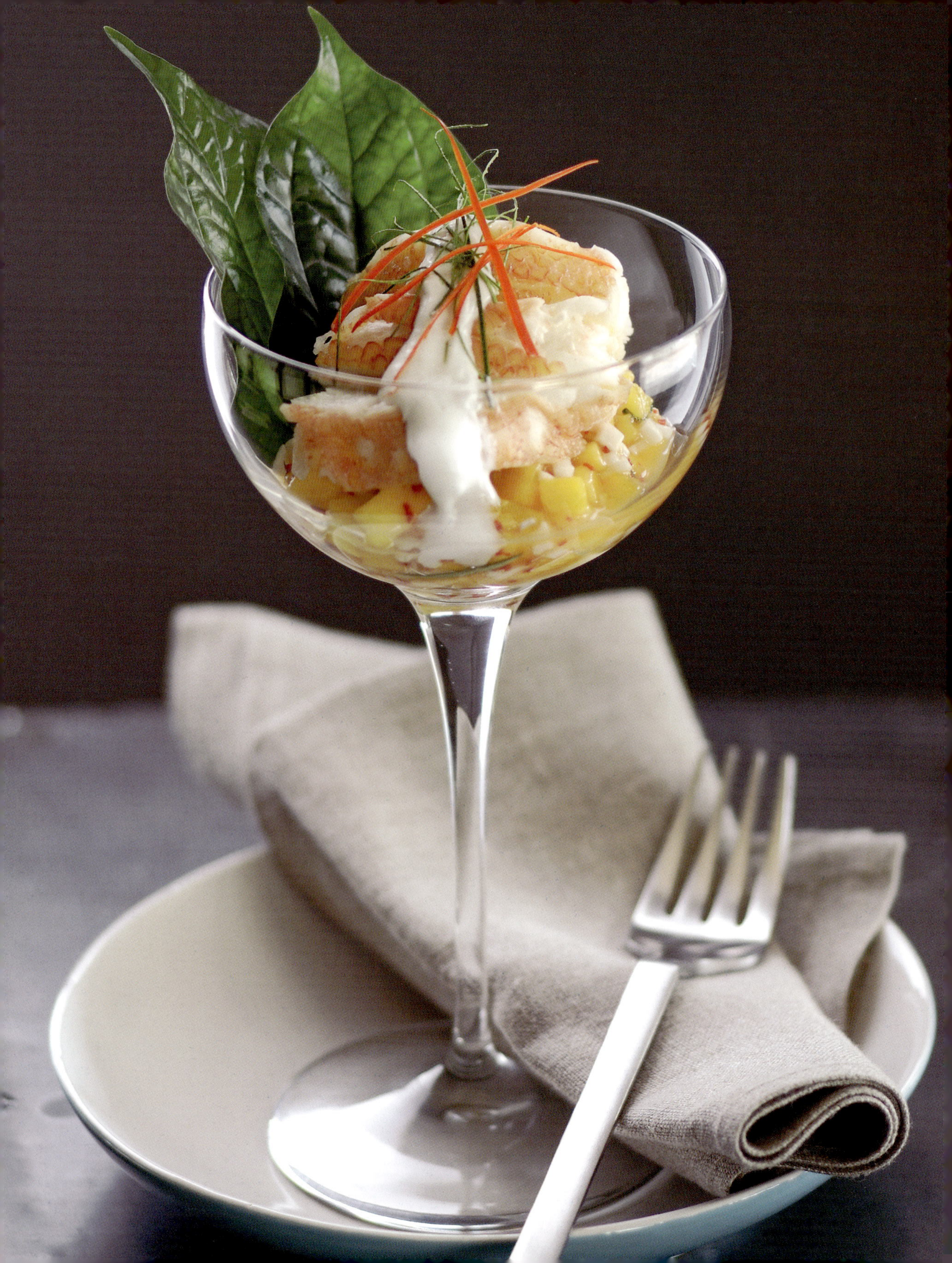

LOBSTER martini

I was invited to cater for the Prince and Princess of Denmark a year or so ago and was quietly scared at the prospect — seven courses, two hundred people, and cooking in someone's mansion. John Pye, my head chef at the time, was tinkering with a variation on prawn cocktail using lobster and mango. When he had finally perfected the dish, I thought we should serve it to the royals — well a girl from Tassie should love a bit of local rock lobster, don't you think?

You could also use PRAWNS, CRAB meat or BUGS

MANGO SALSA
1–2 ripe mangoes, peeled and diced
6 tablespoons finely diced young coconut flesh
1 large red chilli, finely diced
juice of 2 limes
9 Thai basil leaves, julienned

1 x 1 kg (2 lb 4 oz) rock lobster, cooked and shell removed
125 ml (4 fl oz/$1/2$ cup) coconut dressing, page 220
2 kaffir lime leaves, julienned
julienned red chilli and betel leaves, to serve

Have 4 martini glasses ready. Mix the mango, coconut flesh, chilli, lime juice and Thai basil together to make the salsa. Spoon 2 tablespoons of salsa into the bottom of each martini glass.

Slice the lobster into 1 cm ($1/2$ inch) thick medallions (you should have about 12 of them). Put three slices of lobster in each glass, then dress with the coconut dressing. Add a touch more salsa on top and finish with the kaffir lime strips and a garnish of red chilli and betel leaves.

SERVES 4 AS A STARTER

san choy bau of slipper LOBSTER and water chestnuts

If you have never made san choy bau before, I urge you to try it at least once. It is so simple and the flavour is so rewarding. It's very adaptable and is a great dish to start children on if they think they aren't keen on seafood.

You could also use PRAWNS, CRAB meat, SCALLOPS, BUGS or even white-fleshed FISH

200 g (7 oz) slipper lobster tail meat, finely diced
200 g (7 oz) pork loin, finely diced or minced
90 ml (3 fl oz) light soy sauce
3½ tablespoons shaoxing rice wine
2½ tablespoons sesame oil
6 dried Chinese mushrooms
vegetable oil, for stir-frying
2 spring onions, finely sliced
2 tablespoons finely chopped fresh ginger
100 g (3½ oz) water chestnuts, finely chopped
1 teaspoon salt
1 teaspoon sugar
1 teaspoon cornflour
8 iceberg lettuce leaves, shaped to form cups (keep in a bowl of iced water to stay crisp)

Put the lobster and pork in a bowl with half the soy sauce, half the wine and half the sesame oil. Mix together gently and leave to marinate for 30 minutes. Soak the mushrooms in boiling water for 30 minutes, then drain and finely chop, discarding the stalks.

Heat your wok over high heat, add 3 tablespoons vegetable oil and heat until very hot. Add the pork and lobster mix to the wok and stir-fry until browned, then lift out the meat and tip the liquid out of the wok.

Reheat the wok and add a bit more oil. Stir-fry the spring onion and ginger for 10 seconds, then add the mushrooms and fry for 10 seconds. Add the water chestnuts and stir-fry for 10 seconds, then add the remaining soy, wine and sesame oil with the salt and sugar. Mix the cornflour with 125 ml (4 fl oz/½ cup) of water and add to the wok. Stir-fry constantly until the sauce has thickened, then return the cooked lobster and pork to the wok and toss lightly.

Spoon into the lettuce leaf cups, roll up and serve.

SERVES 4 AS A STARTER

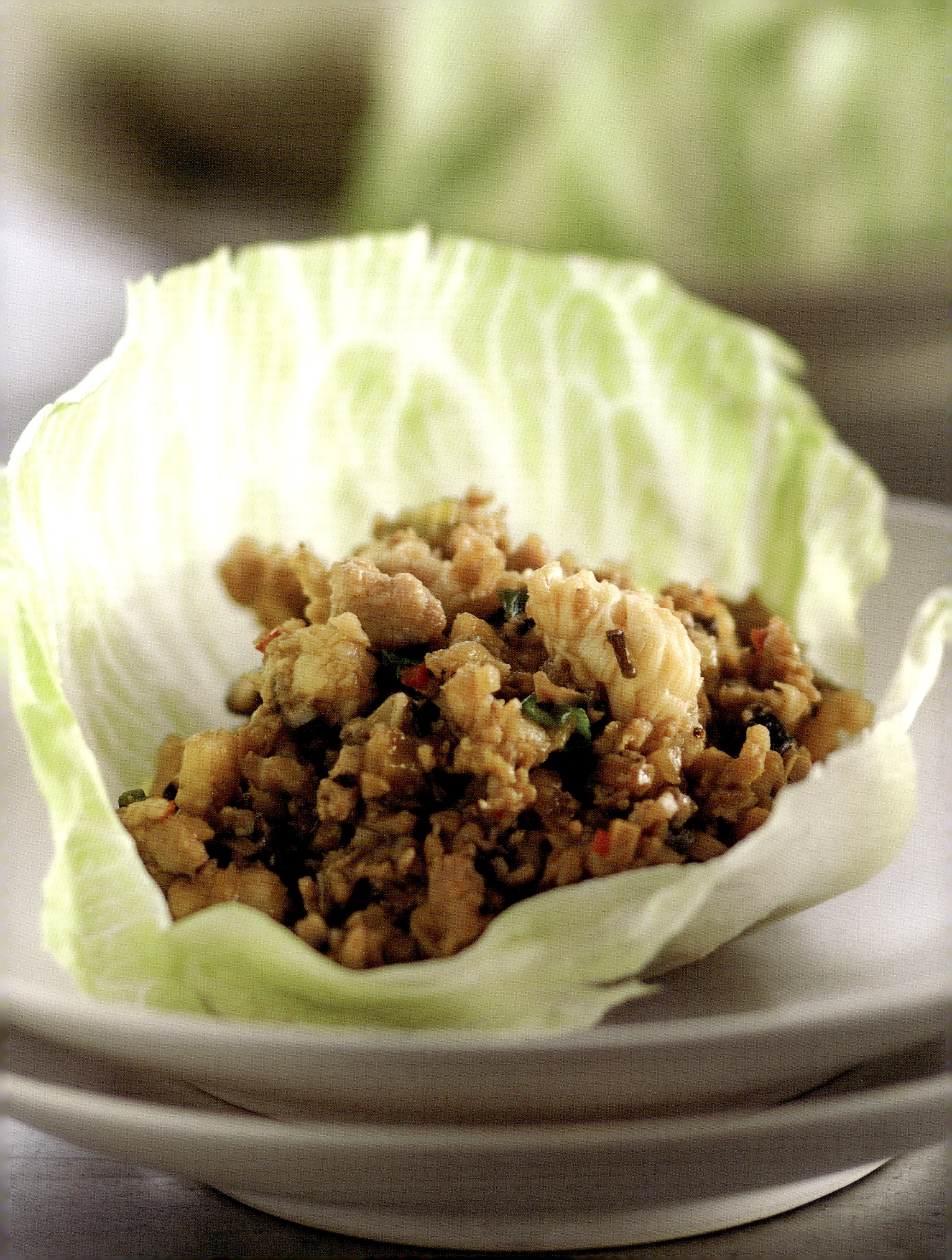

rock LOBSTER with drunken noodles

This delicious Thai noodle dish uses large flat rice noodles. They give the dish a beautiful texture and contrast well with the lobster and vegetables.

You could also use any other FISH or CRUSTACEAN

500 g (1 lb 2 oz) packet fresh rice noodle sheets
meat from 1 rock lobster
2 tablespoons peanut oil
3 garlic cloves, chopped
3 red Asian shallots or 1/4 red onion, chopped
1 banana chilli, chopped
2 eggs, beaten
1/2 red capsicum, sliced
2 tomatoes, chopped
3 Chinese cabbage leaves, roughly chopped
4 tablespoons oyster sauce
2 tablespoons rice wine vinegar
2 tablespoons fish sauce
juice of 1/2 lime
1 tablespoon grated palm sugar
1 teaspoon sambal oelek
3 spring onions, green part only, roughly chopped
a handful of Thai basil leaves
a handful of coriander leaves
3 tablespoons chopped roasted peanuts
sliced pickled garlic and Thai basil, to garnish

Stack your noodle sheets together neatly and cut through all the sheets to make 5 equal portions. Soak the noodles in hot water for 15 minutes. Cut the lobster meat into 2.5 cm (1 inch) pieces.

Heat the peanut oil in a wok until it's smoking. Add the garlic, shallots and chilli and stir-fry for 20 seconds. Add the lobster meat and cook for about 30 seconds to seal on all sides. Push everything to the side of the wok and pour the egg into the middle. Let it set for about 20 seconds, then break it up with tongs.

Toss the wok and add the capsicum, tomato and cabbage. Stir-fry for 10 seconds, then add the oyster sauce, vinegar, fish sauce, lime juice, palm sugar and sambal oelek and toss through. Drain the noodles well and add to the wok. Add the spring onions, basil and coriander and serve immediately, garnished with peanuts, pickled garlic and Thai basil leaves.

SERVES 4

spanish MACKEREL carpaccio with capers and preserved lemon

As far as raw fish goes, Spanish mackerel gets the guernsey. I believe it's the best sashimi fish in the sea, apart from dog-tooth tuna, which is, unfortunately, quite hard to get your hands on. It doesn't have a huge oil content like some of the other sashimi-style fish, so I always incorporate a little into the sauce. I serve it as a carpaccio and team it with lemon four ways — meaning I use four different flavours from the lemon to work on different parts of the palate. I use the juice, the zest, a tiny bit of preserved lemon and some very exquisite lemon-infused extra virgin olive oil. You can buy it at a deli and I would strongly recommend every home has a bottle in the pantry at all times.

You could also use KINGFISH, TUNA, SALMON, OCEAN TROUT, SCALLOPS or OYSTERS

3 tablespoons olive oil
30 baby capers
240 g (7 oz) Spanish mackerel fillet
50 ml (1 3/4 fl oz) lemon-infused olive oil or extra virgin olive oil
grated zest and juice of 1 lemon
12 extra thin slices of preserved lemon rind
mixed baby herbs or torn basil, chopped chives, tarragon or fried sage leaves
1 tablespoon salmon roe

Heat the olive oil in a frying pan and fry the baby capers until crispy. Drain on kitchen paper.

Slice the mackerel as thinly as possible and arrange on a serving plate. Dress the fish with the lemon oil, lemon zest and juice and preserved lemon, then sprinkle with the herbs, salmon roe, capers and some sea salt and cracked pepper.

SERVES 4 AS A STARTER

MAHI MAHI szechuan noodles

Mahi mahi or dolphin fish is one of the most spectacular of all the ocean fish with its bright yellow skin and the strange looking bump on its head. It has the ability to make a grown man or woman howl with glee when they find one on the end of their line. This is an amazing sports fish that anglers dream of catching. Its beautiful white flesh and gaminess go beautifully with Asian flavours. You can use fresh or tinned bamboo shoots for this dish.

You could also use any firm white-fleshed FISH, PRAWNS, BUGS, LOBSTER, PIPIS or VONGOLE

250 g (9 oz) mahi mahi, skin and bones removed, diced
2 teaspoons cornflour
1 egg white
3 tablespoons shaoxing rice wine or dry sherry
3 tablespoons peanut oil
100 g (3½ oz) water chestnuts, finely chopped
50 g (1¾ oz) bamboo shoots, cut into matchsticks
2 spring onions, green part only, finely sliced
2 garlic cloves, minced
1 tablespoon grated fresh ginger
1½ tablespoons chilli bean paste (from Asian delis)
2 tablespoons dark soy sauce
250 ml (9 fl oz/1 cup) chicken stock
400 g (14 oz) fresh (or dried) egg noodles
sliced spring onions and lime wedges, to serve

Mix the fish with the cornflour, egg white and 1 tablespoon of the rice wine. Heat 2 tablespoons of the oil in a hot wok and stir-fry the fish for 1 minute. Pour in any remaining marinade and the rest of the rice wine. Add the water chestnuts and bamboo shoots and stir-fry for a further 30 seconds.

Remove the fish mixture from the wok, give the wok a quick wipe and then heat the remaining oil. Stir-fry the spring onion, garlic and ginger for 20 seconds. Add the bean paste, soy sauce and chicken stock and cook, stirring, for 1 minute. Return the fish mixture to the wok.

Meanwhile, cook the noodles in a large pan of boiling water for 1 minute, then drain well and add to the wok. Toss and heat through.

Serve on a warmed serving platter or in Chinese bowls, garnished with spring onions and lime wedges.

SERVES 4

MANGROVE JACK with spiced spinach and carrot and cardamom sauce

Mangrove jack is a fish you rarely see at the markets, mainly because it isn't commercially fished or farmed in this country. What a shame for the general public, but what a joy for the determined angler in the northern parts of Australia. This really is a superior eating fish with beautiful white flesh and it can stand up to strong flavours like Asian and Moroccan. But I like it best with the touch of sweetness from this carrot sauce.

You could also use SNAPPER, BLUE-EYE, JEWFISH, BARRAMUNDI or MULLOWAY

CARROT AND CARDAMOM SAUCE
750 ml (26 fl oz/3 cups) carrot juice
6 cardamom pods, lightly toasted and bruised
150 g (5^1/$_2$ oz) cold butter, cubed
juice of 1 lime

4 x 160 g (5^3/$_4$ oz) mangrove jack fillets
olive oil, for cooking
2 garlic cloves, finely chopped
1 bird's eye chilli, finely chopped
1 tablespoon finely chopped fresh ginger
200 g (7 oz) English spinach leaves
^{1}/$_2$ lemon

To make the carrot and cardamom sauce, put the carrot juice and cardamom in a saucepan over medium heat and cook until the sauce resembles a thick syrup. Take the pan off the heat and whisk in the butter, a piece at a time, until the sauce has a consistency you like.

Add enough lime juice to balance out the richness of the butter and season with salt and pepper.

Heat a frying pan, brush the fish with a little oil and cook, skin side down, until golden, then turn over and cook the other side until the fish is cooked through.

Meanwhile, in another pan, fry the garlic, chilli and ginger in a touch of olive oil until golden. Add the spinach and cook for 1 minute, then season with salt and pepper and a squeeze of lemon juice. Drain the spinach, squeezing out as much excess moisture as you can.

Spoon the carrot and cardamom sauce into the middle of the plate and add the drained spinach. Top with the fish.

SERVES 4

Udo on the tools.

Catch of the day.

One happy camper.

Pearl perch: "One of the best in the ocean".

Mussel farming in SA.

marron
monkfish moonfish mulloway Murray cod
mussels ocean perch octopus oysters paella
parrot fish pearl meat

pearl perch

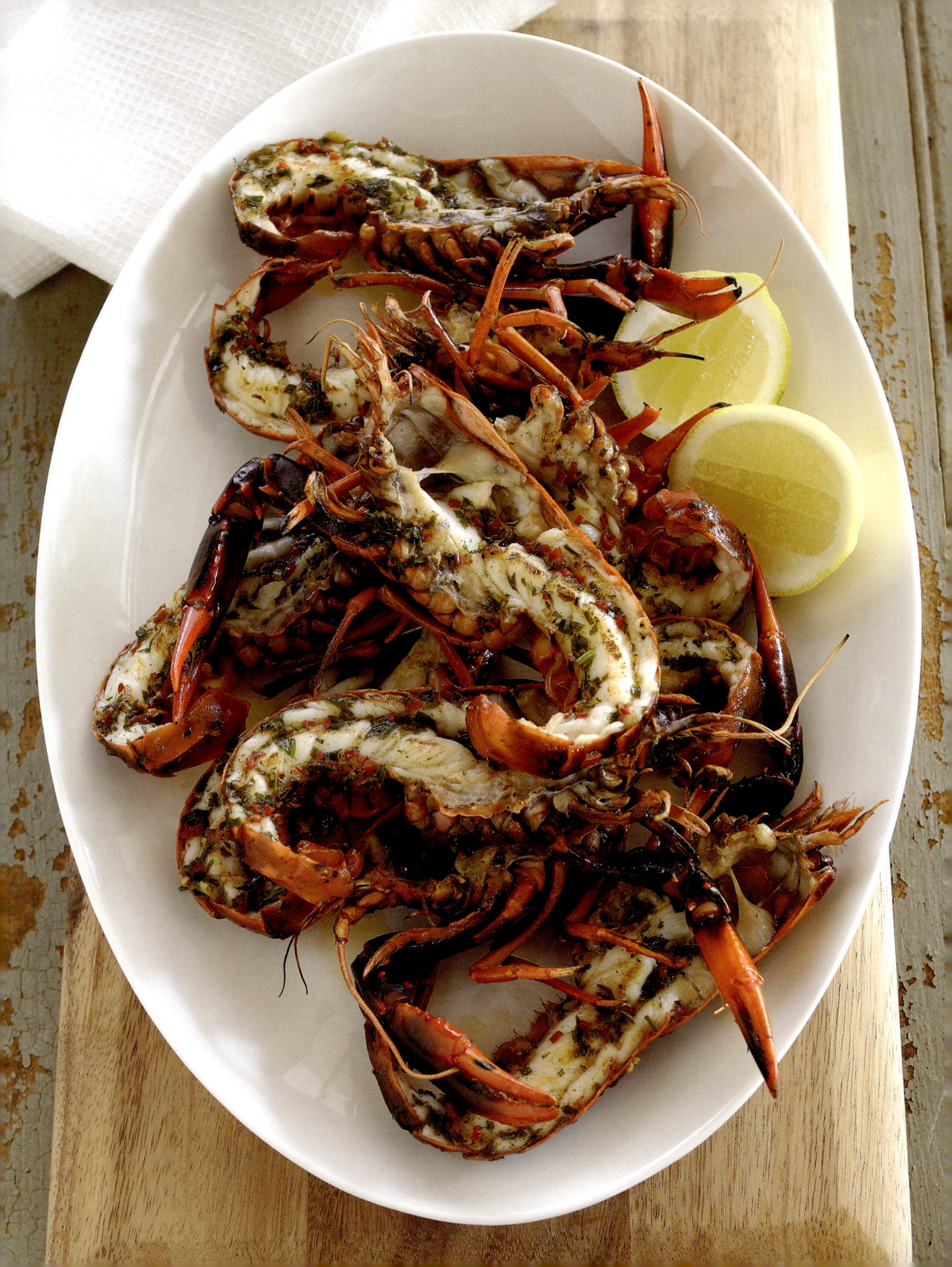

grilled **MARRON** with chilli, rosemary and lemon butter

I love a barbecue — not only for the way food tastes, but for the whole notion of having a good time with friends, enjoying a cold beer or nice wine and really making the most of the outdoors. Whenever I barbecue anything my motto is 'the simpler the better', so some fresh marron grilled with this flavoured butter suits me perfectly. Don't be scared to serve it on paper plates either, then there's no need for washing up.

You could also use PRAWNS, SCAMPI, LOBSTER, SCALLOPS, BUGS, WHITING, or SNAPPER

CHILLI, ROSEMARY AND LEMON BUTTER
100 g (3 1/2 oz) unsalted butter, softened
1 tablespoon chopped rosemary
1 tablespoon chopped flat-leaf (Italian) parsley
1 large banana chilli, finely chopped
grated zest of 1 lemon
1 tablespoon Pernod
1 garlic clove, minced

4 marron, split down the middle
extra virgin olive oil
lemon wedges, to serve

To make the chilli, rosemary and lemon butter, mix all the ingredients together, season with sea salt and cracked pepper and wrap in plastic wrap. Refrigerate until you're ready to use.

Preheat your barbecue. Brush the marron flesh with a touch of extra virgin olive oil and place the marrons, flesh side down, on the barbecue. Cook for 4 minutes, then turn over and spoon a tablespoon of the flavoured butter onto each marron half. Cook for a further 4 minutes, or until the butter has melted and the marron is cooked through. Serve with lemon wedges.

SERVES 4

chu chee curry of MONKFISH

The best curry for seafood would have to be chu chee. Most Thai restaurants team it with prawns, but I love to use monkfish, which is low in fat with a lovely, sweet, lobster-like flesh.

You could also use PRAWNS, LOBSTER, BUGS or any firm white-fleshed FISH

CHU CHEE CURRY PASTE
1/4 teaspoon shrimp paste
5 large dried red chillies
1 teaspoon coriander seeds
10 white peppercorns
6 garlic cloves, chopped
4 red Asian shallots, diced
6 kaffir lime leaves, chopped
2 teaspoons lime zest
1 lemongrass stalk, white part only, finely chopped
2 teaspoons chopped coriander root and stem
1 tablespoon finely chopped fresh ginger
2 tablespoons finely chopped galangal

400 g (14 oz) monkfish fillet
250 ml (9 fl oz/1 cup) coconut cream
250 ml (9 fl oz/1 cup) coconut milk
3 tablespoons fish sauce
3 tablespoons palm sugar
80 g (2 3/4 oz) sugar snap peas
80 g (2 3/4 oz) peas
5 kaffir lime leaves, julienned
a handful of Thai basil leaves
2 banana chillies, julienned

To make the curry paste, preheat the oven to 180°C (350°F/Gas 4). Wrap the shrimp paste in foil and roast in the oven for about 15 minutes. Soak the chillies in hot water for 20 minutes, then drain. Pound the coriander seeds and peppercorns with a mortar and pestle, then add the garlic, chillies, shallots, kaffir lime leaves, lime zest, lemongrass, coriander, ginger, galangal and shrimp paste and pound until you have a paste. You need 3 tablespoons of paste for each curry so store the leftovers in an airtight container in the fridge for up to a week or freeze for 6 months.

Remove the skin and any bones from the monkfish and cut it into bite-sized cubes.

Remove the thick cream from the top of the coconut cream and spoon into a wok over medium heat. Add the 3 tablespoons of curry paste and cook for 3–4 minutes, adding more of the cream if necessary. Add the rest of the coconut cream and milk and bring to a simmer. Add the fish sauce and palm sugar and cook until the sugar has dissolved. Add the sugar snaps and peas and cook for 2–3 minutes, then add the monkfish and cook for a further 2 minutes. Add the kaffir lime leaves, Thai basil and chillies and serve with steamed jasmine rice.

SERVES 4

thai MOONFISH cakes

I love making Thai fish cakes. These work with pretty well any firm white fish, or even tuna if you like. However, if you can get some moonfish (or Opah, as it's also known) give it a try — the flesh is rich, full of flavour and finely textured, suiting the strong flavours in this recipe.

You could also use any firm white-fleshed FISH or TUNA

200 g (7 oz) moonfish fillet, finely diced
1 tablespoon red curry paste
4 coriander roots, finely chopped
1 teaspoon minced fresh ginger
1 egg, lightly beaten
2 tablespoons fish sauce
2 teaspoons caster sugar
150 g (5½ oz) raw prawn meat, finely chopped or minced
2 kaffir lime leaves, julienned
60 g (2 oz/½ cup) finely chopped snake beans or green beans
peanut or grapeseed oil, for frying

NUOC CHAM DIPPING SAUCE
½ garlic clove, finely chopped
1 bird's eye chilli, finely chopped
2 tablespoons caster or grated palm sugar
2 tablespoons fish sauce
1 tablespoon lime juice

In a large bowl, mix the fish, curry paste, coriander root, ginger and egg together and season with the fish sauce and sugar. Add the minced prawn and gather the whole mixture up into a ball, then throw it back into the bowl. Continue doing this until the mixture becomes firmer and stickier (this aerates the fish cakes and helps them puff up when you fry them). Mix in the lime leaves and beans.

Mould the mixture into small discs and shallow-fry in either peanut or grapeseed oil until golden on each side.

Mix together all the dipping sauce ingredients with 1 tablespoon of hot water. Serve with the fish cakes.

SERVES 8 AS A STARTER

olive-crusted **MULLOWAY** with a warm mediterranean salad

This is one of my all-time favourite recipes to cook. I learnt it many years ago when I first moved to Sydney, from Steve Manfredi, a wonderful cook and good friend. Since then I've tried it with numerous varieties of fish. I have found the South Australian mulloway to be my fish of choice, but it is one of those that is tantalisingly elusive to the angler.

You could also use JEWFISH, BLUE-EYE, MURRAY COD, SNAPPER, CORAL TROUT, RED EMPEROR or MANGROVE JACK

olive oil
4 x 160 g (5¾ oz) mulloway fillets, with skin
2 tablespoons olive tapenade, page 226 or ready-made
4 tablespoons butter
juice of 1 lemon
2 good handfuls of English spinach leaves
20 muscatel grapes, deseeded (or you can use raisins or sultanas)
1 tablespoon grated parmesan cheese
1 tablespoon toasted pine nuts
12 pieces tomato confit, page 233, or 24 cherry tomatoes, quartered

Preheat the oven to 180°C (350°F/Gas 4).

Heat a touch of oil in an ovenproof non-stick frying pan and cook the mulloway, skin side down, for 2–3 minutes until golden. Turn the fish over, spread the olive tapenade evenly over the skin and bake in the oven for 5 minutes, or until the fish is just cooked through.

Meanwhile, heat the butter in a pan and cook gently until it turns nut brown. Add the lemon juice, spinach, muscatel grapes, parmesan, pine nuts and tomato confit to the pan with a bit of salt and pepper. Spoon onto plates and serve the fish on top.

SERVES 4

salt-baked MURRAY COD with lime

I love to bake a whole fish and serve it in the middle of the table when family or friends are over. The method is so simple, but it always creates a bit of theatre at the table, which tends to excite people. The best thing about cooking in a salt or dough crust is that it traps in all the flavour of both the fish and the aromatics you put in the cavity. I also think that baking a freshwater fish in a salt crust adds a very subtle element of the sea.

You could also use any whole FISH

1 lime
a small handful of flat-leaf (Italian) parsley, including stems, roughly chopped
3 garlic cloves, thinly sliced
1 x 3 kg (6 lb 12 oz) Murray cod, gutted and scaled
1 tablespoon anchovy oil (the oil that anchovies are packed in)
2 kg (4 lb 8 oz) rock salt
8 egg whites, whisked until stiff
extra virgin olive oil

Preheat the oven to 140°C (275°F/Gas 1). Cut the lime into slices and mix with the parsley and garlic. Rub the inside of the fish with sea salt and black pepper and then pack with the lime and parsley mix.

Use a skewer or toothpicks to close the cavity and then rub the fish skin with the anchovy oil.

Thoroughly mix the rock salt with the egg white. Spread half the salt over the base of a large baking tray. Put the fish on top and cover with the rest of the salt, so the fish is completely covered.

Bake in the oven for 45 minutes, then take out and leave to rest for 10 minutes. Crack the shell with the back of a knife and peel away the salt crust.

Cut portions of fish off the bone and drizzle with extra virgin olive oil. Great with an iceberg lettuce and walnut salad.

SERVES 8

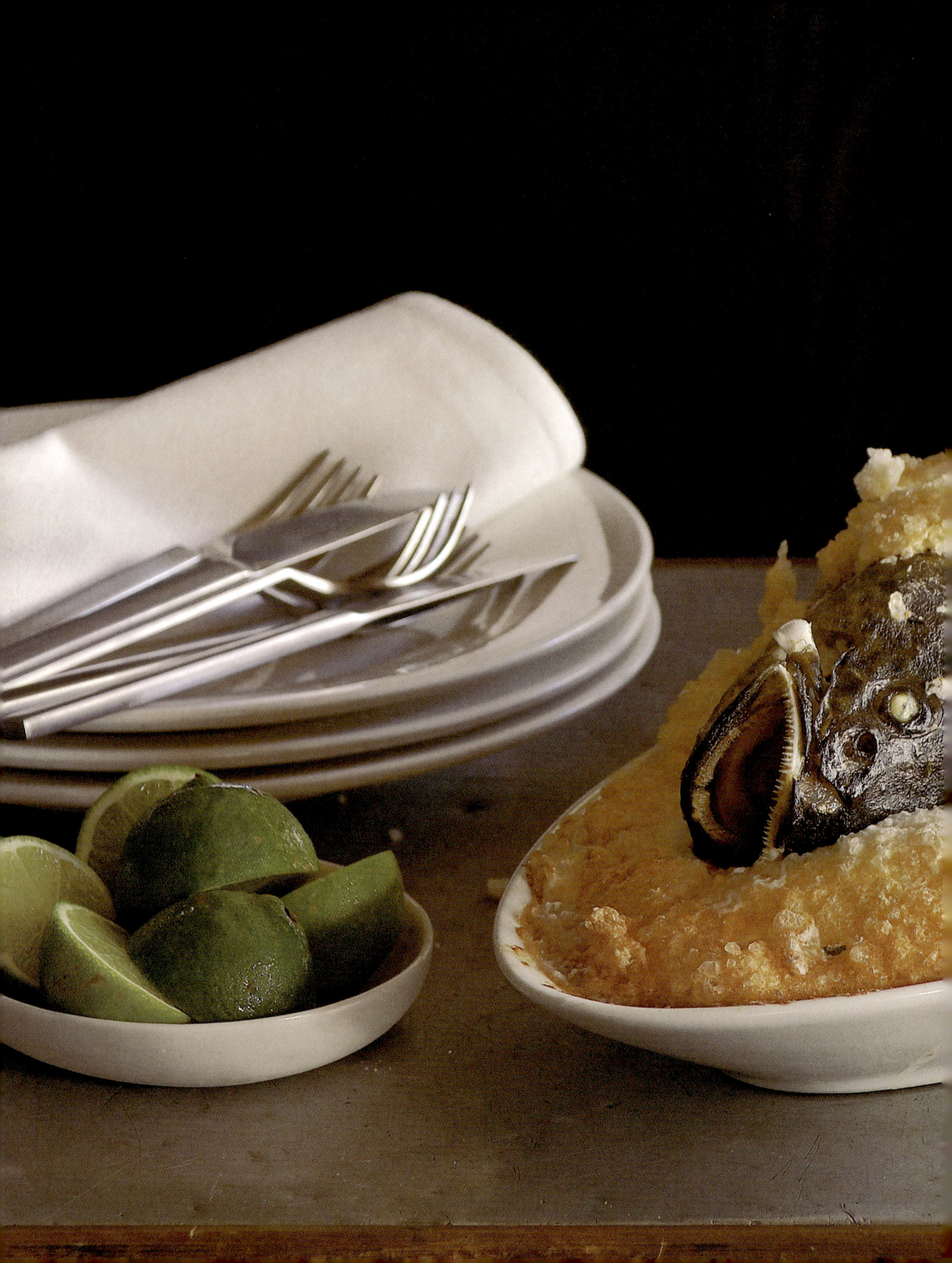

salt-baked Murray cod with lime

thai-style MUSSELS

A few simple rules need to be in place when you buy or cook mussels. Firstly, check that they have a clean smell, secondly, chuck away any open ones that won't close when you give them a firm tap, and thirdly (and probably not so important), discard any that haven't opened once they are cooked (I don't practise what I preach here and actually prise them open anyway, so you can see I'm not a firm believer in this last rule).

You could also use PIPIS, VONGOLE, SQUID, PRAWNS, LOBSTER or BUGS

- 1 tablespoon olive oil
- 2 garlic cloves, finely chopped
- 1 bird's eye chilli, finely chopped
- 1 tablespoon grated fresh ginger
- 1 tablespoon finely chopped coriander roots and stalks
- 30 mussels, cleaned and beards removed
- 250 ml (9 fl oz/1 cup) dry white wine
- 2 tablespoons tamarind pulp concentrate
- 1 quantity Italian tomato sauce, page 223
- 1 tablespoon chilli jam, page 218
- 1 tablespoon fish sauce
- 1 tablespoon grated palm sugar
- a handful of coriander leaves

Heat the oil in your wok and fry the garlic, chilli, ginger and coriander for 30 seconds. Add the mussels and cook for 20 seconds to coat them with the aromatics.

Add the wine and cover the wok with a lid for 2–3 minutes to steam the mussels open. Remove the lid and stir in the tamarind. Add the tomato sauce and chilli jam and bring to a simmer. Add the fish sauce and palm sugar and cook for another minute, or until the sugar dissolves. Remove any mussels that have remained tightly shut. Add the coriander leaves and season with cracked pepper to serve.

SERVES 4 AS A STARTER

orecchiette with **MUSSELS** and Italian sausage ragu

I realise I have quite a few 'surf and turf' recipes in this book that team up meat and seafood. I believe they complement each other in certain dishes, especially in a recipe such as this where the flavour of the Italian sausage permeates the flesh of the mussel. An unusual dish but very more-ish.

You could also use PIPIS, VONGOLE, LOBSTER or BUGS

100 g (3½ oz) fennel, finely sliced
100 ml (3½ fl oz) white wine
1 kg (2 lb 4 oz) mussels, cleaned and beards removed
500 g (1 lb 2 oz) orecchiette
2 tablespoons olive oil
1 large celery stalk, diced
5 garlic cloves, sliced
2 Italian sausages, chopped into small pieces
2 tablespoons lemon juice and zest of ½ lemon
2 tablespoons snipped chives
80 g (2¾ oz) butter

Heat the fennel and wine in a large saucepan. Bring to a simmer, then add the mussels. Put the lid on the pan and leave for 2–3 minutes until the mussels have opened (discard any that remain tightly closed). Take the mussels out of their shells and keep the cooking liquid.

Meanwhile, cook the pasta in a large pan of boiling salted water until al dente, then drain.

Heat the olive oil in a large frying pan and sauté the celery and garlic until softened, then add the Italian sausage and cook for a further minute until browned. Add the mussel cooking liquid, lemon juice and zest and cook until the sauce has a consistency you like. Add the mussels, chives and the butter and heat through. Season with salt and pepper and add the pasta. Toss gently before serving.

SERVES 4

MUSSELS with tomato, white wine and basil

This classic Italian dish doesn't need any explaining — it's one of the best preparations of mussels I have come across.

You could also use VONGOLE, PIPIS, PRAWNS or any firm-fleshed white FISH fillet

2 tablespoons olive oil
32 black mussels, cleaned and beards removed
8 cloves garlic confit, page 222
1 tablespoon chilli confit, page 217
20 basil leaves
100 ml (3$^1/_2$ fl oz) white wine
250 ml (9 fl oz/1 cup) Italian tomato sauce, page 223

Heat the oil in a wok or large saucepan until almost smoking. Add the mussels and cook for 1 minute. Add the garlic, chilli, basil and white wine and cover the wok for 2 minutes. Add the tomato sauce and season with sea salt and black pepper. Let the sauce heat through, discard any mussels that haven't opened, and serve with crusty bread.

SERVES 4 AS A STARTER

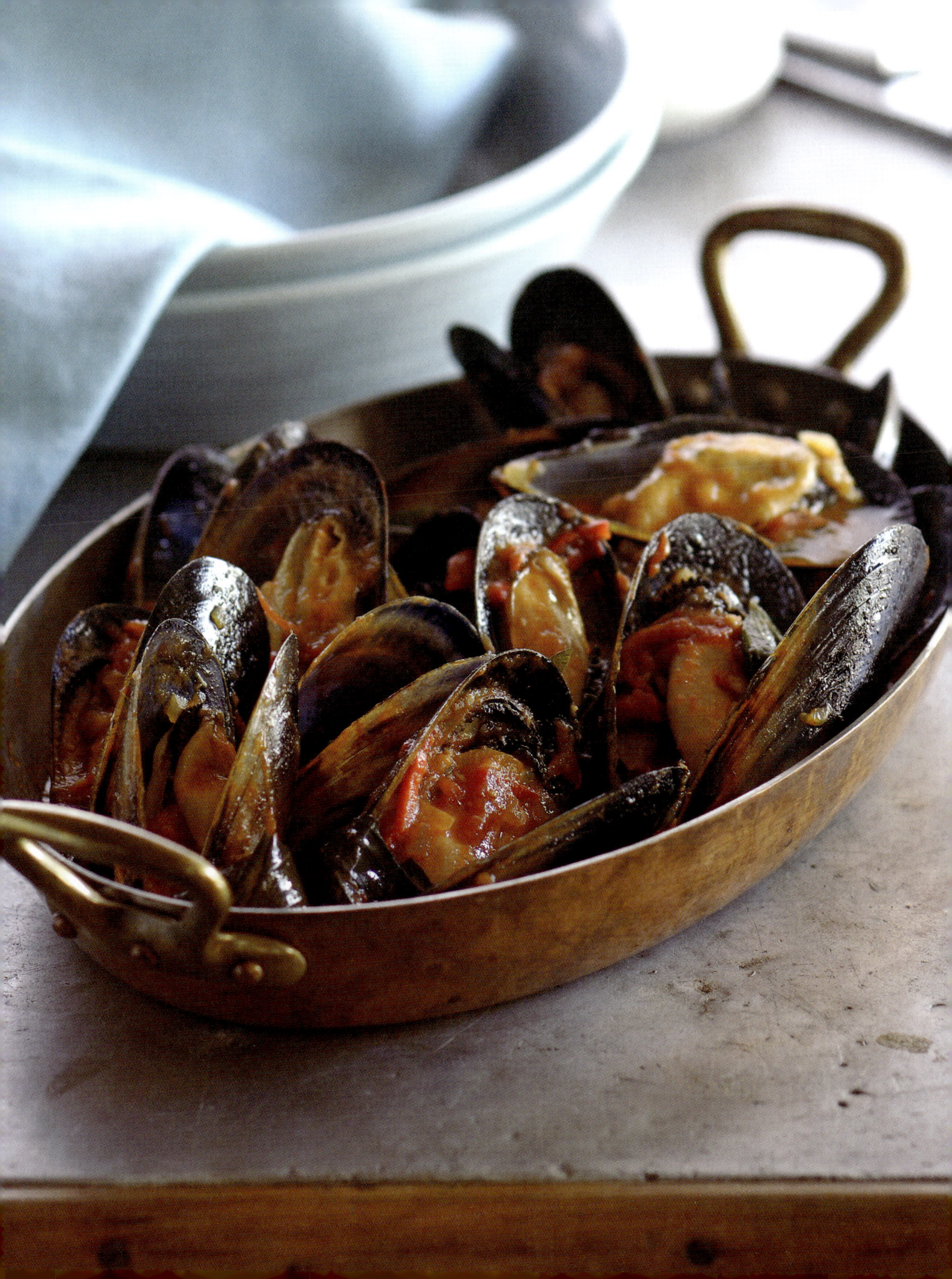

OCEAN PERCH with roasted tomato and fennel sauce

A great way to preserve the delicate flesh of fish is to wrap it in some prosciutto. This acts as a barrier to the intense heat of cooking and, even more importantly, gives a beautiful flavour to the fish. The best accompaniment to prosciutto-wrapped fish is a roasted tomato sauce — this one features fennel to add a lovely hint of aniseed.

You could also use any firm white-fleshed FISH, SARDINES, MACKEREL, HERRING or EEL

ROASTED TOMATO AND FENNEL SAUCE
400 g (14 oz) vine-ripened tomatoes
100 g (3½ oz/1 cup) roughly chopped fennel
50 ml (1¾ fl oz) extra virgin olive oil
a pinch of fennel seeds, dry-roasted and ground
2 cloves garlic confit, page 222
2 teaspoons good-quality red wine vinegar

4 x 160–180 g (6 oz) ocean perch fillets, skin and bones removed
12 slices prosciutto
4 tablespoons extra virgin olive oil
4 tablespoons aioli, page 212

To make the sauce, preheat the oven to 180°C (350°F/Gas 4). Put the tomatoes and fennel on a baking tray with a little sea salt and a dash of the oil and roast until the tomato skins split. Remove from the oven and peel off the skins. If the fennel isn't tender, keep roasting until it is.

Blend the tomatoes, fennel, fennel seeds and garlic until smooth and then put in a pan and cook until the sauce has thickened to a consistency you like. Whisk in the remaining oil and the red wine vinegar and season with sea salt and cracked pepper.

Wrap each ocean perch fillet with 3 slices of prosciutto and place in a roasting tin. Drizzle with the oil and roast for 8–10 minutes. Alternatively, cook on a hot barbecue until golden on all sides.

Spoon some warm tomato and fennel sauce onto each plate, then top with the ocean perch and a dollop of aioli.

SERVES 4

OCTOPUS braised in tomato and garlic

The Greeks and Italians have gone industrial on the octopus front. Some put them in a cement mixer to tenderise, others apparently put them in the washing machine. I am not sold on the idea: I prefer to cook my octopus slowly for a long time to soften the meat and let it soak up the flavours of a really good sauce.

You could also use CUTTLEFISH or SQUID

80 ml (2½ fl oz/⅓ cup) extra virgin olive oil
5 garlic cloves, finely sliced
2 medium-sized octopus (about 200 g/7 oz each), cleaned and cut into 2 cm (¾ inch) pieces
500 g (1 lb 2 oz) ripe tomatoes, diced
small handful of chopped flat-leaf (Italian) parsley

Heat the olive oil in a frying pan and cook the garlic until golden. Add the octopus and cook for 1 minute, then add the tomatoes and parsley, bring to a simmer and cook slowly for about 90 minutes, or until the octopus is tender.

Season with sea salt and pepper and serve with fresh crusty Italian bread.

SERVES 4 AS A STARTER

sydney rock OYSTERS with blood orange bellini granita

Champagne and oysters go hand in hand, so I came up with this recipe for a blood orange bellini. The orange juice is mixed with champagne vinegar and frozen — perfect for celebration drinks on a hot summer's day.

There's no real alternative to the oysters here

30 ml (1 fl oz) champagne, chardonnay or even white wine vinegar
40 g (1½ oz) sugar
100 ml (3½ fl oz) blood orange juice
12 Sydney rock oysters
crushed ice, to serve

Put the champagne vinegar, sugar and orange juice in a pan and warm gently to dissolve the sugar. Pour into a baking tray and put in the freezer. After a few hours in the freezer, run a fork through the mixture so that it resembles ice shavings. Lay your oysters on a plate of crushed ice and serve the granita in a small bowl in the centre.

MAKES A PLATTER OF 12 OYSTERS

angassi OYSTERS with ginger and shallot dressing

There have been many books written entirely about oysters — for most seafood lovers they are the jewels of the ocean. I look at them from a much simpler viewpoint: open, eat as soon as possible, and don't stop until you run out. If you must add anything, a little squeeze of lemon or this simple dressing will make them sing.

There's no real alternative to the oysters here

2 tablespoons mirin
2 tablespoons sherry vinegar
1 teaspoon finely chopped red Asian shallots
1 teaspoon finely chopped fresh ginger
24 angassi oysters
lemon wedges, to serve
crushed ice, to serve

Mix together the mirin, vinegar, shallots and ginger to make a dipping sauce. Serve the oysters and lemon wedges on a bed of crushed ice and, if you're feeling really outrageous, garnish with rose petals and watercress.

MAKES A PLATTER OF 24 OYSTERS

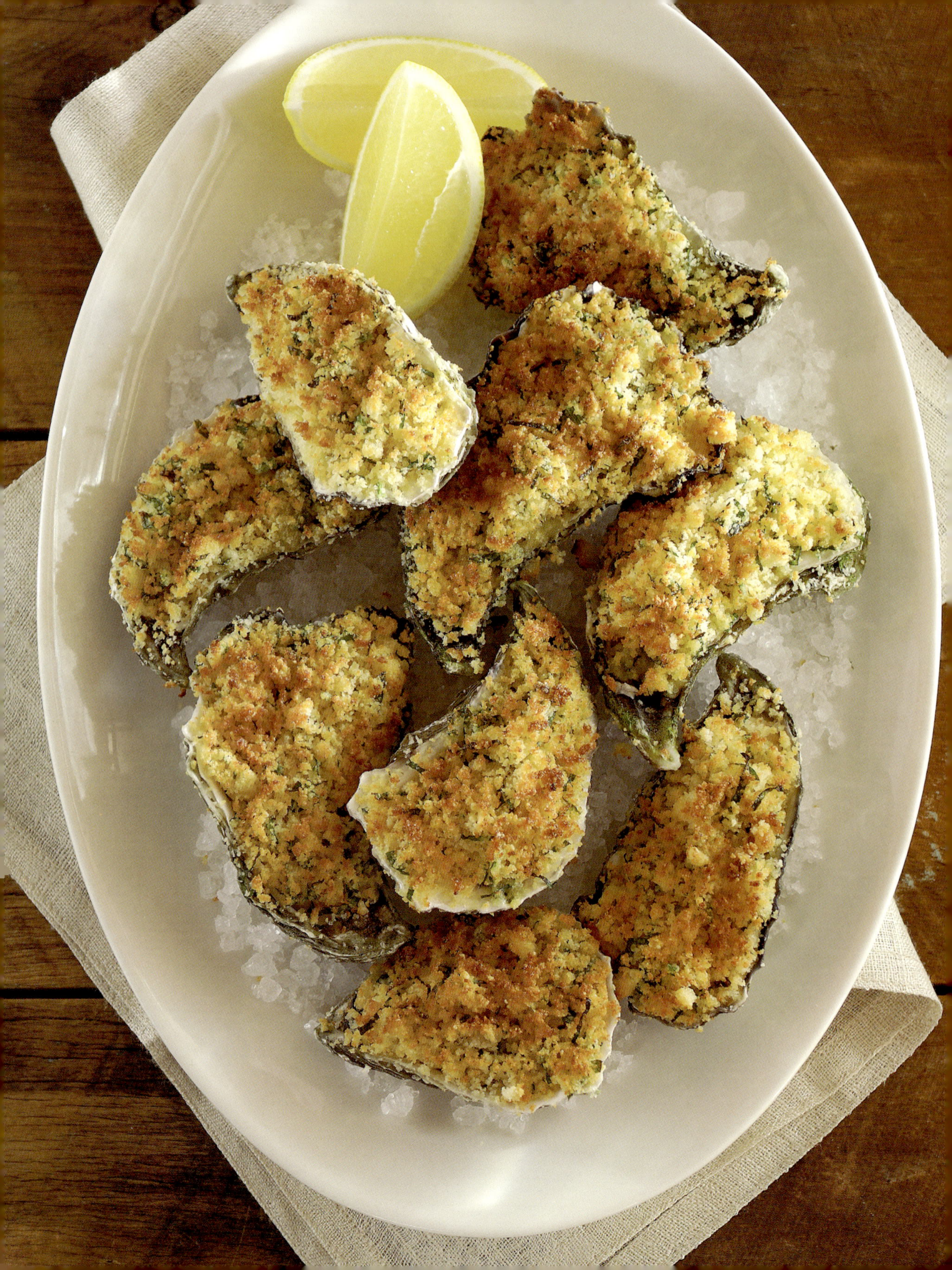

parmesan and horseradish-baked OYSTERS

Horseradish is an ingredient that, in my opinion, was created purely to enhance and enliven seafood. It is one of the staples in my fridge at home and gets used in a multitude of ways. This is a quick and easy recipe that really shows off its fantastic value in the kitchen.

You could also use SCALLOPS in the half shell, SCAMPI, LOBSTER or any firm white-fleshed FISH fillet

HORSERADISH BUTTER
100 g (3½ oz) soft unsalted butter
1 tablespoon finely grated fresh horseradish
1 teaspoon finely chopped flat-leaf (Italian) parsley
1 teaspoon grated lemon zest

12 oysters
3 tablespoons brioche crumbs or breadcrumbs
3 tablespoons finely grated parmesan cheese
rock salt and 1 lemon, to serve

To make the horseradish butter, mix together all the ingredients, roll into a log, wrap in plastic wrap and refrigerate until ready to use.

Preheat your grill to its highest temperature or your oven to 200°C (400°F/Gas 6). Cut the log of horseradish butter into 12 slices and place a slice onto each oyster. Mix together the breadcrumbs and parmesan and sprinkle each oyster with a teaspoonful. Grill or cook in the oven for about 5 minutes until the butter has melted and the parmesan is browning. Serve on a bed of rock salt with lemon wedges.

MAKES A PLATTER OF 12 OYSTERS

OYSTERS with merguez sausage and fennel

You've probably gathered by now that one of my favourite ways to spend an afternoon is around the barbecue with friends. While the barbie's firing up, I like to have a couple of plates of food around for people to dip into — anything that uses simple, no-fuss, good-quality ingredients. Here it's freshly shucked oysters, fresh fennel and great sausages.

There's no real alternative to the oysters here

2 tablespoons sherry vinegar (I like to use Pedro Ximenez)
a few strands of saffron
2 tablespoons Spanish extra virgin olive oil
2 teaspoons finely chopped French shallot or red onion
4 Merguez sausages, cooked
24 Sydney rock oysters
1 baby fennel, stems removed and cut into strips

Mix the vinegar with the saffron, oil, shallot and some salt and pepper to make a dressing. Slice the sausages into quite large pieces and fry in a frying pan with a touch of oil. Serve the oysters with the hot sliced sausage and crisp raw fennel, with the dressing on the side.

MAKES A PLATTER OF 24 OYSTERS

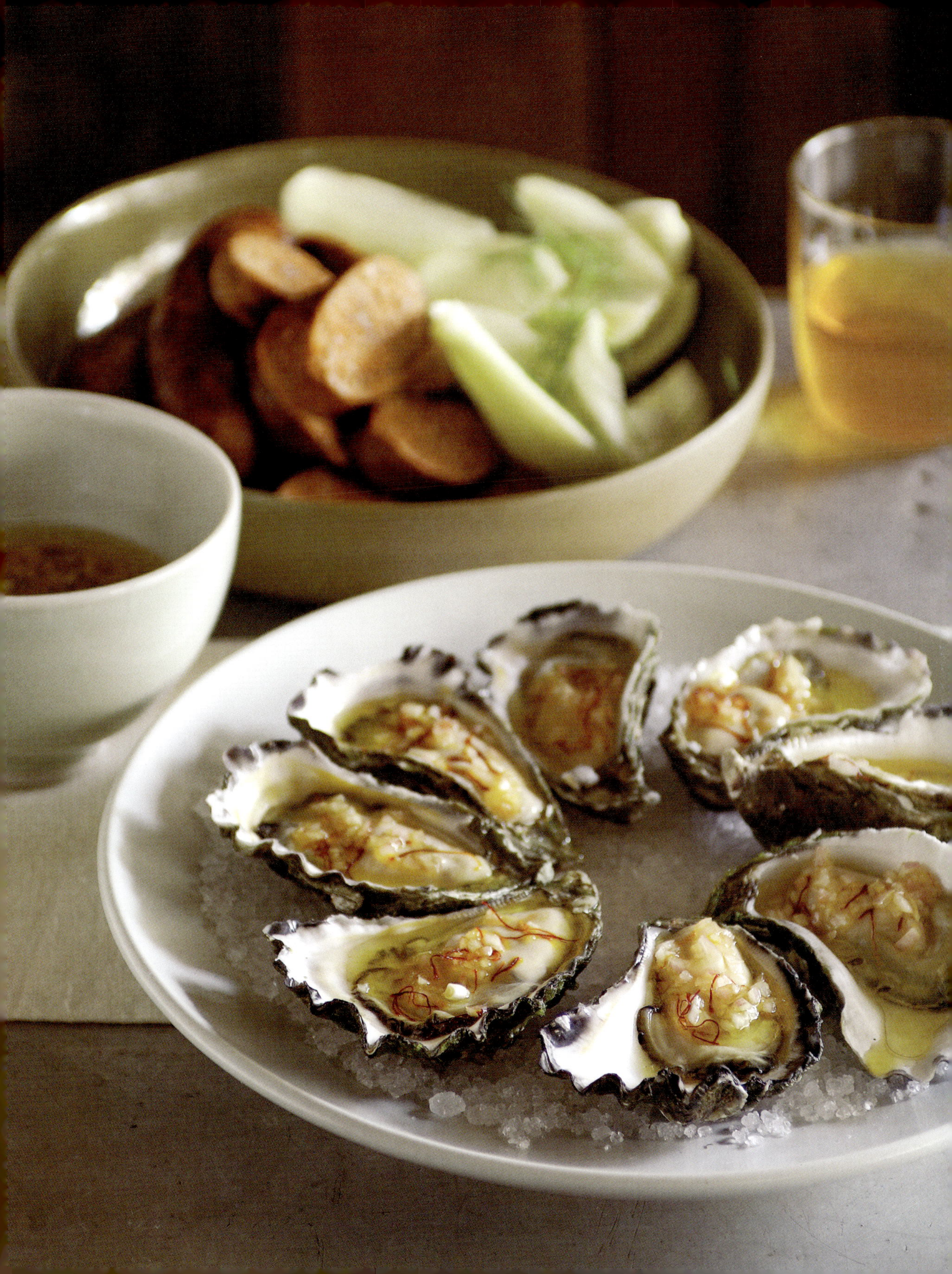

pacific OYSTERS with guanciale, balsamic, goat's cheese and semi-dried tomatoes

I think the first oyster I ever downed was a Kilpatrick and, if that's what it takes to get people to try oysters, well I think the recipe deserves a place in this book. I have used guanciale (cured pork cheek) which has a more subtle flavour than the traditional bacon. I also like to add a touch of goat's cheese, a few semi-dried tomatoes and finish it off with aged balsamic. OK, so it's not a Kilpatrick in the traditional sense, but my twenty-first century Sydney interpretation.

There's no real alternative to the oysters here

24 Pacific oysters

2 cups rock salt

1–2 tablespoons goat's cheese (depending on how much you like)

1 tablespoon chopped semi-dried tomatoes

4 basil leaves, julienned

3 tablespoons chopped guanciale (cured pork cheek) or pancetta, prosciutto or bacon

2 tablespoons aged balsamic vinegar

Preheat your grill to hot. Arrange the oysters on a bed of rock salt in a baking tray. Spoon the goat's cheese, tomatoes, basil and guanciale onto the oysters and drizzle with balsamic vinegar. Place under the grill until the guanciale is crisp, then serve with cracked pepper.

MAKES A PLATTER OF 24 OYSTERS

tempura **OYSTERS** with wasabi tartare

My dad hates oysters (and I mean *really* hates them), but I convinced him to try these tempura-fried oysters years ago and now this is one of his favourites. (He still hasn't progressed to oysters 'au naturel', but if I can get even one avid oyster-hater to love them, I'm happy.) Pacific oysters from Tassie are perfect for this recipe: they retain a lot of their true flavour and moisture as they're larger than the Sydney rocks and native angassi.

You could also use PRAWNS, SEA URCHIN, BUGS, SCALLOPS, EEL or any FISH

2 teaspoons Szechuan peppercorns
2 teaspoons pink peppercorns
2 teaspoons sea salt
1 tablespoon chopped flat-leaf (Italian) parsley
peanut oil, for deep-frying
24 Pacific oysters
plain flour, seasoned with salt and pepper, for dusting
1 quantity tempura batter, page 232
2 tablespoons tartare sauce, page 231
1 scant teaspoon wasabi paste
1 scant teaspoon soy sauce
lime wedges, to serve

Dry-roast the Szechuan and pink peppercorns and salt in a frying pan until fragrant and then grind with a mortar and pestle or spice grinder. Place in a mixing bowl with the parsley.

Heat the oil in your wok to 185°C (365°F) — either measure this with a thermometer or drop a cube of bread into the oil: it should brown in about 10 seconds. Lightly dust the oysters in flour and then dip into the cold tempura batter. Deep-fry the oysters until light and crispy, then drain on kitchen paper and toss with the spice and parsley mix.

Mix together the tartare sauce, wasabi and soy to make wasabi tartare. Serve the oysters with wasabi tartare and wedges of lime.

MAKES A PLATTER OF 24 TEMPURA OYSTERS

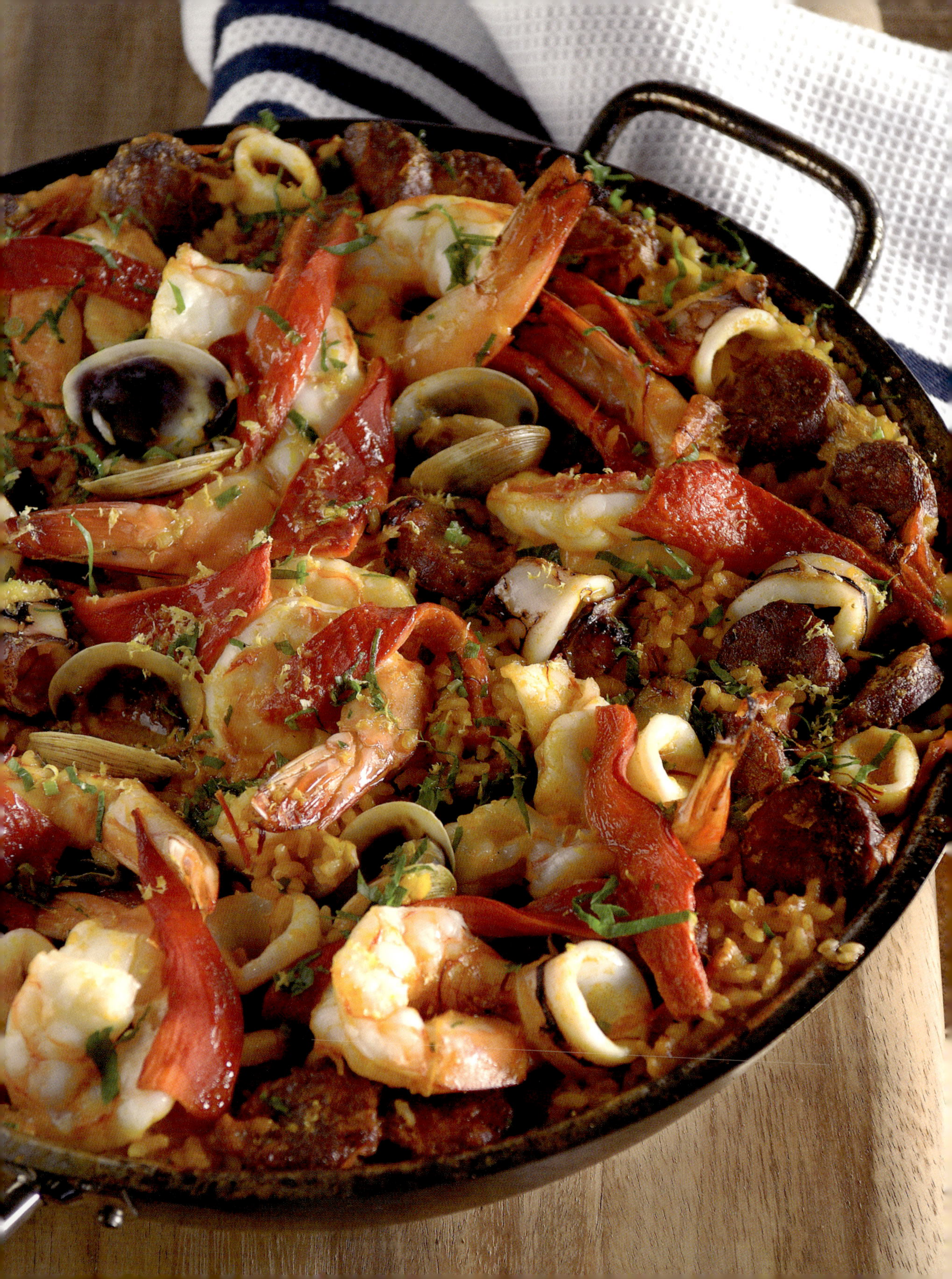

PAELLA

The name paella comes from the two-handled shallow pan in which the dish is cooked. It isn't strictly necessary to cook paella in this pan, but if you're going to make it fairly often they aren't very expensive and do look great on the table.

You could also use MUSSELS or PIPIS instead of the vongole

750 ml (26 fl oz/3 cups) fish or chicken stock
10 flat-leaf (Italian) parsley stalks
250 g (9 oz) peeled prawns (shells and heads kept)
1 lemon, zested and then cut in half
a pinch of saffron threads
2 garlic cloves, minced
2 ripe tomatoes, chopped
1 teaspoon smoked paprika (I like to use La Chinata)
2 tablespoons extra virgin olive oil
1 chorizo sausage, cut into 1 cm ($1/2$ inch) slices
250 g (9 oz) Calasparra or Bomba short-grain rice
150 g ($5^1/2$ oz) cleaned and scored squid, cut into bite-sized pieces
100 g ($3^1/2$ oz) vongole (Italian clams)
75 g ($2^3/4$ oz) pimentos or roasted capsicum, cut into strips
a handful of chopped flat-leaf (Italian) parsley

Preheat your oven to 180°C (350°F/Gas 4). Put the stock in a saucepan over heat and add the parsley stalks, the prawn shells and heads and half the lemon. Bring to a simmer and add the saffron.

Heat a touch of oil in a frying pan and fry the garlic, tomatoes and paprika for a few minutes until soft, then purée with a blender or a mortar and pestle. (This mixture is called picada.)

Heat the oil in a paella pan or large heavy-based frying pan and fry the chorizo on both sides. Add the rice and the picada and cook for a few minutes, stirring well.

Strain the hot stock into the paella pan and stir well. Add a touch of sea salt, bring to the boil for 5 minutes and then stir again.

Add the squid, vongole and prawns to the paella pan, cover with the lid or foil and put in the oven for 15–20 minutes, or until the rice is cooked and the vongole have opened. Arrange the pimento or capsicum strips over the top with the chopped parsley and lemon zest. Season with sea salt and cracked pepper if needed and serve immediately in the paella pan.

SERVES 4

PARROT FISH with three-flavoured sauce

The first time I visited Thailand I must have tried this dish about twenty times in twenty different regions and each time it tasted different. I discovered that the amounts of palm sugar, chilli, tamarind and garnishes were as varied as the provinces of Thailand itself. This is the way I make it at home and it works well with pretty much any fish, but I like it best with a freshly caught parrot fish.

You could also use pretty much any FISH

2 x 800 g (1 lb 12 oz) parrot fish
70 ml (2¼ fl oz) fish sauce
roots from a bunch of coriander
1 bird's eye chilli
3 garlic cloves
3 red Asian shallots
1 knob of fresh ginger
1 teaspoon shrimp paste
peanut oil, for deep-frying
2 tablespoons grated palm sugar
100 ml (3½ fl oz) tamarind pulp concentrate
a large handful of Thai basil leaves
2 kaffir lime leaves, julienned
4 tablespoons roasted cashew nuts
2 limes, cut into wedges

Score three incisions on both sides of each fish and rub all over with fish sauce. Leave for at least 30 minutes in the fridge.

Meanwhile, rougly chop the coriander roots, chilli, garlic, shallots, ginger and shrimp paste, then pound with a mortar and pestle. Heat a touch of oil in a wok and cook the spice mixture until fragrant. Add the palm sugar and cook until caramelised. Then add the tamarind and enough water to give the sauce a consistency you like. Taste, and adjust the seasoning with more fish sauce and palm sugar if necessary.

Fill your wok with enough oil to fully submerge one fish. Heat to 180°C (350°F) — either measure this with a thermometer or drop a cube of bread into the oil: it should brown in about 15 seconds. Deep-fry the fish until cooked through. Lift out and drain on kitchen paper while you deep-fry the other fish. Deep-fry the basil leaves until crispy (be careful: the oil might spit).

Serve the fish topped with a little sauce. Sprinkle with kaffir lime leaves, Thai basil leaves and roasted cashews. Serve with lime wedges.

SERVES 4

PEARL MEAT with lemon and parsley

A lot of people may not have heard of pearl meat, but we should be immensely proud of this truly native Australian product. Most is exported to the Asian market, where they hold it in the sort of high regard we reserve for European truffles or Russian caviar.

You could also use SCALLOPS or ABALONE

200 g (7 oz) pearl meat
2 tablespoons extra virgin olive oil
1 tablespoon finely chopped flat-leaf (Italian) parsley
juice of 1 lemon

Slice the pearl meat very thinly, crossways. Heat the oil in a wok until nearly smoking and add the pearl meat. Toss in the parsley and take off the heat. Add the lemon juice and season to taste with sea salt and cracked black pepper. Ideally, serve in a polished pearl shell.

SERVES 4 AS A STARTER

PEARL meat with ginger and soy

I was filming in Broome and met a great bloke who goes by the name of Salty Dog. He was a hard-hat pearl diver decades ago and knows everything there is to know about pearls. Salty Dog put me in touch with his lovely partner, Colleen — this is her deliciously refreshing recipe.

200 g (7 oz) pearl meat
75 ml (2$^{1}/_{2}$ fl oz) palm or rice wine vinegar
1 tablespoon sugar
75 ml (2$^{1}/_{2}$ fl oz) light soy sauce
1 teaspoon minced garlic
1 teaspoon minced ginger
1 teaspoon finely chopped banana chilli
1 spring onion, green part only, chopped
wasabi paste, to serve

Slice the pearl meat very thinly, crossways. Mix with all the other ingredients and 100 ml (3$^{1}/_{2}$ fl oz) of water. Season with sea salt and cracked black pepper and leave to marinate for 2 hours. Drain and serve with wasabi paste.

SERVES 4 AS A STARTER

chermoula-rubbed PEARL PERCH with yoghurt, coriander and mint sauce

One of the best day's fishing I've ever had was on a charter boat an hour off Noosa Heads. I was with Astrid and a good mate of mine, Hamish, who is also a chef. We left land at 4:45 am and by 7 am we were pulling in bucketfuls of pearl perch, and I mean buckets — the boat we were on must have caught over two hundred. We kept about ten and threw the rest back. The skipper of the boat described them as the best eating fish in the area (and when a skipper tells you that, it's best to take notice). He said the best way to cook them is on the barbie, so, with a little bit of flavour from a spice rub, that's exactly what we did.

You could also use SNAPPER, BREAM, CORAL TROUT, RED EMPEROR, MULLET, MANGROVE JACK or BARRAMUNDI

- 2 tablespoons chermoula spice mix (a Middle-Eastern blend found at delis or spice shops)
- 4 x 160–180 g (6 oz) pieces pearl perch fillet, with skin
- 3 tablespoons olive oil
- 2 chillies, finely chopped
- 2 garlic cloves, finely chopped
- 1 kg (2 lb 4 oz) English spinach leaves
- 2 tablespoons lemon juice
- 1 quantity yoghurt, coriander and mint sauce, page 233

Rub the chermoula spice over the fish fillets. Heat half the oil in a frying pan and cook the fish, skin side down, until blackened but not burnt, then flip over and cook the other side. Remove from the pan.

Heat the remaining oil in the frying pan, toss the chilli and garlic in the pan for 1 minute to release the flavour, then add the spinach and cook for another minute before adding the lemon juice. Strain the spinach to remove all the excess moisture, then serve with the fish, topped with a little yoghurt, coriander and mint sauce.

SERVES 4

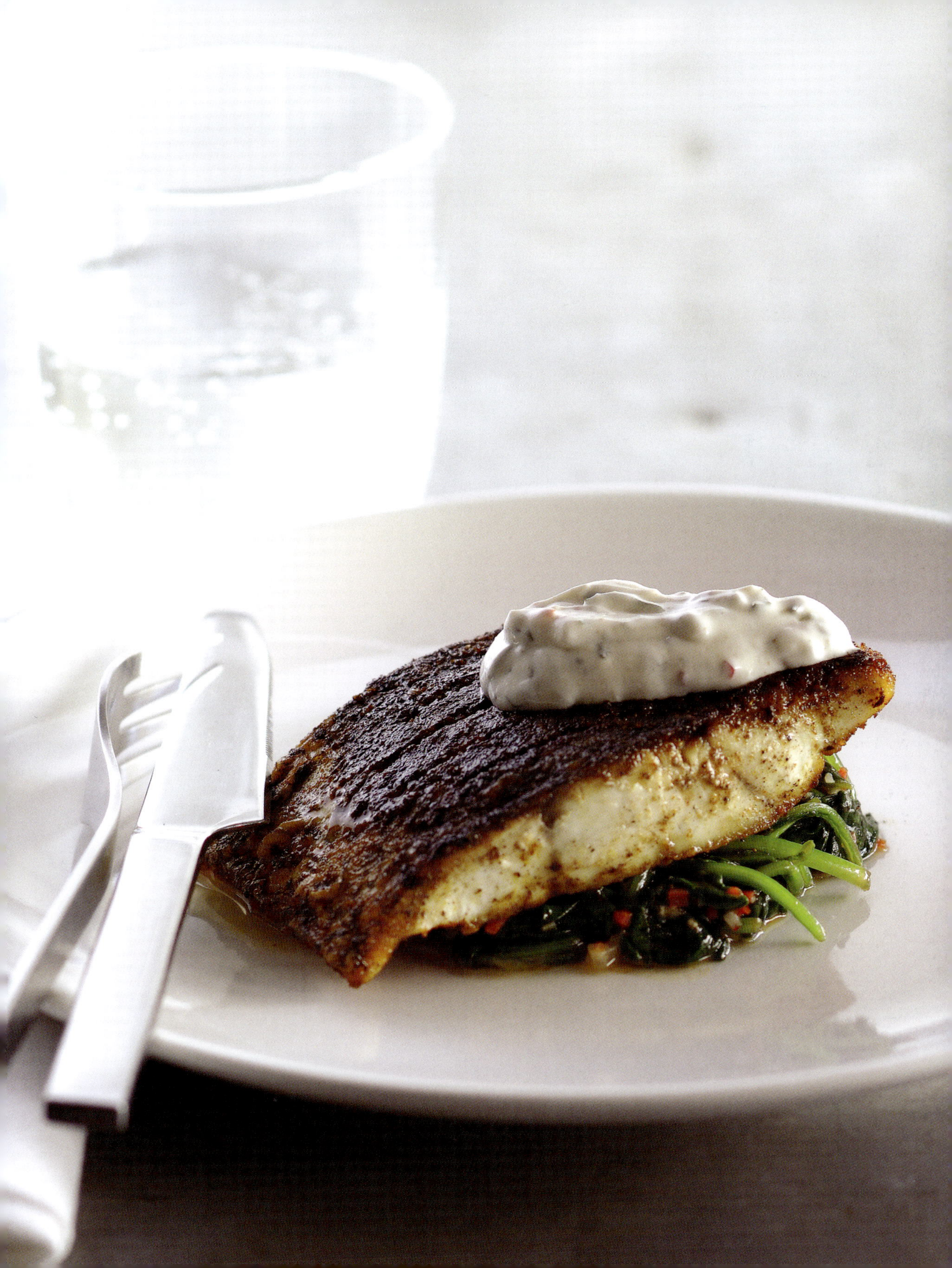

A great day on the reef. Far North QLD.

What a view!

It doesn't get much better than this.

My mate Steve from NT, keeping us out of reach of the crocs.

Cape Leveque, beyond Broome. God's country.

pipis
prawns red emperor red mullet
salmon

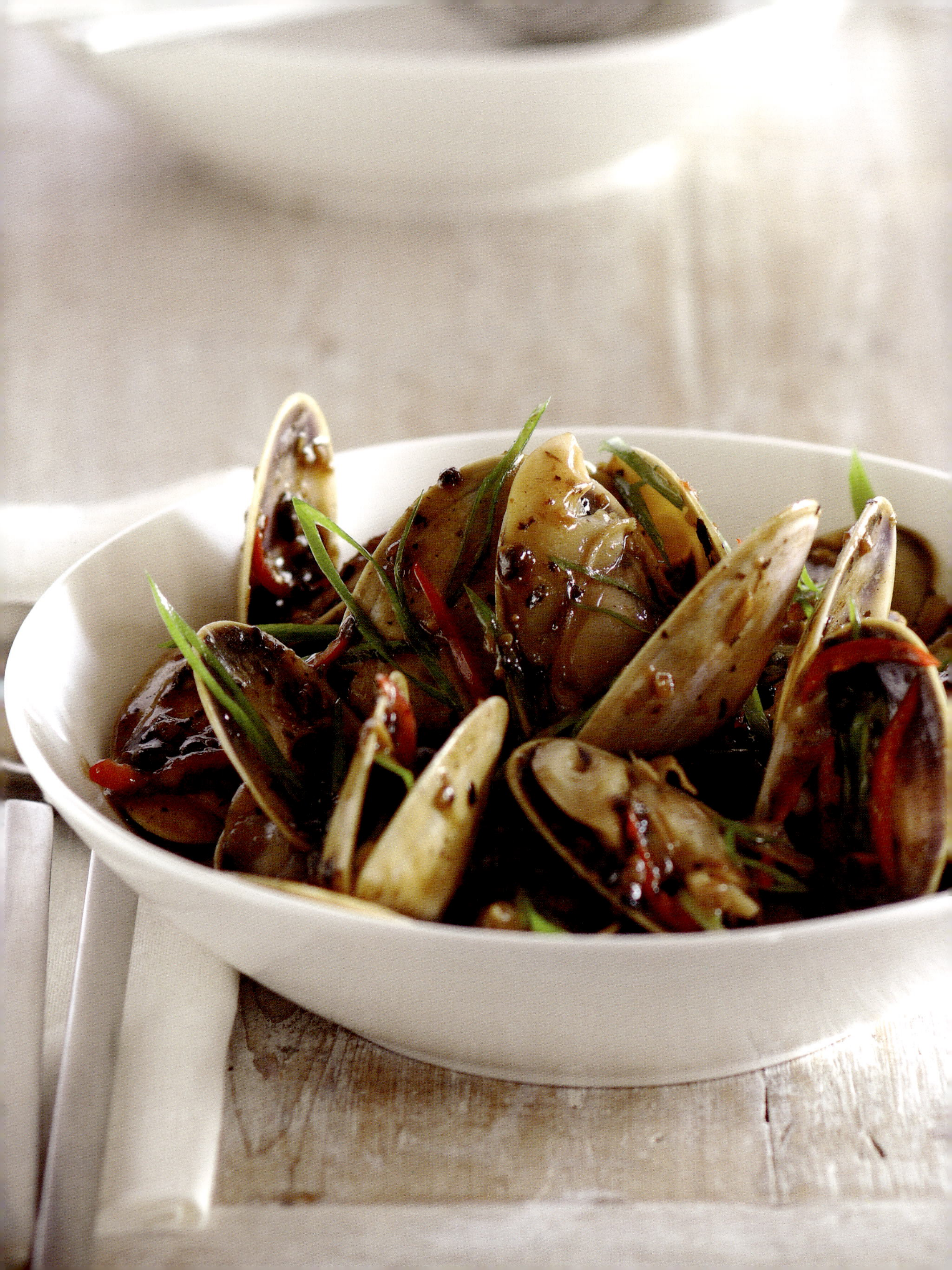

PIPIS with black beans

The Chinese have honed their seafood-cooking skills to a fine art and, luckily for us, we have access to all their special ingredients and cooking secrets. This is a wonderfully simple dish that is full of flavour and really a joy to prepare.

You could also use LOBSTER, MUSSELS or VONGOLE

800 g (1 lb 12 oz) pipis
1 tablespoon grapeseed oil
2 teaspoons sesame oil
1 tablespoon Chinese salted fermented black beans, chopped
2 garlic cloves, finely chopped
1 tablespoon finely chopped fresh ginger
1 tablespoon sliced banana chilli
4 tablespoons shoaxing rice wine
1 tablespoon dark soy sauce
sugar, to taste
3 thinly sliced spring onions, green part only

Wash the pipis in plenty of cold water and drain well (they should have already been purged of sand, see page 251).

Heat the grapeseed oil and sesame oil in a large wok, add the black beans, garlic, ginger and chilli and stir-fry for 20 seconds. Add the pipis to the wok and stir-fry for 1 minute. Add the wine and soy sauce and cover with a lid until the pipis open. Add sugar, to taste, and the spring onions and serve with steamed rice.

SERVES 4

tandoori PRAWNS

The name comes from the brick and clay tandoor ovens that are used in Indian cooking; traditionally these bake the food over intense heat to create a smoky flavour. Without a tandoor, we make a marinade or sauce to coat the food and create a similar flavour.

You could also use any firm white-fleshed FISH, SCALLOPS, LOBSTER, CRAB or BUGS

- 2 tablespoons paprika
- 2 tablespoons cumin seeds
- 2 tablespoons coriander seeds
- 6 garlic cloves
- 2 tablespoons grated fresh ginger
- 4 large chillies, deseeded and chopped
- 2 teaspoons grated lime zest and juice of 2 limes
- 375 ml (13 fl oz/1 1/2 cups) yoghurt
- 20 raw king prawns, unpeeled
- 2 tablespoons peeled, seeded and finely diced cucumber
- 1 quantity yoghurt, coriander and mint sauce, page 233, to serve

Dry-roast the spices in a frying pan until fragrant, then pound in a mortar and pestle with the garlic, ginger, chillies and lime zest. Transfer to a large bowl, mix with the yoghurt and lime juice and add the prawns. Cover and leave to marinate for 24 hours in the fridge.

Heat your oven to 220°C (425°F/Gas 7) and cook the prawns on a baking tray for 10 minutes, or until they are cooked through. Stir the cucumber through the yoghurt, coriander and mint sauce and serve with the prawns.

SERVES 4 AS A STARTER

PRAWN won tons with hot English mustard

I discovered these simple but tasty morsels in a Japanese restaurant. The idea of won tons deep-fried then dipped into hot English mustard had me wondering at first, but then they arrived at the table and I still don't think I've ever tasted anything so addictive in all my life. Be warned though — hot English mustard didn't get its name for nothing. Use just a tiny bit.

You could also use BUGS, LOBSTER or any firm-fleshed white FISH

300 g (10½ oz) raw prawn meat, minced or finely chopped
1 teaspoon chopped garlic chives
grated zest of 1 lemon
20 won ton wrappers
1 egg, lightly beaten
peanut oil, for deep-frying
2 tablespoons hot English mustard

Season the prawn mince with sea salt and cracked white pepper. Add the garlic chives and lemon zest and mix well.

Lay the won ton wrappers on the work surface and spoon a teaspoon of prawn filling onto each one. Brush around the edge with the egg. Bring the corners together and give a little twist to seal.

Heat the oil in a deep-fat fryer or large wok to 180°C (350°F) — either measure with a thermometer or drop a cube of bread into the oil: it should brown in about 15 seconds. Deep-fry the won tons in batches until golden. Serve with the hot English mustard (not for the faint-hearted).

MAKES 20 TO SERVE AS CANAPES

garlic PROWNS

This is probably the most widely loved seafood dish in the world — the Chinese have their own version, as do the French, Spanish and Portuguese. This is the Italian method, because the thing I love most of all is the crusty ciabatta bread that soaks up all the lovely flavours.

You could also use SCALLOPS, BUGS, SCAMPI, SARDINES, CRAB, MUSSELS, VONGOLE or PIPIS

3 tablespoons olive oil
8 garlic cloves, thinly sliced
2 anchovies
4 tablespoons chilli confit, page 217
3 tablespoons chopped flat-leaf (Italian) parsley
16 raw king prawns, peeled and deveined, leaving the tails intact
250 g (9 oz/1 cup) tinned tomatoes, crushed in the hand
2 thick slices ciabatta bread, toasted and then torn into pieces

Put the oil, garlic and anchovies into a cold frying pan and cook until the garlic starts to turn golden. Add the chilli confit, parsley and prawns and toss for 20 seconds. Add the tomato and season with sea salt and cracked black pepper, then cook until the prawns are just cooked. Add the ciabatta toast and let it soak up the sauce a little before serving.

SERVES 4 AS A STARTER

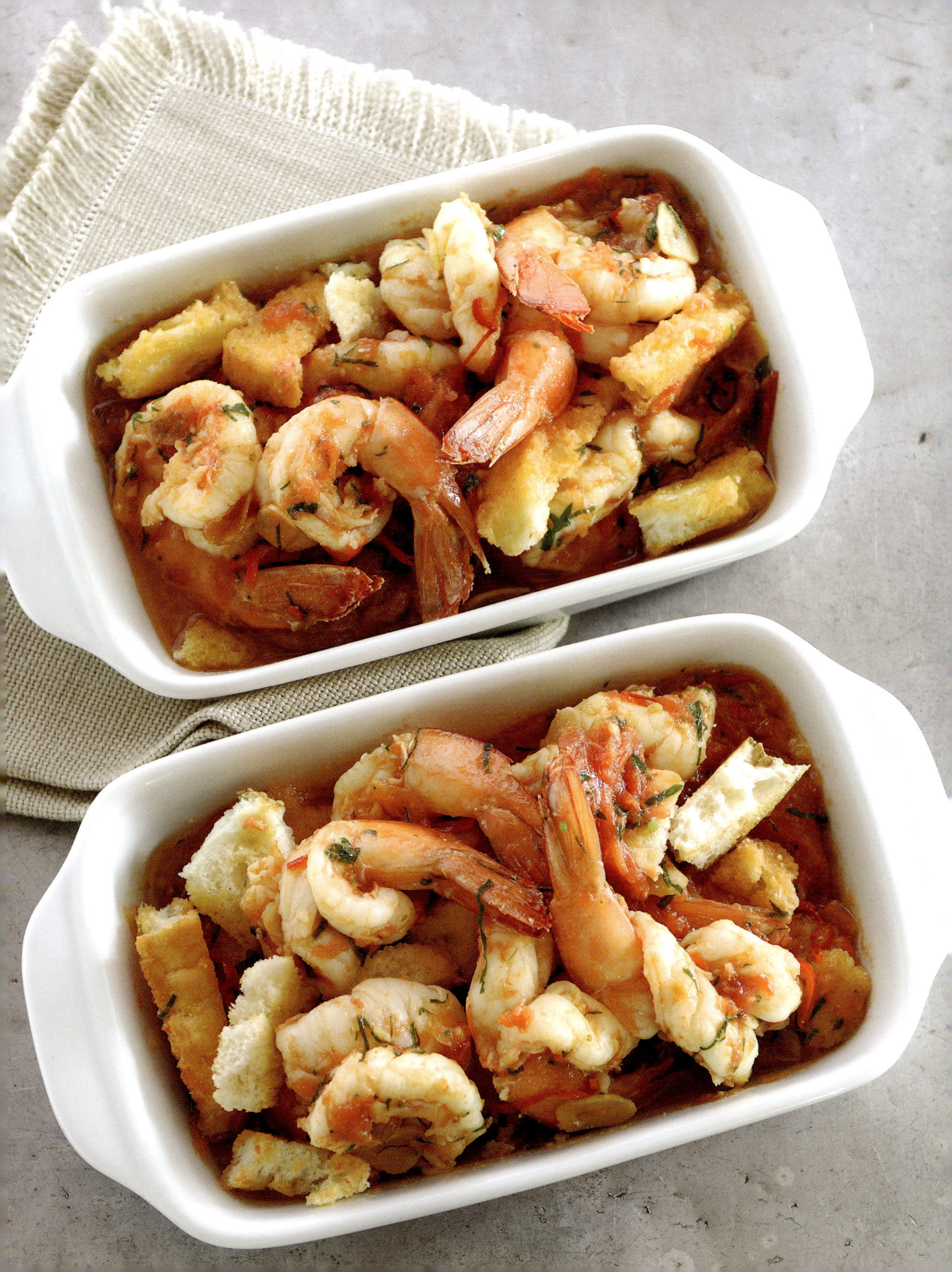

PRAWN and corn fritters

We have a catering business in Sydney called Hugo's Catering and, much as I try to steer the menu away from too many deep-fried dishes, these fritters are what everyone begs for when the platter is empty. (I suspect this greediness has something to do with the free alcohol people consume at parties.) They are incredibly yummy and fantastic for just about any celebration.

You could also use CRAB, SCALLOPS, LOBSTER or BUG meat

200 g (7 oz/1 cup) corn kernels, cut from the cob
1/2 teaspoon white pepper
2 teaspoons sea salt
2 garlic cloves
2 red Asian shallots
2 coriander roots
85 g (3 oz/2/3 cup) plain flour
2 eggs
250 g (9 oz/1 cup) tinned creamed corn
500 g (1 lb 2 oz) raw prawn meat, finely minced
2 tablespoons chopped coriander leaves
2 kaffir lime leaves, julienned
500 ml (17 fl oz/2 cups) vegetable oil
2 quantities chilli caramel dipping sauce, page 217
lime wedges, to serve

Put two-thirds of the corn kernels in a blender and mix until smooth. Add the pepper, salt, garlic, shallots and coriander roots and purée again. Add the flour and process for 1 minute, then add the eggs and process for a further 30 seconds.

Pour the mixture into a bowl and fold through the remaining corn kernels and the creamed corn. Add the prawn meat, chopped coriander and kaffir lime leaves.

Form the mixture into small patties and heat the oil in a frying pan. Cook the fritters for 2–3 minutes until just browned. Drain well on kitchen paper and serve with chilli caramel dipping sauce and lime wedges.

SERVES 8 AS A STARTER

chinese vermicelli noodles with **PRAWNS** and pork

This is a terrific noodle dish that is ridiculously easy to prepare — a great meal for a big family dinner.

You could also use SCALLOPS, LOBSTER, CRAB, SQUID, ABALONE or any firm white-fleshed FISH

100 g (3½ oz) vermicelli rice noodles
125 ml (4 fl oz/½ cup) peanut oil
2 eggs, whisked
2 teaspoons minced garlic
2 teaspoons minced fresh ginger
3 spring onions, finely chopped, white and green parts kept separate
1 tablespoon curry powder
150 g (5½ oz) raw prawn meat, cut into bite-sized pieces
5 shiitake mushrooms, sliced
100 g (3½ oz) barbecued Chinese pork neck, thinly sliced (available from Chinese barbecue shops)
½ red capsicum, sliced
75 g (2¾ oz) bean sprouts
7 snow peas, finely sliced
1 tablespoon sambal oelek
2 tablespoons shaoxing rice wine
100 ml (3½ fl oz) soy sauce
lemon wedges, to serve

Cook the noodles in boiling salted water for 1–2 minutes until they are soft and cooked through. Drain and keep warm.

Heat half the oil in a wok and add the eggs as if you were making an omelette. When the eggs are just set, slide the omelette out of the wok and cut it into thin ribbons.

Heat the rest of the oil in the wok over high heat and then add the garlic, ginger, white spring onions, curry powder and prawns and cook for 1 minute. Add the mushrooms and cook for a further 30 seconds, then add the pork, capsicum, bean sprouts and snow peas and cook for a further minute.

Add the noodles, omelette, sambal oelek, rice wine and soy sauce and toss together. Cook for a further minute or two and then scatter with green spring onions and serve with lemon wedges.

SERVES 4

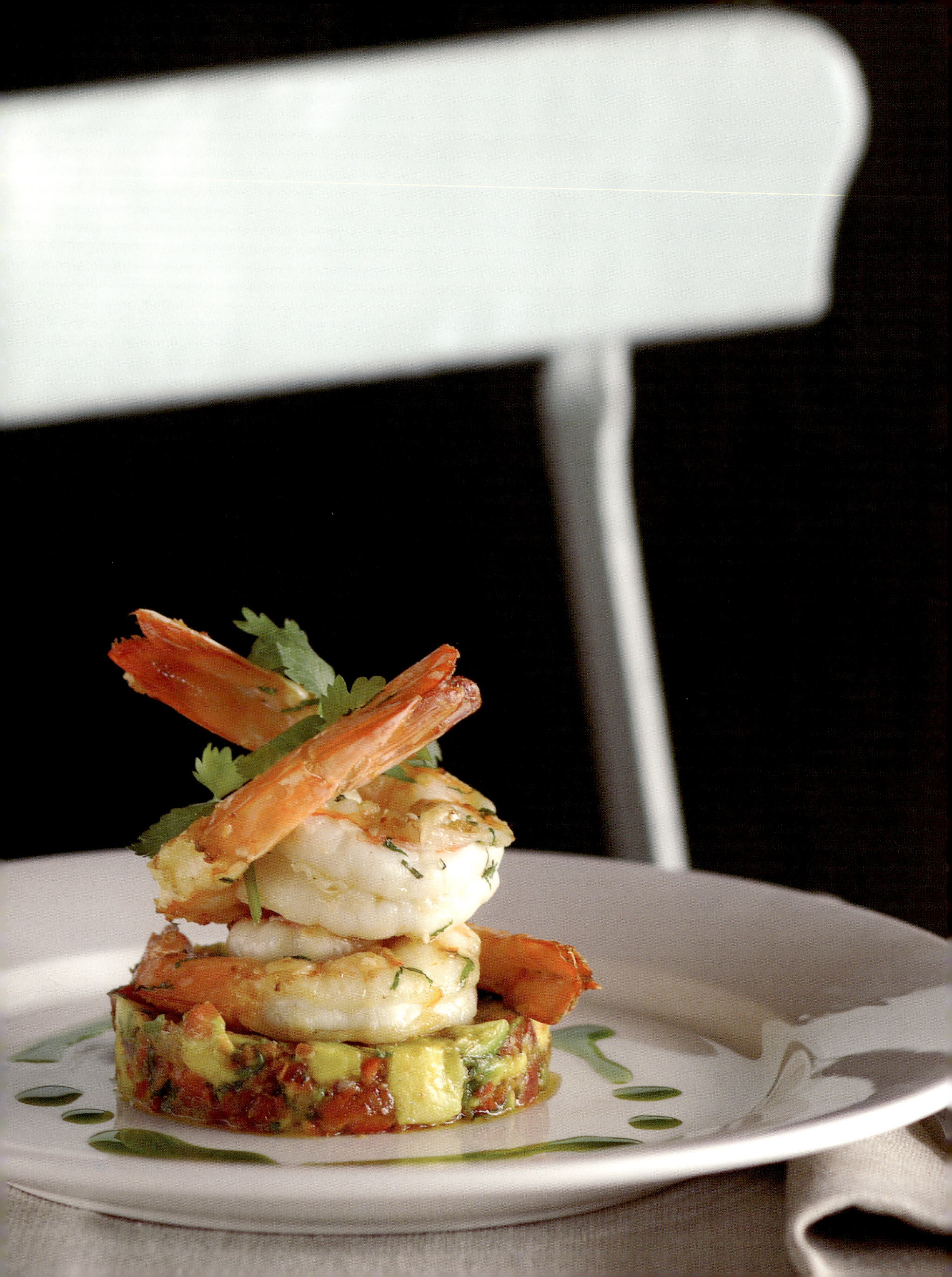

PRAWNS on avocado salsa

If you like easy recipes that are perfect for a weekend barbecue, then try this. It is basically a Mexican guacamole with barbecued prawns on top. I have yet to find anyone who doesn't love it.

You could also use BUGS, LOBSTER, SCAMPI, MARRON or raw TUNA

2 avocados, cubed
1 semi-dried tomato, diced
1 roasted capsicum, diced
1 bird's eye chilli, finely chopped
1 tablespoon chopped coriander
1 tablespoon extra virgin olive oil
2 teaspoons diced red onion
2 tablespoons lemon juice
4 tablespoons basil oil, page 213
4 tablespoons chilli oil, page 219
16 raw prawns, peeled and deveined, with tails intact
2 tablespoons olive oil
2 garlic cloves, minced
coriander sprigs, to garnish

Gently mix the avocado, tomato, capsicum, chilli, coriander, extra virgin olive oil, onion and 1 tablespoon of the lemon juice in a bowl with some sea salt and cracked pepper. Put a biscuit cutter in the centre of each plate and spoon the avocado salsa into it. Lift the biscuit cutter away to leave a neat pile of salsa.

Spoon a little of the basil and chilli oils around the salsa.

Season the prawns with sea salt and pepper. Heat 1 tablespoon of the olive oil on the barbecue plate or in a frying pan and cook the prawns until golden on one side. Turn them over and cook until almost done, and then scatter with the garlic (the prawns should still be a little opaque in the middle).

Toss the prawns in the remaining lemon juice and olive oil and arrange on top of the salsa. Garnish with sprigs of coriander.

SERVES 4

tom yum soup with **PRAWN** dumplings

This hot and sour soup is possibly the most famous of all the Thai dishes. You can drop whole prawns into the soup to make tom yum goong, but these dumplings are a little special.

You could also use CRAB meat, any firm white-fleshed FISH or SCALLOPS

5 garlic cloves, chopped
3 red Asian shallots, sliced
2 coriander roots, chopped
1 tablespoon chopped spearmint leaves
grated zest of 1 lime
2 teaspoons minced fresh ginger
2 teaspoons minced galangal
1 lemongrass stalk, sliced
2 red bird's eye chillies, roughly chopped
2 kaffir lime leaves, shredded
12 raw king prawns
1 tablespoon vegetable oil
2 litres (70 fl oz/8 cups) fish stock or water
80 ml ($2^{1}/_{2}$ fl oz/$^{1}/_{3}$ cup) fish sauce
85 ml($2^{3}/_{4}$ oz) lime juice
24 gow gee or wonton wrappers
1 cup chestnut mushrooms (or other mushrooms)
2 tomatoes, peeled, deseeded and sliced
12 Vietnamese mint leaves
shredded kaffir lime leaf and sliced red chilli, to serve

Pound the garlic, shallots, coriander roots, spearmint leaves, lime zest, ginger, galangal, lemongrass, chillies and kaffir lime leaves with a mortar and pestle.

Peel and devein the prawns, keeping the shells and heads, and mince or finely chop the prawn meat. Keep the prawn meat in the fridge until you need it. Heat the oil in a wide saucepan and fry the prawn heads and shells over moderate heat until they are pinkish, then remove from the pan.

Tip the mixture from your mortar into the same pan and cook until fragrant and just beginning to colour. Return the prawn heads and shells to the pan and stir together well. Add the stock and bring to a simmer over gentle heat, then cook for 45 minutes. Strain through a fine meshed sieve and throw away the solids.

Return the strained stock to the clean pan. Stir in the fish sauce and lime juice while the stock is very hot. Taste and adjust the seasoning if necessary.

Lay out half the gow gee or wonton wrappers on a lightly floured work surface and place 2 teaspoons of minced prawn in the centre of each one. Season with sea salt and white pepper, lightly brush around the edge with water and place the other 12 wrappers on top, sealing firmly around the edge with your finger.

Gently lower the prawn wontons and mushrooms into the simmering soup and cook for 2 minutes before spooning into bowls. Add the tomato slices and scatter with Vietnamese mint leaves, shredded kaffir lime leaves and chilli to serve.

SERVES 4

light **PRAWN** curry with bok choy and shiitakes

This is a beautifully fragrant curry sauce that isn't so rich that it smothers all the glorious flavour of the prawns. I especially like the contrast of the soft shiitakes and crisp bok choy.

You could also use BUGS, SCALLOPS, LOBSTER, SALMON, TROUT or any firm white-fleshed FISH

LIGHT CURRY SAUCE
1/2 teaspoon coriander seeds
1/4 teaspoon cumin seeds
5 white peppercorns
seeds of 1 cardamom pod
3 dried chillies
2 red Asian shallots, sliced
2 garlic cloves, minced
1/2 lemongrass stalk, chopped
2 coriander roots, chopped
1/2 teaspoon sea salt
2 teaspoons curry powder
30 ml (1 fl oz) vegetable oil
750 ml (26 fl oz/3 cups) coconut milk
2 tablespoons fish sauce
2 tablespoons palm sugar
lime juice, to taste

16 large raw king prawns
6 shiitake mushrooms, stalks removed, sliced into four
3–4 heads bok choy or choy sum, cut into quarters
375 ml (13 fl oz/1 1/2 cups) light curry sauce, above
20 Thai basil leaves
1 kaffir lime leaf, julienned
1 banana chilli, julienned

To make the curry sauce, dry-roast the coriander and cumin seeds in a frying pan until fragrant but not burnt. Transfer to a grinder or mortar and pestle and grind with the peppercorns and cardamom seeds. Add the chillies, shallots, garlic, lemongrass, coriander root, sea salt and curry powder and blend to a smooth paste.

Heat the vegetable oil in a wok and cook the paste until fragrant. Add the coconut milk and simmer for 10 minutes (do not boil or the coconut milk will split). Remove from the heat, add the fish sauce, palm sugar and lime juice to taste. Blend with a hand blender and then strain through a fine sieve.

This will make enough to prepare two curries — you can store the leftover curry sauce in the freezer for up to 6 months or keep it in the fridge for 2 days.

Heat a wok with a touch of grapeseed oil, add the prawns and cook on one side, then flip the prawns over, add the mushrooms and cook for a minute.

Blanch the bok choy in some boiling salted water for 30 seconds, then add to the wok with the curry sauce and Thai basil. Cook for 2–3 minutes, or until the sauce has a consistency you like. Serve with steamed rice, with the kaffir lime and chilli scattered over the top.

SERVES 4

chilli PRAWN pizzas with salsa verde

I have always steered very far clear of seafood pizzas, as the quality of the produce can be a bit dodgy. However, when we opened up Hugo's Bar Pizza I wanted to create some beautiful recipes highlighting seafood on pizza, and this is one of my favourites. (Not boasting — well, not much — but we also went on to win 'best pizza in the world' at the New York Pizza competition in 2005 with a seafood pizza using scallops and bottarga.)

You could also use LOBSTER, BUGS, MUSSELS

1 quantity pizza dough, page 228
1 quantity Italian tomato sauce, page 223
160 g (5¾ oz) mozzarella cheese, shredded
40 cherry tomatoes, cut into thirds
120 g (4¼ oz) roasted capsicum, peeled and cut into strips
320 g (11¼ oz) raw king prawn meat, chopped
1 teaspoon hot chilli flakes
2 balls Italian buffalo mozzarella
4 tablespoons salsa verde, page 228

Preheat your oven to its hottest temperature.

Divide the pizza dough into four portions and, using a rolling pin, roll out each portion on a work bench dusted with either flour or semolina. Lift each dough base onto a 30 cm (12 inch) pizza tray and prick holes all over it with a fork.

Spread the tomato sauce over the pizza bases and top with shredded mozzarella, then tomatoes and capsicum. Sprinkle the prawn meat over the top and scatter with salt, pepper and chilli flakes. Tear the buffalo mozzarella into pieces and arrange on the pizzas.

Cook the pizzas for 6–10 minutes (depending on how hot your oven is) or until the dough is crispy and golden brown. When the pizzas come out of the oven, drizzle them with the salsa verde.

SERVES 4

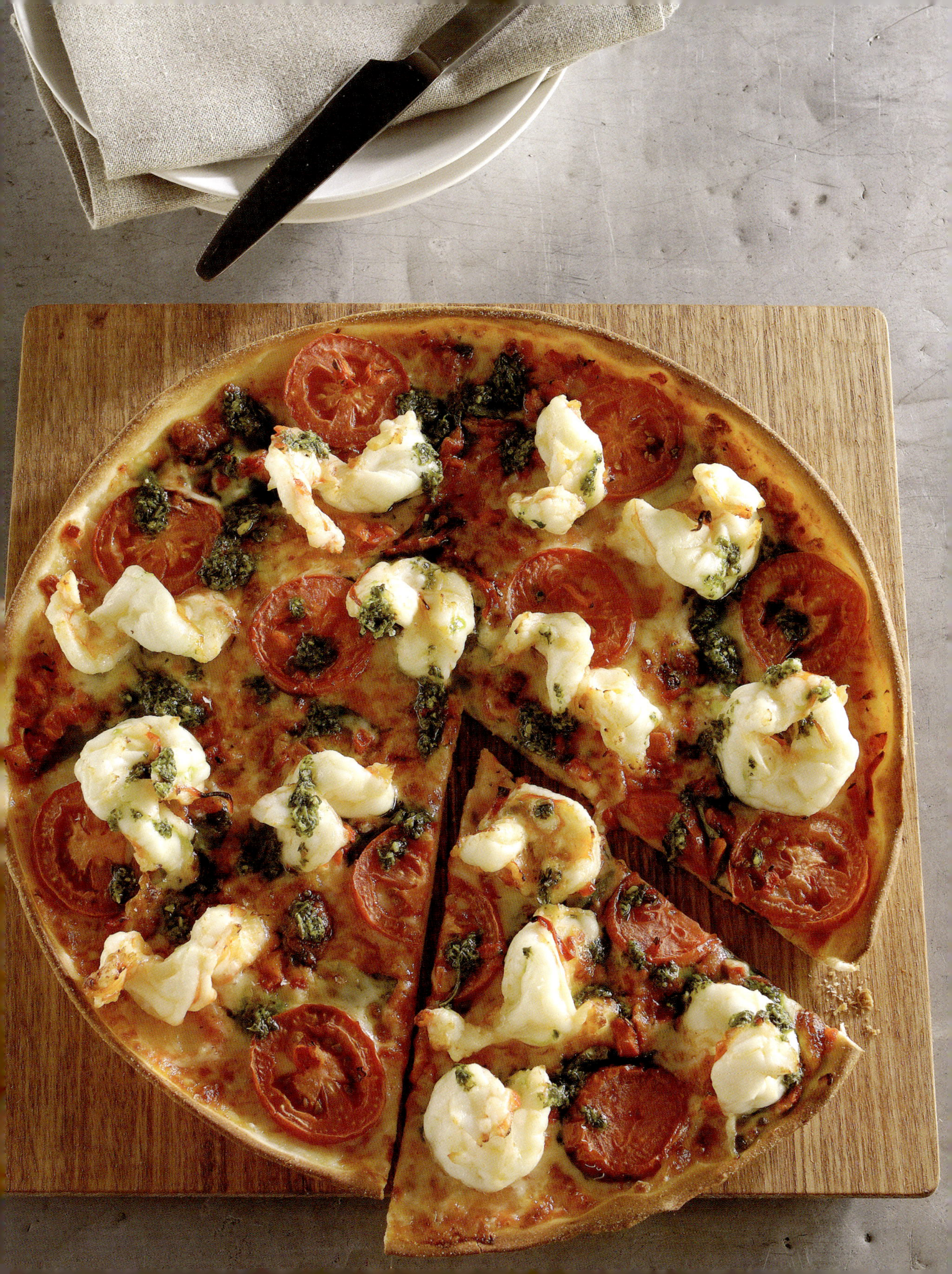

PRAWN, radicchio and red wine risotto

I love cooking risotto in the colder months. Just as red wine is my drink of choice in autumn and winter, it becomes my favourite flavour base for risotto then, as well. This is a lovely combination of flavours — the warming, earthy qualities of the wine, the sweetness from the prawns and the slight bitterness of the radicchio. And the best thing is that it only takes about 15 minutes from start to finish.

You could also use BUGS, any white-fleshed reef FISH, SQUID or MUSSELS

2 tablespoons olive oil
4 French shallots, finely chopped, or
2 tablespoons finely chopped onion
4 garlic cloves, finely chopped
1 tablespoon chopped flat-leaf (Italian) parsley
16 large raw prawns, peeled and each cut into 6 pieces
300 g (10 1/2 oz/1 1/2 cups) arborio rice
250 ml (9 fl oz/1 glass) pinot noir or other red wine
400 ml (14 fl oz) hot fish or chicken stock
1 tablespoon butter
2 large handfuls of thinly sliced radicchio
lemon wedges, to serve
1 teaspoon hot chilli flakes

Heat the oil in a wide heavy-based saucepan and gently fry the shallot or onion and garlic until soft but not coloured. Add the parsley and cook for 30 seconds. Season with salt and pepper. Add the prawns and cook for 30 seconds.

Add the rice and cook for another 30 seconds, stirring well to coat all the grains with the oil. Add the wine and stir for about 2 minutes until it has almost evaporated. Add the hot stock and stir well. Put the lid on the pan. Turn down the heat to its lowest setting and leave the risotto for 12–15 minutes, or until the rice is cooked. Stir in the butter and radicchio and leave to rest for 5 minutes. Serve with lemon wedges and chilli flakes.

SERVES 4

sweet and sour **RED EMPEROR**

It's funny how a recipe comes together... The red emperor is regarded as one of the best eating reef fish in the world, with its firm white flesh and slightly meaty taste. So, I'm using a Chinese recipe for sweet and sour that is usually served with pork or chicken, but I think works even better with fish. If you're pickling your own vegetables, don't forget to do that beforehand.

You could also use PRAWNS, SCALLOPS, BUGS or any firm white-fleshed whole FISH or fillets

peanut oil, for deep-frying
4 plate-sized red emperor, or 600 g (1 lb 5 oz) fillet cut into 2.5 cm (1 inch) pieces
flour, for dusting
8 baby pearl onions, cut into quarters
125 ml (4 fl oz/½ cup) of your favourite brand of sweet and sour sauce
1 quantity pickled vegetables with vinegar, page 227
12 snow peas, blanched in boiling salted water and then refreshed
20 garlic chives, cut into short batons
4 tablespoons diced fresh pineapple
2 handfuls julienned spring onions

If you're using whole fish, heat the peanut oil in a wok to 185°C (365°F) — either measure this with a thermometer or drop a cube of bread into the oil: it should brown in about 10 seconds. Dust the fish lightly in flour, shaking off the excess, and then fry until golden brown. Lift out and drain on kitchen paper, then arrange on plates.

Clean the wok, return to the heat and add a few tablespoons of oil. Stir-fry the onions until just starting to brown and then add the sweet and sour sauce.

Add the pickling vinegar and let it cook for a couple of minutes until you have a sauce consistency that you like. If you're using pieces of fish, add them to the wok now. Add the snow peas, garlic chives, pineapple and spring onions to the wok, give a quick stir and pour over the whole fish on the plates. (If you're using pieces of fish, serve over steamed rice.) Garnish with the pickled vegetables.

SERVES 4

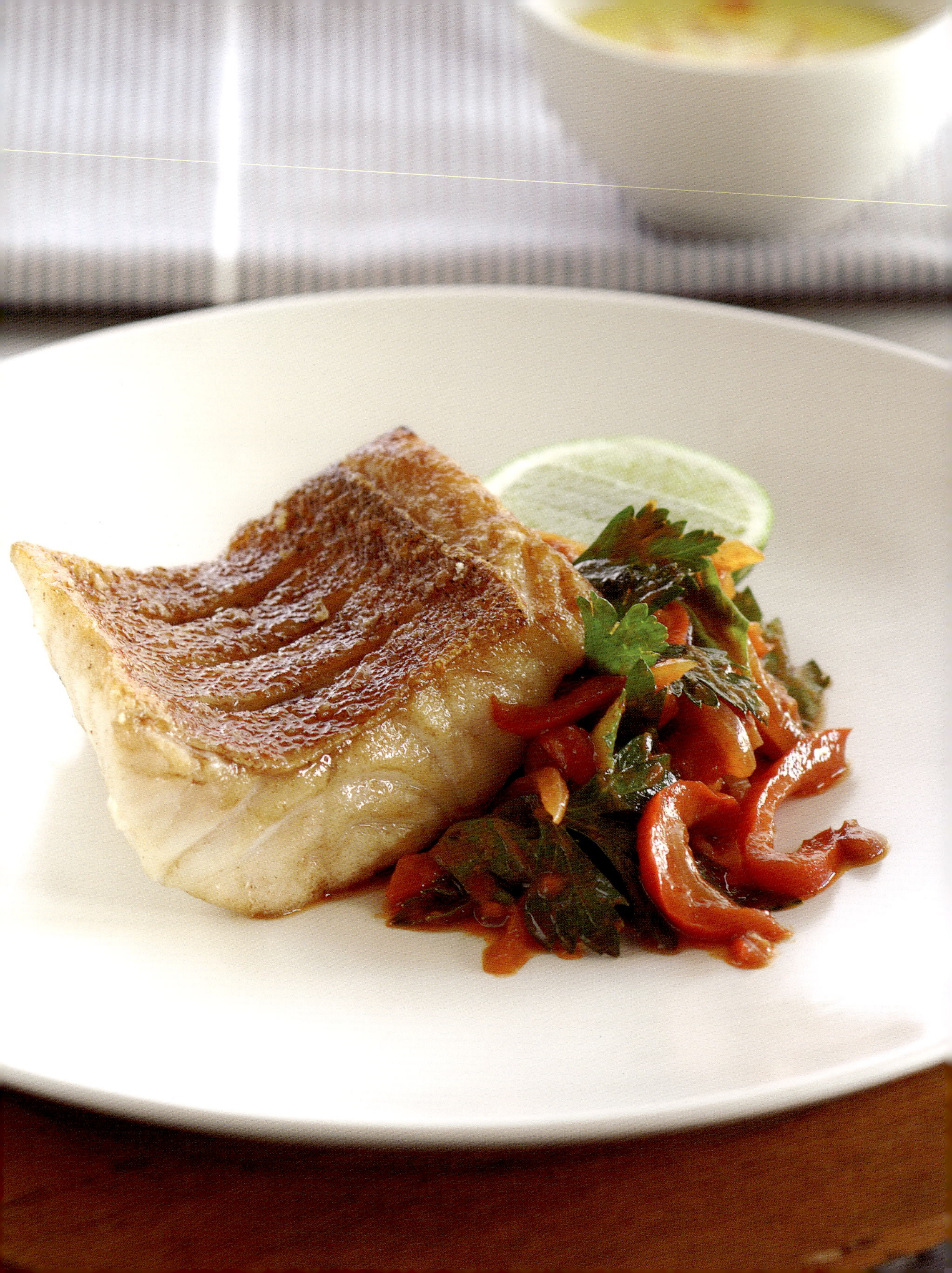

RED EMPEROR with basque peppers

These capsicums are cooked in the basque manner, using smoked paprika, garlic, olive oil and Spanish onions. They are delicious served with almost any variety of seafood, but put them on a plate with a lovely piece of red emperor and some creamy saffron aioli and you're in culinary heaven.

You could also use PRAWNS, LOBSTER, SWORDFISH, SALMON, TUNA, KINGFISH, SARDINES, MACKEREL, HERRING or any firm white-fleshed FISH

2 red capsicums, roasted and peeled
1 yellow capsicum, roasted and peeled
1 green capsicum, roasted and peeled
3 roma tomatoes
100 ml (3 1/2 fl oz) extra virgin olive oil
1 red onion, thinly sliced
2 garlic cloves, chopped
1 teaspoon smoked paprika
2 teaspoons tomato paste
a handful of flat-leaf (Italian) parsley leaves
4 x 160–180 g (6 oz) red emperor fillets

SAFFRON AIOLI
1 teaspoon sherry vinegar
a couple of saffron threads
2 tablespoons aioli, page 212

Cut the capsicums into strips 1–2 cm (about 3/4 inch) wide, discarding the seeds and membrane. Score a cross on the base of each tomato, plunge the tomatoes into boiling water for 10 seconds, then transfer to cold water and peel the skin away from the cross. Cut into quarters, scoop out the seeds and roughly chop the flesh.

Heat the olive oil in a pan and cook the onion and garlic until soft but not coloured. Add the paprika and fry for 30 seconds. Add the tomato paste and cook for 1 minute. Add the capsicum and tomatoes and cook for 10 minutes. Stir in the parsley and season to taste with sea salt and cracked black pepper.

Brush the fish with olive oil and salt and cook on a barbecue, under a hot grill or in a frying pan until just cooked through. Leave to rest for 5 minutes before serving.

To make the saffron aioli, warm the sherry vinegar and saffron together and fold through the aioli.

Spoon the capsicums onto a plate and serve with the fish and a little saffron aioli.

SERVES 4

pan-fried RED MULLET with lentils

I find lentils to be very grounding. Whenever I feel as if I'm going at a hundred miles an hour I always try to incorporate some lentils into my diet to bring me back to earth and calm me. This is a lovely combination of beautiful red mullet served with lentils enriched with veal jus. If you like theatrics at the dinner table, roast the red mullet whole.

You could also use JOHN DORY or STRIPEY TRUMPETER

3 tablespoons puy (blue/green) lentils
1 bouquet garni
1 teaspoon olive oil
1 teaspoon diced carrot
1 teaspoon chopped leek, white part only
1 teaspoon diced celery
1 teaspoon chopped flat-leaf (Italian) parsley
125 ml (4 fl oz/$^1\!/_2$ cup) veal jus
2 teaspoons lemon juice
4 x 160–180 g (6 oz) red mullet fillets, bones removed

Soak the lentils for 1 hour in cold water, then drain and put in a saucepan. Cover the lentils with cold water, add the bouquet garni and bring to a simmer. Cover the pan and cook for 20 minutes, or until the lentils are tender, and then drain.

Heat the olive oil in a saucepan and sauté the carrot, leek and celery until softened. Add the parsley and lentils and season with salt and pepper. Add the veal jus and cook until the sauce reaches the consistency you like, then add the lemon juice.

Heat a touch of oil in a frying pan and pan-fry the red mullet, skin side down, until golden. Flip over and cook for a further minute until the fish is just cooked through. Serve with the lentil sauce spooned over the top.

SERVES 4

gnocchi with RED MULLET

Red mullet isn't as popular in Australia as it is in Europe, mainly because it tends to be very seasonal and hard to come by. This is a shame because it is one of the tastiest of the sea fishes and a perfect accompaniment to pasta or gnocchi.

You could also use SNAPPER, WHITING, CRAB meat or EEL

POTATO GNOCCHI
600 g (1 lb 5 oz) desiree potatoes, unpeeled
30 g (1 oz) unsalted butter, softened
30 g (1 oz) parmesan cheese, grated
1 egg yolk
10 g ($1/4$ oz) sea salt
about 60 g ($2^{1}/4$ oz) 00 (baker's) flour

4 x 100 g ($3^{1}/2$ oz) fillets red mullet with skin on, bones removed
2 garlic cloves, finely chopped
$1/2$ bird's eye chilli, chopped
12 basil leaves
$1/2$ punnet cherry tomatoes
500 ml (17 fl oz/2 cups) sparkling mineral water
50 g ($1^{3}/4$ oz) unsalted butter

To make the gnocchi, simmer the potatoes in water until cooked through. Cool a little, then remove the skins and dry out the potatoes in a warm oven to remove any moisture. Purée the potatoes in a mouli or ricer, or just mash well.

Put in a mixer with a paddle blade on slow speed (or mix by hand on your work surface) and add the butter, cheese, egg yolk and salt. Add flour until the dough doesn't stick to your fingers.

Knead and roll the dough on a work surface dusted with flour into 1 cm ($1/2$ inch) thick logs. Cut at 2.5 cm (1 inch) intervals with a spatula. Cook the gnocchi, a few at a time, in boiling salted water until they float to the surface, then lift them out quickly with a slotted spoon.

Meanwhile, heat a frying pan with a touch of oil and put the fish in the pan, skin side down. Add the garlic, chilli, basil and cherry tomatoes. Flip the fish over, add the mineral water and cook until it has reduced by half. Break up the fish in the pan and add the butter. Place the gnocchi in the pan and toss together gently. Serve immediately.

SERVES 4

slow-poached atlantic SALMON with cauliflower purée, apple balsamic and roasted pancetta

Cooking is a science, and over the last ten years there have been great discoveries made regarding cooking times, temperatures and the molecular make up of food. This recipe uses a technique for slow-cooking salmon so that the internal temperature reaches 45°C, which means the fish just melts in your mouth.

You could also use any firm white-fleshed FISH, SCALLOPS, LOBSTER, CRAB or BUGS

2 x 200 g (7 oz) Atlantic salmon fillets, skin and bones removed
4 slices pancetta
½ cup cauliflower purée, page 216
2 tablespoons salmon roe (Yarra Valley is the best)
2–3 tablespoons apple balsamic vinegar (available at good delis)

Roll out about 50 cm (20 inches) plastic wrap but do not cut it from the roll. Place one piece of salmon across the cling film, then generously season the top of that fillet with sea salt. Take the other fillet and place it on top, facing the opposite way to the first so they are head to tail so to speak (what you are after is a uniformly thick side of salmon).

Roll up the salmon very tightly in the plastic wrap about 10 times, and then tie at the ends so the parcel is airtight.

Pour water into a roasting tin (enough water to cover the fish parcel when you put it in) and heat the water to 55°C (use a thermometer). Place the fish in the water and leave for 20–30 minutes or until the internal temperature of the fish reaches 45°C. (You will need to insert a thermometer to check — if the temperature hasn't reached 45°C, you'll need to rewrap the fish to ensure it's watertight and return it to the water.) Remove from the water and leave the fish to sit for 5 minutes.

Meanwhile, preheat the oven to 180°C (350°F/Gas 4). Put the pancetta on an oven tray and roast until just starting to go crispy (but not all the way there). Drain on kitchen paper.

Slice the salmon into four equal pieces. Spoon 2 tablespoons of cauliflower purée into the centre of each plate, top with the salmon, then the pancetta and salmon roe and finally drizzle some apple balsamic around the plate.

SERVES 4 AS A STARTER

crisp-skinned king SALMON with celery sauce and salt cod mash

This is a simplified version of a dish we used to serve at Hugo's in the early years — it still has the same wonderful flavours but is presented in a simpler form. If you did want to get fancy with the presentation for a large group of people, take two sides of salmon from the same fish, remove the pin bones and skin and spread one fillet with the cold salt cod mash. Put the other fillet on top, then truss the salmon with some butcher's twine and let it sit overnight in the fridge to set. You can either bake it whole or cut it into medallions and pan-fry them, as below. You could use ordinary potato mash, but the salt cod adds a depth of flavour that is sublime.

You could also use OCEAN, RAINBOW or BROWN TROUT or JOHN DORY

CELERY SAUCE
olive oil, for cooking
2 French shallots, sliced
150 ml (5 fl oz) white wine
8 peppercorns
1 bay leaf
250 ml (9 fl oz/1 cup) chicken stock
375 ml (13 fl oz/1½ cups) cream
2 large handfuls dark green celery leaves

4 x 160–180 g (6 oz) king salmon fillets, with skin on, bones removed
8 pencil leeks (baby leeks), blanched and refreshed
1½ cups warm salt cod mash, page 229

To make the celery sauce, heat a little olive oil in a saucepan and cook the shallots until soft but not coloured. Add the white wine, peppercorns and bay leaf and cook until reduced by about two-thirds. Add the chicken stock and cook until reduced to about half a cupful. Add the cream and cook until it has reduced by half. Pass through a fine sieve and season with salt and pepper.

When the sauce is cool enough to put your finger in without being burnt, blend the celery leaves into it with your blender.

Heat a touch of oil in a non-stick frying pan until hot. Put the salmon in the pan, skin side down, and cook over medium heat for 4–5 minutes until the skin is golden and crisp. Season with sea salt and turn the fish over. Add the leeks to the pan and continue cooking until the fish is medium-rare.

Pour the celery sauce into four shallow bowls, spoon some hot salt cod mash into the centre of each bowl and top with the crisp-skinned salmon and sautéed leeks.

SERVES 4

eggs benedict with smoked SALMON

This is without a doubt one of the best-ever breakfast recipes for eggs and seafood. Hollandaise sounds scary but it is really quite simple to make — you just need to remember that the water in the pot should be barely simmering, so that you don't overheat the yolks and scramble them, and you must add the butter slowly to prevent the sauce separating. It is also important to use the sauce within about half an hour.

For a real extravagance, try whisking some SEA URCHIN roe into the hollandaise. This sauce is glorious on just about any grilled or poached seafood.

HOLLANDAISE SAUCE
2 egg yolks
1–2 tablespoons tarragon or white wine vinegar
125 ml (4 fl oz/½ cup) melted butter
1 teaspoon chopped chives

a couple of drops of vinegar for poaching the eggs
8 free-range eggs
4 English muffins
butter for the muffins
200 g (7 oz) baby English spinach leaves
8 slices smoked salmon
salmon roe or caviar (if you're feeling indulgent)

To make the hollandaise sauce, half-fill a saucepan with water and bring to the boil. Turn off the heat. Put the egg yolks and vinegar in a stainless steel mixing bowl and put that over the saucepan. Start whisking fast until when you lift up your whisk the ribbons that run off it into the bowl 'sit' on top of the mixture for about 3 seconds (this is the ribbon stage). Slowly add the melted butter in a thin stream, still whisking fast. Season with some salt and white pepper, chives and a touch of lemon juice if you like.

Bring about 1 litre (35 fl oz/4 cups) of water to the boil in a large wide pan and add a few drops of vinegar to the water (this helps the eggs hold their shape when you poach them). You might find it easier to bring two pans of water to the boil and cook 4 eggs in each.

When the water comes to the bowl, crack the eggs into a bowl first (so they are all ready to cook at exactly the same moment), slide them into the water and turn the water temperature down to a simmer. Cook to your own taste (I like my eggs runny, so 3–4 minutes). Toast and butter your muffins while the eggs are cooking.

Meanwhile, blanch the spinach in boiling salted water and then drain, or alternatively heat a little olive oil in a pan and quickly cook the spinach leaves, then drain and season.

Lay smoked salmon over the muffins, spoon spinach onto the salmon, pop your eggs on top of the spinach, ladle some of your hollandaise over the eggs and finish with some salmon roe or caviar.

SERVES 4

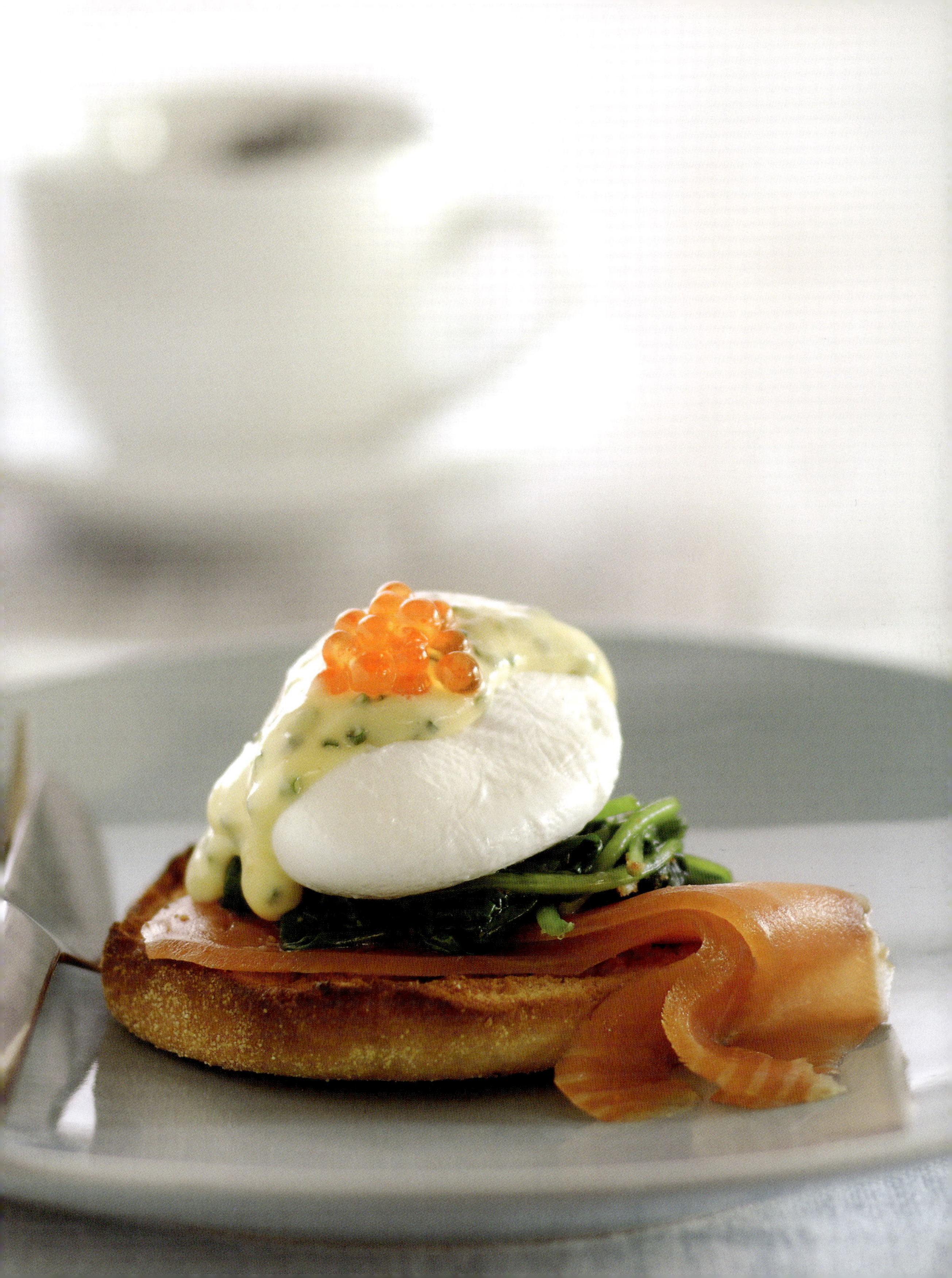

Our hut, Snowy Mountains, NSW.

Barry, Udo and me with a healthy catch.

Dinner.

Astrid on to a fighter.

The man from Snowy River.

salt cod
sardines scallops scampi sea urchin skate
snapper

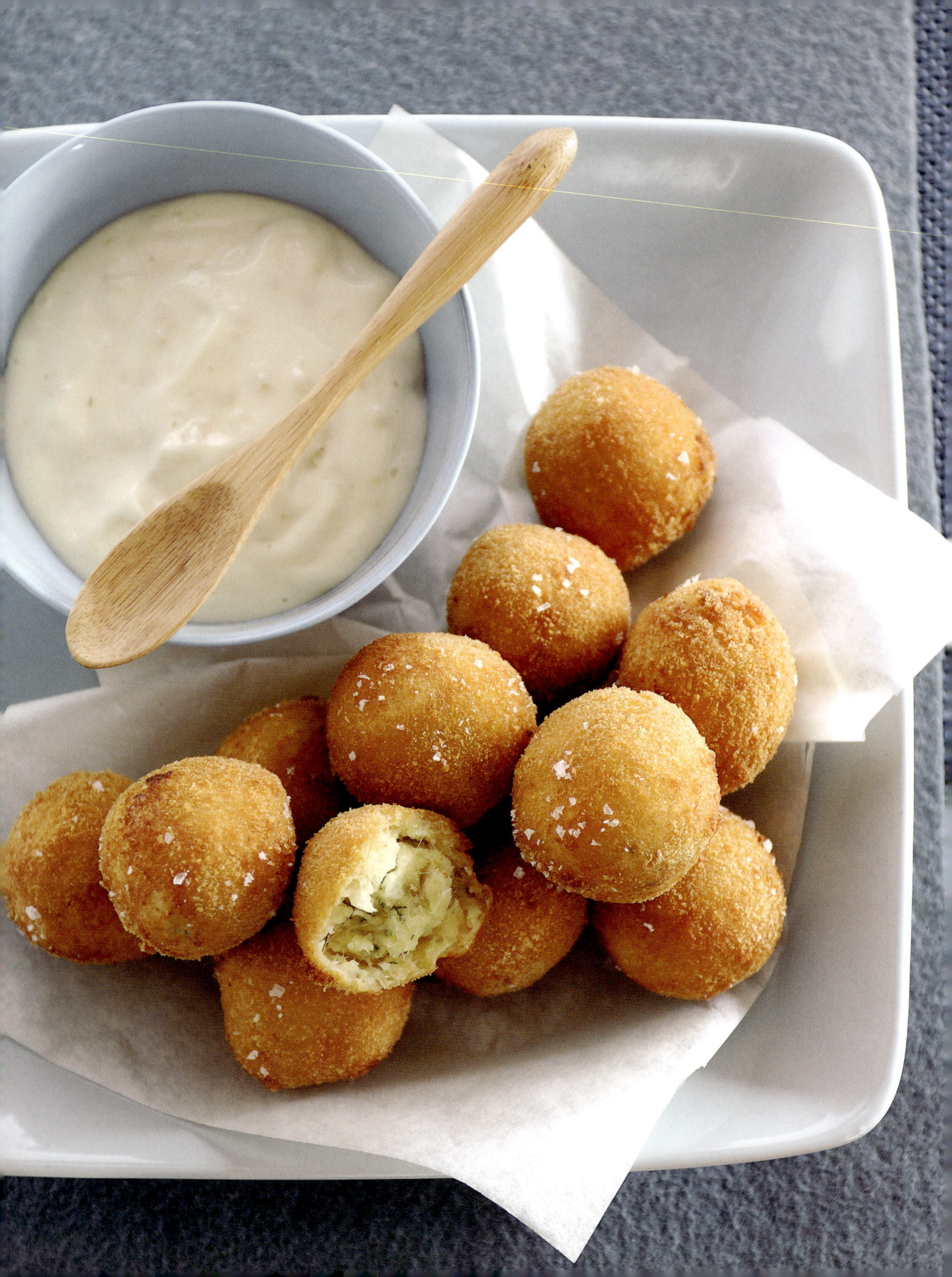

SALT COD fritters with preserved lemon aioli

Salt cod (baccala) is one ingredient we do have to get from overseas. There is a bit of work that goes into making these fritters, but I dare say they would have to be my all-time favourite snack food (the kids love rolling them, too). You can make lots in one batch and freeze them prior to crumbing.

There's no substitute for the flavour of SALT COD, but you could also use any other firm white-fleshed FISH instead of the blue-eye

250 g (9 oz/¼ side) salt cod, soaked in cold water for 48 hours (change the water every 24 hours)
750 g (1 lb 10 oz) potatoes
500 ml (17 fl oz/2 cups) milk
grated zest of ½ orange
1 bay leaf
1 French shallot, sliced
1 garlic clove, peeled but left whole
160–180 g (6 oz) blue-eye trevalla
3 cloves garlic confit, page 222, mashed
2 tablespoons chopped flat-leaf (Italian) parsley
grated zest of 1 lemon
1 tablespoon dijon mustard
flour, for dusting
2 eggs, lightly beaten with a splash of milk
120 g (4 oz/1½ cups) breadcrumbs
½ cup aioli, page 212
1 tablespoon finely chopped preserved lemon rind

When the salt cod has been soaked, cut it into cubes. Peel and boil the potatoes until soft, then put through a mouli or grater.

Heat the milk, orange zest, bay leaf, shallot and garlic in a pan and add the salt cod. Bring to a gentle simmer and poach the fish for 15–20 minutes until half cooked.

Add the blue-eye and cook for another 10–15 minutes, until the salt cod starts to come off the bone and the blue-eye is cooked through. Lift the fish out of the milk and leave to cool. Remove the flesh from the bones (making sure no bones are left in).

Finely shred the salt cod and blue-eye and mix with the potato, garlic confit, parsley, lemon zest, mustard and some sea salt and white pepper. Roll into balls, using about 1 tablespoon of mixture for each, and dip in flour, then beaten egg and then breadcrumbs. Heat the oil in a deep-fat fryer or large pan to 180°C (350°F) — either measure this with a thermometer or drop a cube of bread into the oil: it should brown in about 15 seconds. Deep-fry the fritters until golden and heated through.

Mix the aioli with the preserved lemon and serve with the fritters.

MAKES 30

grilled SARDINES with saffron dressing

Acidity creates an important balance in seafood cooking, especially with seafood that is high in oil and fat (those wonderful omega 3s). Sardines supposedly take their name from the young pilchards caught off the coast of Sardinia, but for me the most amazing are those found off the coast of Western Australia. Sardines are high in oil, and this simple Spanish dressing of saffron and vinegar complements that oiliness to perfection. Any leftover dressing can be kept in a screw-top jar in the fridge for a month or so.

You could also use HERRING, MACKEREL, SCALLOPS, SCAMPI, MARRON, TUNA, TROUT or SQUID

SAFFRON DRESSING
1 tablespoon Madeira or port
a pinch of saffron threads
1 garlic clove, finely chopped
a pinch of hot chilli flakes
a pinch of paprika
1 tablespoon dijon mustard
3 tablespoons sherry vinegar
250 ml (9 fl oz/1 cup) Spanish olive oil

8 whole sardines, gutted and bones removed
olive oil
1 tablespoon chopped flat-leaf (Italian) parsley

To make the saffron dressing, heat the Madeira with the saffron, then transfer to a blender with the other ingredients, except the oil. Blend until smooth and then slowly drizzle in the oil while you mix until the dressing is emulsified. Season with a pinch of salt.

Rub the sardines with the olive oil and roast on a barbecue or in a 200°C (400°F/Gas 6) oven until cooked. Season well, lay on a serving platter and scatter with chopped parsley and the saffron dressing. Great with a bowl of roast potatoes.

SERVES 4 AS A STARTER

barbecued panata-crumbed SARDINES

Sardines... one smell I can distinctly remember from growing up is the freshly opened tin of sardines. Dad, I haven't completely forgiven you for those torturous Sunday teatimes: I think they were the reason I was put off seafood as a youngster. Thankfully, these days we've discovered that some of the best sardines in the world come out of the waters of Western Australia. I love them just dusted with some homemade breadcrumbs, flavoured with a bit of chopped parsley and chilli, and thrown on the barbecue.

You could also use BUTTERFLIED PRAWNS, WHITING or GARFISH

40 g (1½ oz/½ cup) fresh breadcrumbs
a pinch of chilli flakes
1 tablespoon chopped flat-leaf (Italian) parsley
8 butterflied sardines, fins, heads and bones removed
2 tablespoons olive oil
grated zest of 2 lemons
2 large handfuls of watercress leaves, dressed with olive oil and lemon juice
lemon wedges, to serve

Mix together the breadcrumbs, chilli and parsley and season with sea salt and black pepper. Rub the sardines with the olive oil and then dip into the breadcrumb mixture, pressing the crumbs on firmly.

Heat a barbecue or frying pan with a touch of oil and cook the sardines, turning once, until golden on both sides. Transfer to a plate and sprinkle with lemon zest. Serve with lemon wedges and watercress.

SERVES 4 AS A STARTER

seared SCALLOPS with angel hair pasta and truffle dressing

Truffles are a luxury item and rightly so: they are very rare and very expensive (and, like fine Champagne, not to everyone's taste). This dressing uses a truffle salsa or paste that you can buy in jars or tins at good delis, which makes it less expensive than using fresh. Once you've bought some, you'll probably start putting it in everything from scrambled eggs to mushroom risotto.

You could also use BUG meat, LOBSTER, PRAWNS, SCAMPI, MARRON or TUNA

4 paper-thin slices prosciutto
200 g (7 oz) angel hair pasta
2 tablespoons balsamic truffle dressing, page 213
12 scallops with roe
4 tablespoons warm cauliflower purée, page 216
a handful of chervil or baby herbs

Preheat the oven to 200°C (400°F/Gas 6). Lay the prosciutto on a wire rack over a baking tray and cook in the oven until crispy. Drain on kitchen paper.

Cook the angel hair pasta in a large pan of boiling salted water until al dente, then drain and tip into a mixing bowl. Add half the balsamic truffle dressing and toss to coat.

Heat a touch of oil in a non-stick frying pan and sear the scallops for about 30 seconds on each side until they are medium-rare in the centre and golden on the outside.

Using a carving fork, twirl a portion of pasta onto the side of each plate. Arrange a line of cauliflower purée beside the pasta and arrange 3 scallops on the purée. Lay a slice of crispy prosciutto between the scallops and pasta, garnish with herbs and drizzle the remaining dressing around the plate.

SERVES 4 AS A STARTER

SCALLOPS with leek and potato soup

The fancy name for leek and potato soup is vichyssoise and it is traditionally served chilled. However, I think in the colder months it makes a fantastic starter, served hot and teamed with plump, juicy seared scallops and a dollop of caviar cream.

You could also use OYSTERS with chilled soup

50 g (1³/₄ oz) unsalted butter
200 g (7 oz) leek, white part only, finely sliced
½ onion, finely sliced
100 g (3½ oz) potatoes, thinly sliced
600 ml (9 fl oz/21 fl oz) fish stock
150 ml (5 fl oz) thick cream
1 tablespoon salmon caviar
4 tablespoons whipped cream
20 scallops
2 teaspoons snipped chives

Heat the butter in a large pan and cook the leek and onion gently until softened but not coloured. Add the potatoes.

Meanwhile, bring the fish stock to the boil and then add to the leek and onion pan. Boil for 10 minutes, then add the thick cream and cook for another couple of minutes.

Purée in a food processor or blender and then pass through a fine sieve. Season to taste with sea salt and white pepper.

Mix the caviar into the whipped cream. Season the scallops with sea salt and white pepper.

Heat the tiniest amount of olive oil in a non-stick frying pan until the oil starts to smoke. Add the scallops and sear for about 20 seconds on each side, until golden on the outside but soft inside.

Put five scallops in each warm soup bowl and cover with the hot soup. Sprinkle with chives, then spoon a little of the whipped caviar cream on top.

SERVES 4

SCALLOP and szechuan duck omelette

Scallops and duck are a beautiful combination in Asian cookery, and this is a very impressive dish to make for a dinner party. Buy yourself a roast Peking duck from Chinatown and shred the meat from the bones (you can ask for this to be done for you). You then make a very simple stir-fry that is served in a fine omelette with a light broth poured over the top.

You could also use CRAB meat

- 1 tablespoon grated palm sugar
- 1 tablespoon fish sauce
- 6 eggs
- 3 tablespoons peanut oil
- 8 shiitake mushrooms, sliced
- 8 Queensland sea scallops, roe removed, cut in half crossways
- 1 cup roasted Peking duck meat, shredded
- a handful of bean sprouts, roughly chopped
- a handful of snow pea sprouts, roughly chopped
- 1 quantity miso broth, page 225
- 4 tablespoons kecap manis
- spring onions, julienned

Heat the palm sugar and fish sauce in a small pan until the sugar dissolves. Crack the eggs into a mixing bowl and whisk in the melted palm sugar and fish sauce.

Heat a touch of peanut oil in a non-stick frying pan and pour in just enough of the egg mixture to cover the bottom of the pan. Cook until just golden on the bottom but still moist on top. Slide the omelette out onto a plate and cook another three, using the rest of the eggs.

Heat some peanut oil in a wok and stir-fry the mushrooms. Add the scallops and cook for 10 seconds, then stir in the duck meat. Take off the heat and spoon this filling into the centre of each omelette. Add a few bean sprouts and snow pea sprouts, then roll up the omelette and place in a warm bowl. Ladle hot miso broth over the top, drizzle with kecap manis and sprinkle with spring onions to serve.

SERVES 4

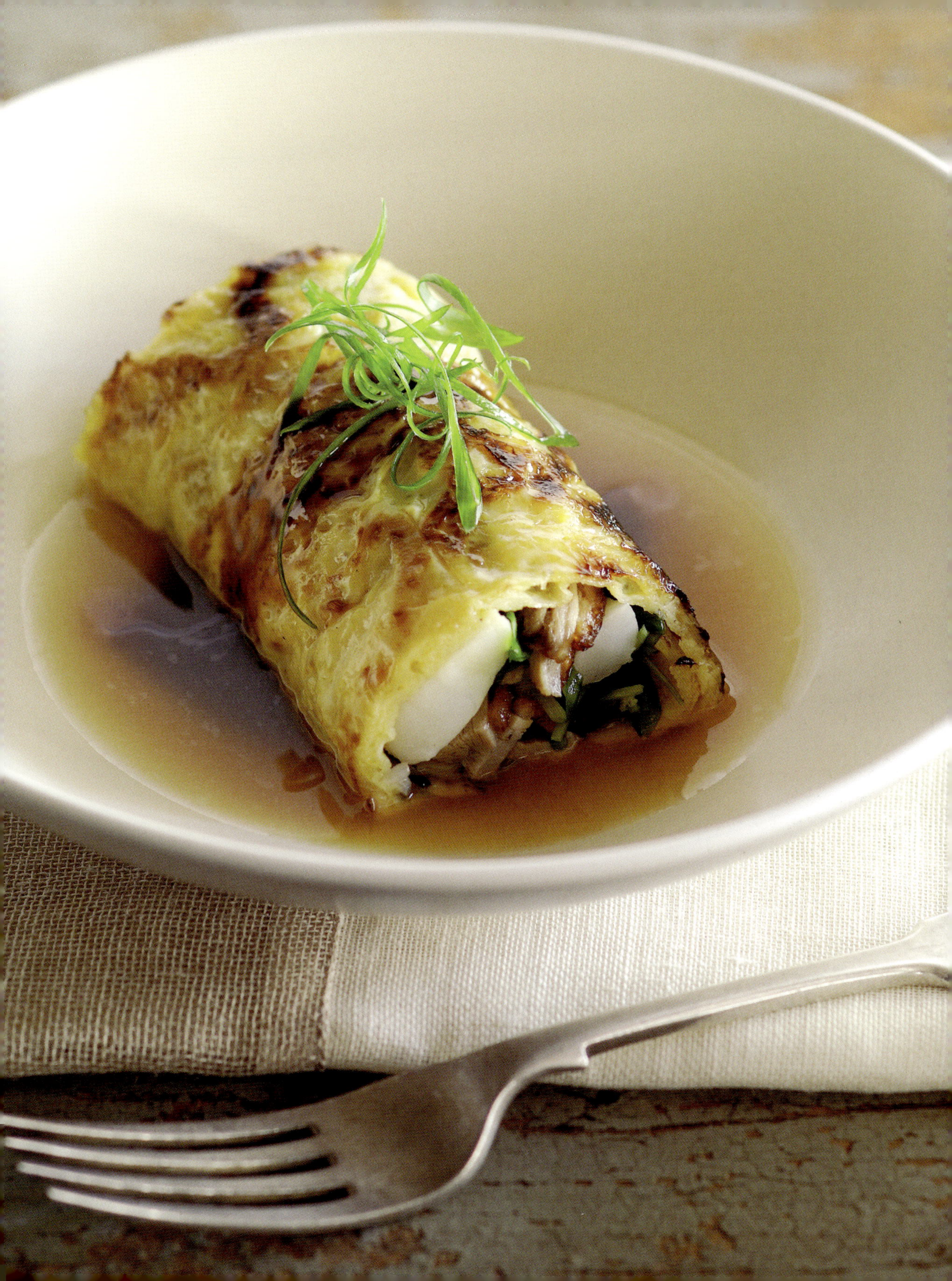

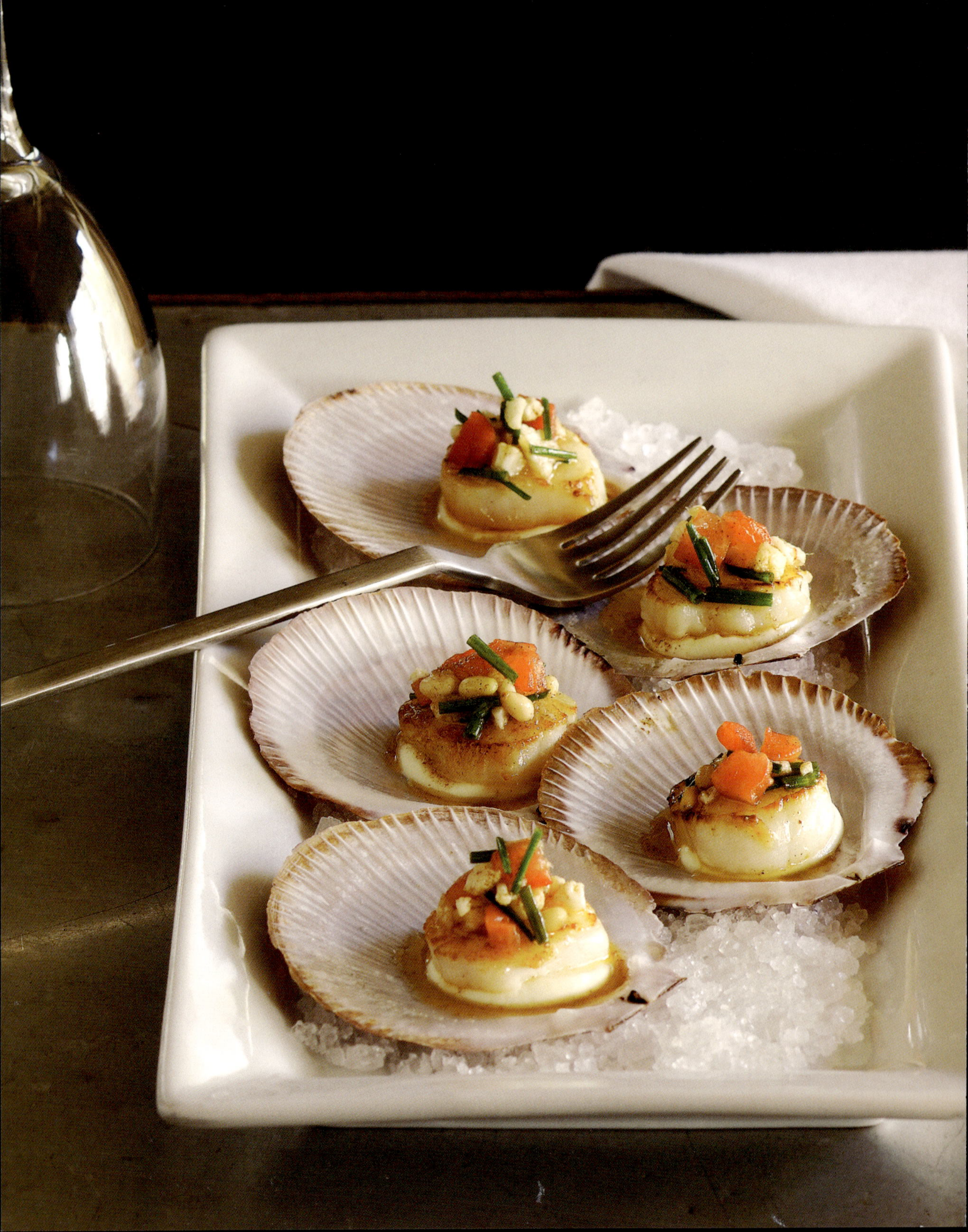

SCALLOPS with cauliflower purée and pine nuts

There are few foods more visually satisfying than scallops served in their shells. And, with this velvety cauliflower purée, a touch of acidity from a lime, the texture of pine nuts and the sheer indulgence of the brown butter sauce, I have never come across a better way to serve grilled scallops. If you want a truly dramatic meal, fry a few tablespoons of diced black pudding until crisp and then add to the sauce.

You could also use any firm white-fleshed FISH fillet

20 scallops in the half shell
1/2 cup cauliflower purée, page 216
4 tablespoons unsalted butter
8 lime segments, diced
100 g (3 1/2 oz) cauliflower, finely diced
2 tomatoes, peeled and deseeded, diced
1 tablespoon chopped chives
1 tablespoon toasted pine nuts

Preheat the oven to 180°C (350°F/Gas 4). Remove the scallops from their shells and set aside. Spoon the cauliflower purée into the scallop shells and heat in the oven until warm.

To make the sauce, put the butter in a cold pan and place over medium heat until it turns nut brown. Add the lime, cauliflower, tomato, chives and pine nuts and season with salt and pepper.

Heat a touch of oil in a pan and fry the scallops for 1 minute until golden, then turn over and cook for 15 seconds. Put the scallops back in their shells on top of the purée and spoon the sauce over them.

SERVES 4 AS A STARTER

Fettucine with SCALLOPS and tomato pesto

Tomato, basil and scallops are a classic combination. This takes it one step further to produce a very moreish dish that is great for a winter supper.

You could also use PRAWNS, CRAB meat, BUG meat, MUSSELS, PIPIS or any firm white-fleshed FISH fillet

4 vine-ripened tomatoes
500 g (1 lb 2 oz) fettucine
3 tablespoons sun-dried tomatoes
1 tablespoon grated pecorino cheese
1 tablespoon toasted pine nuts
4 cloves of garlic confit, page 222
8 anchovies
12 purple basil leaves (or use ordinary basil)
1 tablespoon lemon juice
125 ml (4 fl oz/$1/2$ cup) extra virgin olive oil
20 scallops with roe

Preheat the oven to 180°C (350°F/Gas 4). Put the tomatoes on a baking tray and roast for 20–30 minutes until soft. Let them cool.

Cook the pasta in a large pan of boiling salted water until al dente. Meanwhile, blend the tomatoes, sun-dried tomatoes, cheese, pine nuts, garlic, anchovies, basil, lemon juice and olive oil until smooth.

Heat a touch of oil in a frying pan and sear the scallops on one side until golden. Season the scallops and turn over, then add the tomato sauce to the pan to heat through. Drain the pasta (saving some of the cooking water), add to the pan with the sauce and toss well. Add a little of the cooking water if you need to thin the sauce down. Serve immediately on warm plates.

SERVES 4

SCAMPI and saffron risotto

Saffron is the stigma of the crocus flower and is quite expensive because it takes about 14,000 stigma to produce one ounce of saffron. This is a lot when you consider that each flower produces about three stigma. Fortunately you don't need much saffron in your dish to produce that wonderful flavour (and I'm far more concerned with the flavour than the characteristic golden colour). Keep the saffron in its container in the freezer to extend its shelf life.

You could also use PRAWNS, LOBSTER, MUSSELS, VONGOLE or any firm white-fleshed FISH

a pinch of saffron threads
400 ml (14 fl oz) hot fish or chicken stock
1 teaspoon butter
2 teaspoons olive oil
1 garlic clove, finely diced
1/4 onion, finely diced
300 g (10 1/2 oz/1 1/2 cups) arborio rice
125 ml (4 fl oz/1/2 cup) white wine
3 tablespoons chopped semi-dried tomatoes
1 tablespoon chopped chervil leaves
1 tablespoon grated parmesan cheese
8 scampi, cut in half
1 quantity capsicum sauce, page 216

Add the saffron threads to the hot stock. Heat the butter and olive oil in a large heavy-based pan and cook the garlic and onion until softened but not coloured.

Add the rice and cook for another 30 seconds, stirring well to coat all the grains with the oil. Add the wine and stir for about 2 minutes until it has almost evaporated. Add the hot stock and tomatoes and stir well. Put the lid on the pan, turn down the heat to its lowest setting and leave for 12–15 minutes, or until the rice is cooked. Stir in the chervil and parmesan and a touch more butter if you like, to give the risotto a great shine.

Brush the scampi with a touch of olive oil or clarified butter, season with sea salt and pepper and cook under a hot grill, on your barbie or in a hot pan until they are just cooked.

Spoon the risotto onto plates, top with the hot scampi and pour the capsicum sauce around.

SERVES 4

steamed SCAMPI sandwiches

Finger food should be eye-catching, tasty and neat and these little sandwiches are just the thing to really impress. They are cut into perfect little rounds with a biscuit cutter and filled with a lovely combination of creamy champagne leek and steamed scampi. The black caviar topping is pure indulgence.

You could also use LOBSTER, PRAWNS, CRAB meat, SMOKED EEL, SALMON, TROUT or OYSTERS

CHAMPAGNE CREAMED LEEK
1 tablespoon olive oil
1 leek, white part only, thinly sliced
250 ml (9 fl oz/1 cup) champagne
170 ml (5^1/$_2$ fl oz/^{2}/$_3$ cup) cream

8 whole scampi
16 slices of buttered white bread
1 tablespoon lemon-infused olive oil
1 tablespoon salmon roe
1 tablespoon chopped chervil leaves
2 teaspoons black caviar

To make the champagne creamed leek, put the olive oil and leek in a saucepan and cook over medium heat for 3–4 minutes until the leek is softened but not coloured. Add the champagne and cook until nearly evaporated, then add the cream and cook until reduced by half. Season with sea salt and white pepper.

Cook the scampi in a steamer or in barely simmering water for about 6 minutes until they are just cooked. Remove the meat from the shells and cut in half lengthways, then leave to cool in the fridge.

Lay 8 slices of the bread on your work surface and top with the other slices to make empty sandwiches. Use a 5 cm (2 inch) biscuit cutter to cut out the middle of the bread so you have neat little round sandwiches (chuck away the crusts). Now take the tops off all the sandwiches and spread them with 2 teaspoons of champagne creamed leek.

Toss the scampi with lemon-infused oil, salmon roe, chervil and some sea salt and cracked pepper and put two halves of scampi on each sandwich. Now put the tops back on your sandwiches (press them down firmly), place a small amount of black caviar on top and serve with a flourish.

MAKES 8 MINI SANDWICHES

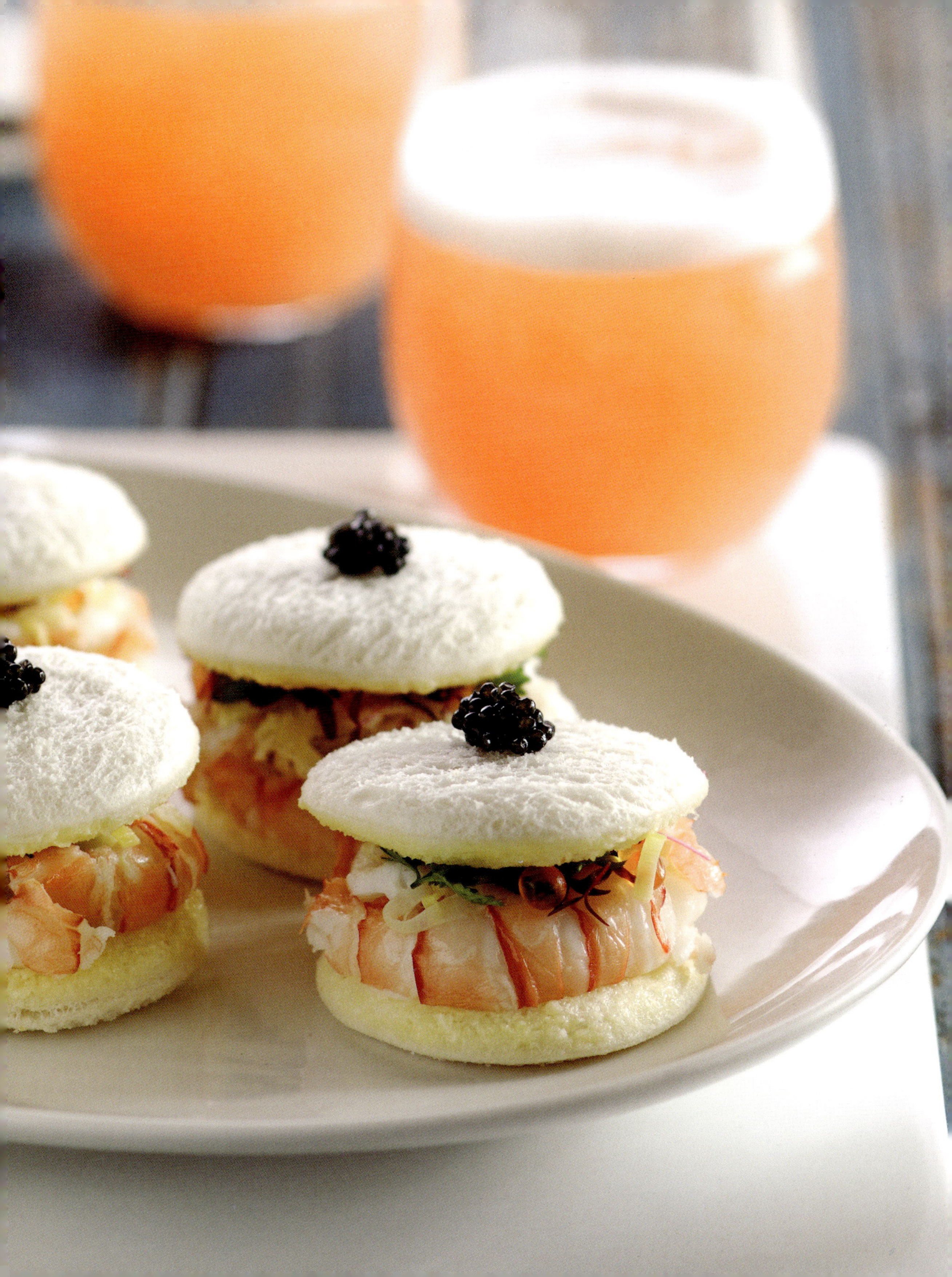

japanese steamed egg custard with SCAMPI (chawan-mushi)

This is a remarkably simple recipe that is great as a dinner party starter — there is hardly anything to do, but your guests will be intrigued as to how you made it. You can substitute other types of seafood (below) but, because this is a light and luxurious dish, only use those that will marry well in both taste and texture.

You could also use CRAB meat, SMOKED EEL, PRAWNS or SEA URCHIN

4 scampi, peeled and cut into 1 cm ($1/2$ inch) pieces
2 shiitake mushrooms, thinly sliced
2 teaspoons sake
grated zest of $1/2$ lemon
3 teaspoons light soy sauce
250 ml (9 fl oz/1 cup) chicken stock or dashi-flavoured stock
$1/2$ teaspoon sea salt
2 teaspoons mirin
1 egg, beaten

Put the scampi in a bowl with the mushrooms, sake, lemon zest and 1 teaspoon of the soy sauce. Toss together gently and leave to marinate for 15 minutes, then strain.

Mix together the stock, salt, mirin and remaining soy sauce in a mixing bowl. Carefully add the beaten egg and mix gently (you don't want any air bubbles). Strain the mixture.

Spoon the scampi, mushrooms and lemon zest into four heatproof cups or small bowls (you can buy special chawan-mushi bowls with lids in Japanese stores). Pour the egg mixture over the scampi, to fill about 2.5 cm (1 inch) from the top of the cup. Cover with foil, plastic wrap or a fitted lid and then place in a steamer and steam gently over barely simmering water for about 15 minutes, or until a skewer poked into the middle comes out clean. The custard should be just set but still wobbly and moist. Delicious served hot or cold.

SERVES 4 AS A STARTER

SEA URCHIN sandwiches

I have attended many cooking schools over the past fifteen years and picked up a lot of handy tips and recipes along the way. This recipe is from a New Zealand chef called Lee Hokianga, who worked with the great Janni Kyritsis at Sydney's MG Garage. I attended her class and she made these sandwiches... I can still remember that first bite and my amazement at the subtle flavour and unique texture. Tasmania's sea urchins are some of the best in the world and most are exported to Japan, but if you're lucky enough to find some very fresh sea urchin roe, please try these sandwiches. And try to use French or Danish butter, or the best quality you can find.

There is absolutely no substitute for fabulous fresh SEA URCHIN

100 g (3^1/$_2$ oz) softened butter
8 slices of white bread
grated zest of 3 lemons
40 sea urchin roe (or roe from 8 live sea urchins)

Butter the bread and sprinkle half the slices with the lemon zest. Top with the sea urchin roe and season with sea salt and cracked pepper. Make into sandwiches with the rest of the bread, cut off the crusts and cut into finger sandwiches.

SERVES 4 AS A STARTER OR WITH DRINKS

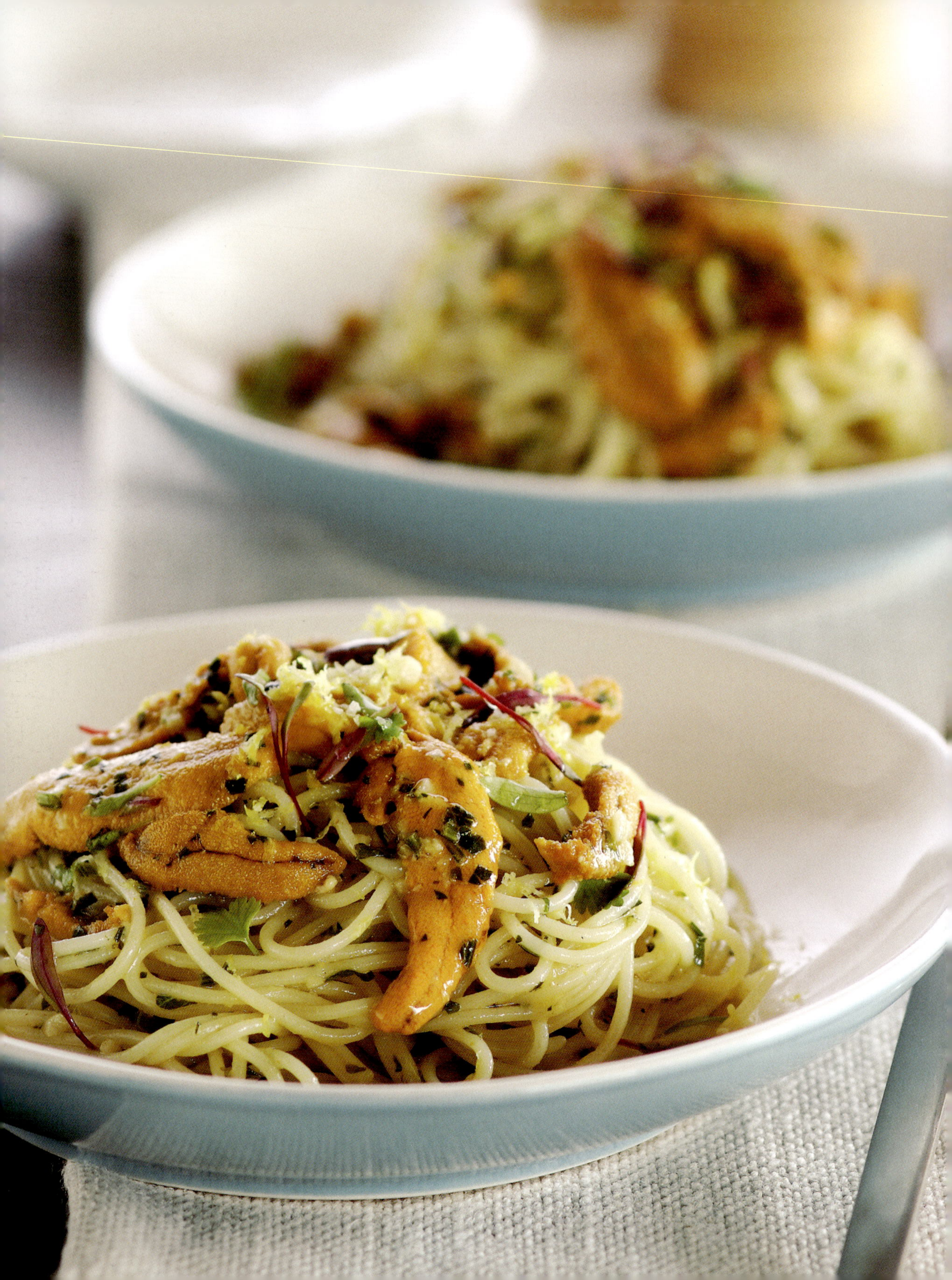

SEA URCHIN with angel hair pasta and lemon

I know sea urchins aren't everyone's cuppa, but prepare them this way and people might just change their minds. Serve this as a starter when you feel like wowing your guests... it will certainly get the conversation going.

You could also use SCALLOPS, OYSTERS, SCAMPI, MARRON or CRAB

250 g (9 oz) angel hair pasta
4 tablespoons olive oil
1 garlic clove, finely chopped
2 tablespoons chopped flat-leaf (Italian) parsley
20 sea urchin roe (or roe from 4 live sea urchins)
125 ml (4 fl oz/1/2 cup) dry white wine
170 ml (5 1/2 fl oz/2/3 cup) fish stock
1 tablespoon butter
grated zest of 1 lemon

Cook your pasta in a large pan of boiling salted water until al dente, then drain.

Meanwhile, heat the oil and garlic in a saucepan until the garlic starts to turn golden. Add the parsley and cook for 10 seconds. Add the sea urchin roe, then immediately add the wine and heat until it has almost disappeared. Add the fish stock and cook until it has reduced by about half. Add the hot cooked pasta and the butter to the pan, season with sea salt and cracked pepper and toss well. Serve immediately, sprinkled with lemon zest.

SERVES 4 AS A STARTER

SKATE with brown butter, lime and capers

In Australia we are not huge eaters of stingray, also known as skate. It has amazing texture, the flavour is really sublime and it's also quite cheap and generally of very high quality. The classic method for cooking skate is with brown butter and capers — and I have to admit it's one of the best.

You could also use any firm white-fleshed FISH fillet

4 tablespoons butter
grated zest of 2 limes and 2 tablespoons lime juice
1 tablespoon tarragon leaves
2 tablespoons capers
4 x 160 g (5^{3}/$_{4}$ oz) stingray wings, skin off and filleted (I like to use eagle ray or skate)
flour, for dusting
olive oil, for frying

Heat the butter in a saucepan over moderate heat until it turns nut brown. Remove from the heat and add the lime zest, juice, tarragon and capers. Season with sea salt and cracked pepper.

Season the ray very lightly and dust with a little flour, shaking off any excess. Heat the oil in a frying pan and fry the ray for 2–3 minutes on each side. Lift out onto plates and dress with the sauce.

SERVES 4

SNAPPER carpaccio with blood orange and lemon thyme

I think snapper would have to be one of the most popular fish in Australia and New Zealand, yet most people aren't aware how good it is to eat raw. This simple recipe uses interesting ingredients that really show off the snapper's 'natural talents'.

You could also use SWORDFISH, TUNA, SALMON, OCEAN TROUT, KINGFISH or SCALLOPS

125 ml (4 fl oz/½ cup) blood orange juice (or navel orange juice)

½ teaspoon roasted fennel seeds

300 g (10½ oz) snapper fillet, skin and bones removed

1 teaspoon lemon thyme leaves

6 lime segments, chopped into pieces

3 tablespoons extra virgin olive oil

a few drops of chilli oil, page 219

Bring the orange juice to a simmer in a saucepan and cook until reduced by half. Pound the fennel seeds to a powder with a mortar and pestle.

Slice the snapper very thinly and arrange over four plates. Season with sea salt, lemon thyme, lime pieces and a sprinkling of the fennel powder. Dress the fish with the olive oil, orange juice and a few drops of chilli oil.

SERVES 4 AS A STARTER

SNAPPER ceviche with coconut, mint and cucumber

As you might have gathered by now, I am fascinated by anything raw. It was a little over a decade ago that my curiosity got the better of me and I tried my first raw prawn at a very fine Japanese restaurant. Since then I have read about and studied many different preparations of raw food around the world — I don't necessarily have a favourite but ceviche (especially of snapper) is definitely up there near the top of my raw food ladder.

You could also use KINGFISH, WHITING, TREVALLY, PRAWNS, SCALLOPS or SCAMPI

240 g (9 oz) sashimi-grade snapper fillet, skin and bones removed
2 tablespoons peeled, seeded and diced cucumber
2 tablespoons julienned mint
100 ml (3 1/2 fl oz) coconut dressing, page 220
1 tablespoon diced tomato confit, page 233 (or diced peeled tomato)
1 tablespoon seeded and diced cucumber, extra
2 tablespoons extra virgin olive oil

Cut the snapper into very thin strips and place in a chilled bowl. Add the cucumber, mint and coconut dressing and season with sea salt and white pepper. Mix together lightly and then spoon into four small martini glasses.

Mix the tomato confit, extra cucumber and olive oil together and place a small amount into each glass.

SERVES 4 AS A STARTER

SNAPPER aqua pazza (fish in crazy water)

This dish really defines my preferred cooking style — super-easy but full of flavour. Originally, the Italians cooked the fish in seawater, which is where the name crazy water or 'aqua pazza' comes from. Today we use sparkling mineral water and salt.

You could also use BREAM, MULLET, GARFISH, WHITING, PRAWNS, MUSSELS or VONGOLE

4 frying-pan or plate-sized snappers
12 cloves garlic confit, page 222
4 tablespoons chilli confit, page 218
20 cherry tomatoes
20 ligurian olives (or marinated small olives)
1.5 litres (52 fl oz/6 cups) sparkling mineral water
3 tablespoons butter
24 basil leaves

Make three cuts down to the bone on both sides of each fish and then cook each fish separately, using a quarter of the ingredients for each one. (You might want to keep the cooked fish in a warm oven as you go.)

Heat a touch of olive oil in a frying pan, add the fish and cook for 3–4 minutes until golden on one side. Turn the fish over and add some garlic, chilli, tomatoes and olives and season with sea salt and cracked pepper. After 30 seconds add the mineral water (just enough to cover the fish), butter and basil and cook for another couple of minutes until the fish is just cooked through.

Lift out onto a serving plate and pour the sauce over the top.

SERVES 4

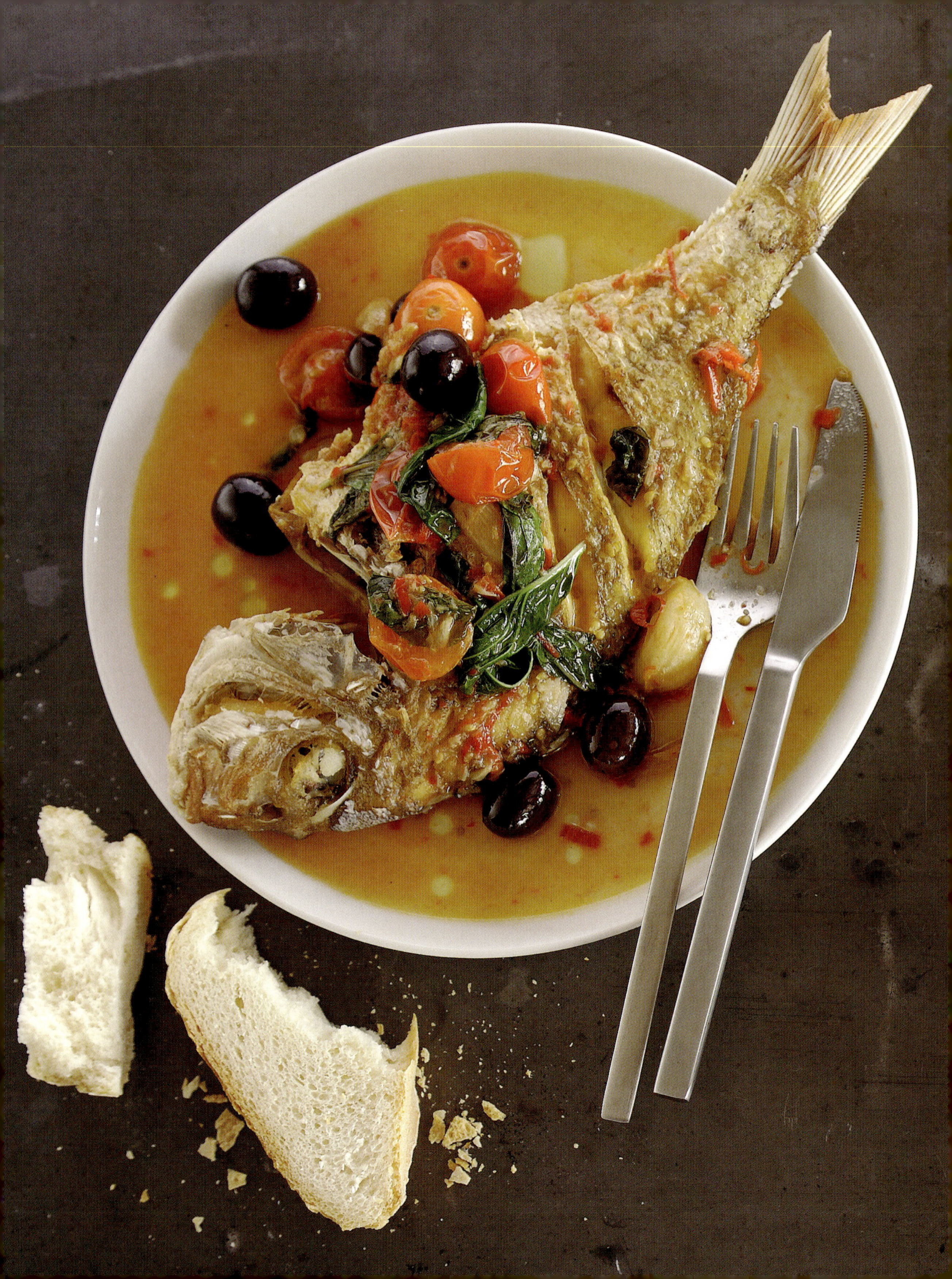

snapper aqua pazza (fish in crazy water)

udo's whole SNAPPER in foil on the barbie

My brother-in-law, Udo Edlinger, has been a huge influence on me. He has a never-say-die attitude and is one of the most adventurous and generous people I have ever had the privilege to meet. The only downside to Udo's personality is that he's an appallingly fussy eater. This is how he cooks fish whenever he has me over for dinner, and it is just glorious.

You could also use just about any type of FISH

4 plate-sized snapper, scaled and gutted
2 tablespoons butter
2 tablespoons julienned fresh ginger
1 tablespoon finely chopped garlic
1 bird's eye chilli, chopped
1 tablespoon finely chopped lemongrass stem
1 tablespoon chopped coriander root
juice of 1 lemon
125 ml (4 fl oz/½ cup) light soy sauce

Cut three incisions into the flesh on both sides of each fish.
Tear off four large pieces of foil and rub them with butter so the fish doesn't stick. Put the fish in the middle of the foil with the ginger, garlic, chilli, lemongrass, coriander, lemon juice and soy sauce and wrap up the foil like an envelope.
Put the parcels on the hot barbecue for 5 minutes and then turn over and cook for another 3 minutes (the fish is cooked when the flesh is white, so you may need to unwrap one parcel and check).
Serve with steamed jasmine rice and bok choy.

SERVES 4

SNAPPER pizza pie

This is a fantastic interpretation of a fish pie, using pizza dough instead of pastry for the base. This makes four individual pies — it's useful to have a couple of frying pans so you can cook them two at a time.

You could also use PRAWNS or any firm white-fleshed FISH

- 1 quantity pizza dough, page 228
- 600 g (1 lb 5 oz) snapper fillet, skin and bones removed
- 1 quantity baccala sauce, page 212
- 85 g (3 oz) shredded mozzarella cheese
- 1 tablespoon lemon juice
- 1 teaspoon seeded mustard
- 3 tablespoons extra virgin olive oil
- 2 handfuls of rocket leaves

Preheat the oven to 220°C (425°F/Gas 7) and grease an ovenproof frying pan with a little olive oil. Divide the pizza dough into four portions. Roll out one portion very thinly and line the pan so that the dough comes just over the edge.

Slice the snapper very thinly crossways (like sashimi) and mix with the baccala sauce. Pour a quarter of this into the frying pan and sprinkle with mozzarella. Put in the oven for about 15 minutes, or until the dough is crispy and the top of the pie is golden. Keep warm while you make the others.

Mix together the lemon juice, mustard and oil and use to dress the rocket leaves. Serve over the pies.

SERVES 4

Tasmanian lobster boat.

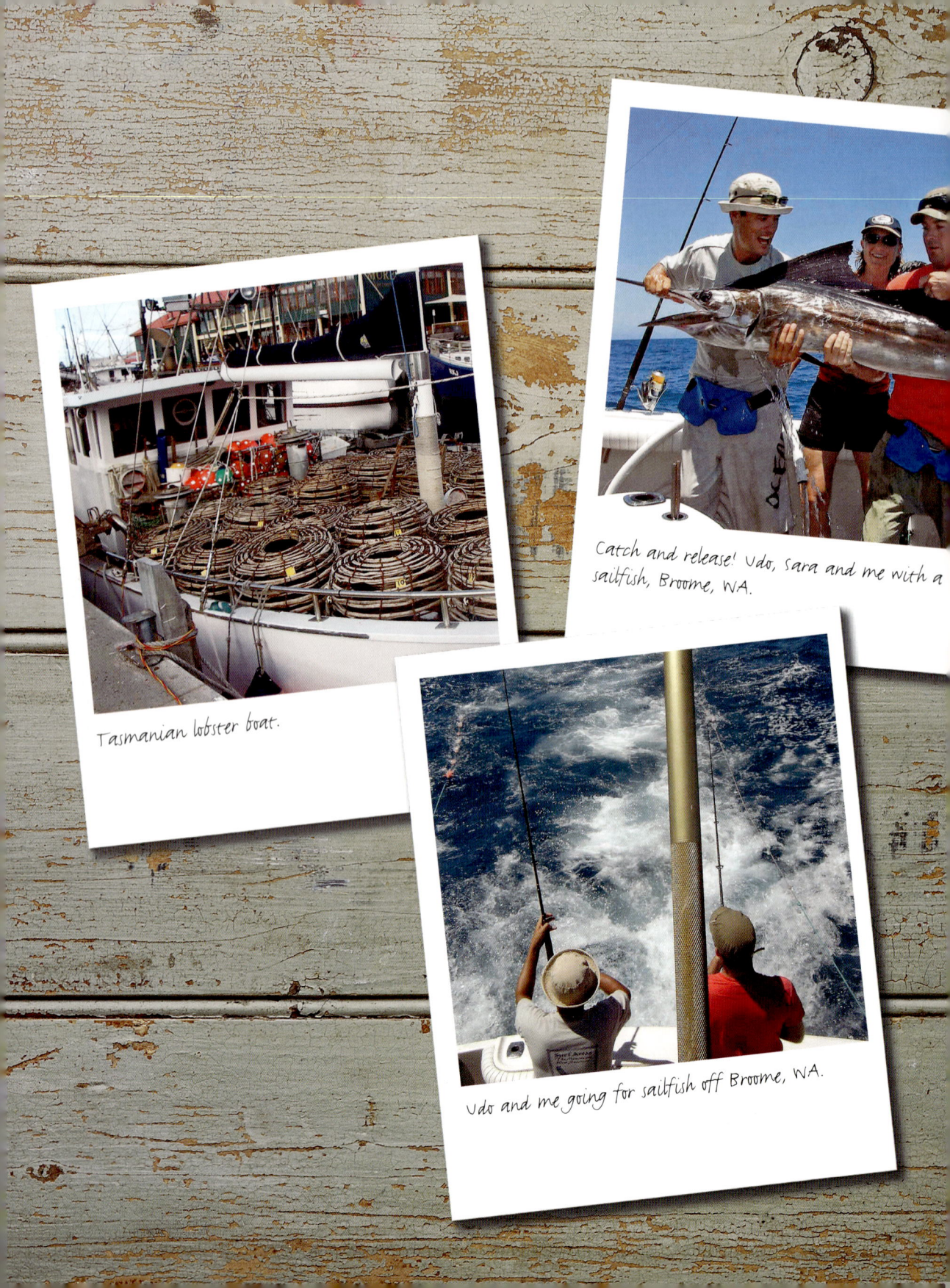

Catch and release! Udo, sara and me with a sailfish, Broome, WA.

Udo and me going for sailfish off Broome, WA.

The only way to travel. Far north WA.

A nice queenfish. Weipa, QLD.

sole
squid stripey trumpeter sushi swordfish
threadfin salmon

pan-fried SOLE with salmoriglio

Salmoriglio is an Italian dressing of lemon, garlic and oregano. It complements just about any seafood and works extremely well with anything chargrilled.

You could also use PRAWNS, LOBSTER, TUNA, SWORDFISH, MACKEREL or SARDINES

SALMORIGLIO
2 tablespoons lemon juice
2 tablespoons extra virgin olive oil
2 teaspoons finely chopped oregano leaves
grated zest of 1 lemon
½ garlic clove, finely chopped

4 whole sole, scaled and gutted
flour, for dusting
olive oil, for cooking

Whisk together all the salmoriglio ingredients and season with sea salt and white pepper.
    Score three incisions on both sides of each sole. Season the fish with sea salt and pepper and dust lightly with flour. Heat some olive oil in a large heavy-based frying pan and cook the sole on both sides until golden and crispy. Lift the fish onto plates and spoon the salmoriglio over the top.

SERVES 4

barbecued thai **SQUID** salad

A barbecue should be about kicking back, having a beer or wine, and eating some lovely food with friends and family. There should be no stress associated with it at all. This dish fits the bill perfectly: it can all be prepared beforehand and takes just a few minutes to cook. What more could you want?

You could also use PRAWNS, LOBSTER, SMOKED TROUT, CUTTLEFISH or OCTOPUS

400 g (14 oz) squid tubes
1 cucumber, thinly sliced lengthways
2 handfuls of bean sprouts
3 banana chillies, julienned
4 tablespoons crushed roasted peanuts
a large handful of Thai basil leaves
a small handful of Vietnamese mint leaves
a large handful of mint leaves
2 kaffir lime leaves, julienned
20 coriander sprigs
3 tablespoons Thai salad dressing, page 232

Remove the skin from the squid and take out the cartilage from the inside. Cut open the squid lengthways and then score incisions in the flesh in a criss-cross pattern (being careful not to cut all the way through). Cut into large pieces.

Fry the squid in a touch of oil on the barbecue or in a frying pan until curled. Mix quickly with all the other ingredients, tossing to coat with the Thai dressing.

SERVES 4 AS A STARTER

tagliatelle with SQUID and pesto

Everyone seems to have their own special way of making pesto — some say they would never make it in a blender as it bruises the basil leaves and makes them bitter; others like it to be all finely chopped and folded together, while still others will only make it in a mortar and pestle. I go with the last crowd, as the pestle is where the name pesto actually comes from (meaning 'pounded' in Italian). Pesto is a great accompaniment to seafood and this simple pasta recipe is one of my favourites.

You could also use PRAWNS, SWORDFISH, KINGFISH, SCALLOPS or SEA URCHIN

500 g (1 lb 2 oz) tagliatelle (or spaghetti or linguine)
olive oil
2 tablespoons chopped garlic confit, page 222
1 tablespoon chilli confit, page 218
400 g (14 oz) cleaned squid, cut into thin strips or rings
1 quantity pesto, page 227

Cook the pasta in a large pan of boiling salted water until al dente. Heat a few tablespoons of olive oil in a frying pan and add the garlic and chilli confit. Once this is hot, add the squid and cook for 30 seconds. Remove from the heat, add the pesto and the drained pasta to your pan and toss it all together well, so the pasta is coated. Serve immediately.

SERVES 4

SQUID, chorizo, white bean and fennel salad

The Spanish love to team seafood with chorizo sausage and, to be honest, I don't blame them, especially when the seafood is squid. Chorizo is a strongly seasoned, coarsely ground pork sausage flavoured with garlic, chilli and other spices. The pork in Spanish chorizo is generally smoked, while Mexican chorizo is made with fresh pork. This recipe is perfect for an outdoor lunch — I would serve just this one dish in the middle of the table, with some crunchy bread and a couple of ice cold beers.

You could also use PRAWNS, CUTTLEFISH or MUSSELS

185 g (6^1/$_2$ oz/1 cup) tinned white beans, rinsed
2 baby fennel, very thinly sliced
a large handful of flat-leaf (Italian) parsley leaves
1 bird's eye chilli, julienned
grated zest of 1 lemon
1 tablespoon sherry vinegar
4 tablespoons extra virgin olive oil
500 g (1 lb 2 oz) squid tubes, cleaned, cut into pieces and scored
1 teaspoon fennel seed and pepper spice mix, page 222
^{1}/$_2$ chorizo sausage, skin removed, thinly sliced
1^1/$_2$ teaspoons harissa (a North African chilli paste available from good delis)
4 tablespoons mayonnaise, page 224

Mix together the white beans, fennel, parsley, chilli, lemon zest, vinegar and olive oil in a salad bowl and season with sea salt and pepper.

Toss the squid in the fennel spice mix with some sea salt and just enough olive oil to coat. Heat a frying pan or barbecue plate and cook the squid in batches for about 1 minute each batch until coloured and curled, then add to the salad.

Cook the chorizo in the same pan or on the barbecue until nicely coloured and then toss into the salad. Stir the harissa into the mayonnaise and serve with the salad.

SERVES 4

sautéed SQUID with malaysian water spinach

This is a wonderfully simple but extremely flavoursome recipe. If you can't buy the kang kong (water spinach), just use English or baby spinach. And don't be put off by the smell of the shrimp paste — you do need to use the amount it says, but it mellows during the cooking and becomes quite an integral part of the dish.

You could also use CUTTLEFISH, PRAWNS, BUGS, any firm white FISH, SALMON or TROUT

4 garlic cloves
6 dried red chillies, soaked for 20 minutes in hot water, drained and chopped
4 macadamia nuts or candlenuts
5 red Asian shallots or French shallots
2 teaspoons dried shrimp paste (blachan)
300 g (10½ oz) water spinach ('kang kong' from Asian grocers) or English spinach
4 tablespoons grapeseed oil
400 g (14 oz) squid tubes, cleaned and scored
1 teaspoon sugar
lime wedges, to serve

Pound the garlic, chillies, macadamia nuts, shallots and shrimp paste with a mortar and pestle until you have a paste. Cut the stems off the water spinach and save them.

Heat the oil in a wok until it is smoking. Add the paste and cook for 30 seconds, add the squid and cook for 20 seconds, then add the water spinach stems and cook for 1 minute. Season with sea salt and the sugar. Add the water spinach leaves and cook until wilted. Squeeze some fresh lime juice over the top and serve.

SERVES 4

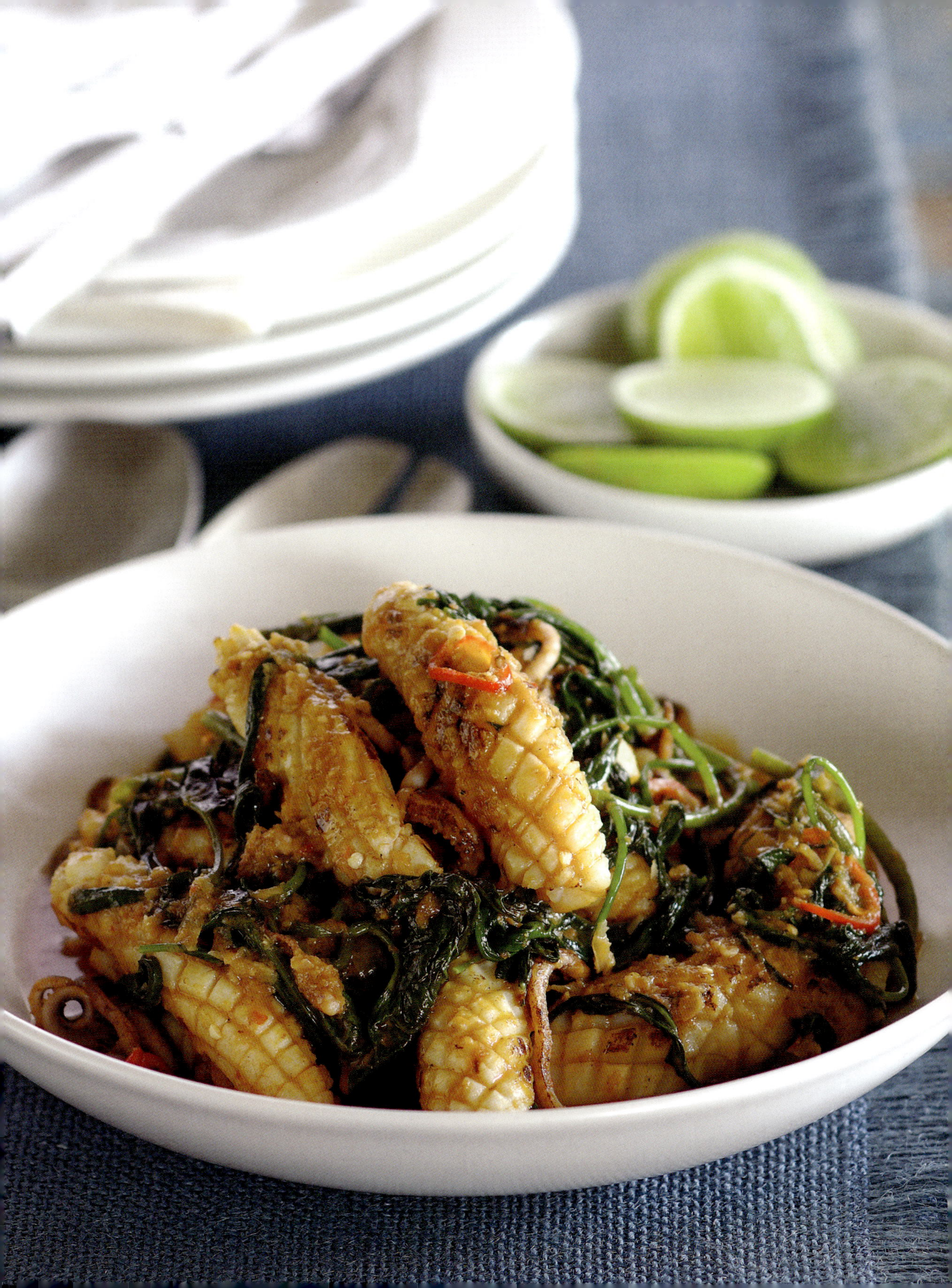

chilli salt SQUID

The main ingredients here are salt and chilli. For the chilli you can use chilli powder, ground-up chillies (fresh or dried) or even buy some chilli salt at good delis. I sometimes serve this with a wedge of lemon or lime as a snack, but more often these days I really like to use it as an 'extra' textural component to jazz up other dishes.

You could also use OYSTERS, PRAWNS, CRAB, BUGS or any firm white-fleshed FISH

peanut oil, for deep-frying
400 g (14 oz) squid tubes, cleaned
175 g (6 oz/1 cup) rice flour or tempura flour
3 tablespoons chilli salt spice, page 219
2 tablespoons chopped coriander
lime wedges, to serve

Heat the peanut oil to 185°C (365°F) in a deep-fat fryer or large wok — either measure this with a thermometer of drop a cube of bread into the oil: it should brown in about 10 seconds.

Cut the squid into thin strips (or score lightly with a knife and cut into larger pieces), keeping the tentacles whole.

Mix the rice flour with 2 tablespoons of the chilli salt spice. Dust the squid lightly with the spiced flour and cook in small batches so the oil stays hot and the squid gets crunchy. Drain on kitchen paper and serve sprinkled with coriander and the remaining chilli salt spice and some lime wedges for squeezing.

SERVES 4 AS A STARTER

pan-roasted STRIPEY TRUMPETER with romesco sauce

Romesco is a remarkable sauce that is usually served with pork or other meats but also goes surprisingly well with seafood. When you look at the list of ingredients that go into the making, it sounds quite rich, but it is one of my favourites to serve with some perfectly cooked fish.

You could also use SQUID, BUGS, PRAWNS or any firm white-fleshed FISH

ROMESCO SAUCE
2 red capsicums
2 ripe tomatoes
olive oil, for cooking
2 slices crusty white bread, cut into cubes
12 almonds
12 roasted hazelnuts, peeled
1 teaspoon sweet paprika
$1/2$ bird's eye chilli
3 garlic cloves, finely chopped
2 tablespoons white wine vinegar
100 ml ($3^{1}/_{2}$ fl oz) Spanish extra virgin olive oil

olive oil, for frying
4 x 160 g ($5^{3}/_{4}$ oz) stripey trumpeter fillets, skin on
4 handfuls of baby English spinach leaves
16 thin julienne slices of preserved lemon

To make the romesco sauce, preheat the oven to 180°C (350°F/Gas 4) and roast the capsicums and tomatoes on a baking tray with a sprinkling of salt and a little olive oil for about 30 minutes, until the capsicums are coloured and the tomatoes soft. Cool a little, then peel the capsicums and remove the seeds.

Meanwhile, heat a little olive oil in a pan and fry the bread until golden and crunchy to make croutons. Put the capsicum, tomato, almonds and hazelnuts in a blender and mix until smooth. Add the croutons and season with the paprika, chilli, garlic and vinegar, then mix again. Add more olive oil until you like the consistency.

Reduce the oven to 160°C (315°F/Gas 2–3). Heat 1 tablespoon olive oil in an ovenproof frying pan and cook the fish, skin side down, for 3–4 minutes until golden on one side. Turn the fish over, season with sea salt and pepper and put the pan in the oven for about 4 minutes, or until the fish is just cooked through. Lift the fish out onto a plate.

Put the spinach leaves and 1 teaspoon olive oil into the pan with the fish juices and season with salt and pepper. Cook until just wilted, then strain to remove the excess moisture.

Arrange romesco sauce on each plate and top with a mound of spinach. Lay the preserved lemon over the spinach and then top with the fish.

SERVES 4

SUSHI of scampi

It was about fifteen years ago that I ate in a sushi bar for the first time. On that first visit I wanted to try everything, so I asked the chef to just keep bringing out food until I was full. I loved every moment of the dinner until I was presented with raw scampi on top of sushi rice. I was dubious, but I took the plunge and what followed was a revelation that has shaped the way I eat and cook ever since.

1 quantity sushi rice, page 230
8 whole scampi
1/4 teaspoon wasabi paste
a pinch of grated fresh ginger
1 teaspoon extra virgin olive oil
tamari soy sauce, to serve

Squeeze the rice into 8 blocks, each about 5 cm (2 inches) long and 2 cm (3/4 inch) high. Take the scampi meat from the shell, leaving just the last part of the tail joined. Butterfly the scampi down the back and remove the intestinal tract (clean with a damp cloth if necessary).

Rub a small amount of wasabi paste over the sushi rice and top with the scampi and a touch of grated ginger. Drizzle some olive oil over the top of the scampi and serve with tamari soy sauce.

MAKES 8 PIECES

cuttlefish SUSHI with lemon, sesame and shiso

I am a huge fan of Japanese food — I'd have to say it's my favourite cuisine — and this is a dish I have eaten too many times to count at a Sydney restaurant called Azuma. Chef Kimitaka Azuma buys the best-quality seafood and somehow makes it taste about a hundred times better than the local sushi train. This is my favourite of his sushi recipes.

1 quantity sushi rice, page 230
1 teaspoon wasabi paste
8 x 20 g (3/4 oz) pieces cuttlefish
4 shiso leaves (a Japanese herb), cut in half
juice and grated zest of 1 lemon
1 teaspoon toasted white and black sesame seeds

Squeeze the rice into 8 blocks, each about 5 cm (2 inches) long and 2 cm (3/4 inch) high and spread with a touch of wasabi.

Score the cuttlefish lengthways with your knife without cutting all the way through. Lay a piece of shiso leaf on each block of sushi rice (just enough to cover the top), then lay the cuttlefish on top and squeeze a little lemon juice over it. Top with the sesame seeds and lemon zest and a little sea salt.

MAKES 8 PIECES

SUSHI of seared salmon belly

One of the easiest and most impressive ways to present sushi is a piece of lightly seared seafood over sushi rice (it is also a good way to get people who won't try raw fish to appreciate sushi). You can cook the fish on a wire rack over a naked flame, or even use a blow torch to lightly cook one side — the trick is to briefly sear one side so that the other is raw.

1 quantity sushi rice, page 230
1 teaspoon wasabi paste
8 x 20 g ($3/4$ oz) pieces salmon belly
juice of $1/2$ lemon

Squeeze the rice into 8 blocks, each about 5 cm (2 inches) long and 2 cm ($3/4$ inch) high, and spread with a touch of wasabi.

Place a wire rack over a naked flame and, once hot, lay the salmon belly on the rack until it gets that lovely charred mark and slightly burnt smell. Cook it on one side only, then place the raw side of the fish down on the rice. Squeeze some lemon juice over the fish and season with a little sea salt. No soy sauce required!

MAKES 8 PIECES

SUSHI of toro (tuna belly)

I was in Tokyo a few years ago and visited a fantastic sushi restaurant with some Japanese friends. I had never tried toro (also known as fatty tuna belly), but it is highly regarded as the best part of the tuna and commands an exhorbitant price. It is one of the most fascinating things I have ever eaten: it is so full of oil that it coats your tongue when you eat it. You don't need to add anything but a touch of soy sauce or a squeeze of lemon.

1 quantity sushi rice, page 230
8 x 25 g (1 oz) pieces tuna belly
$1/4$ teaspoon wasabi paste
tamari soy sauce, to serve

Squeeze the rice into 8 blocks, each about 5 cm (2 inches) long and 2 cm ($3/4$ inch) high.

Lightly score the tuna in a criss-cross pattern without cutting all the way through. Rub a little wasabi onto the rice, place the tuna on top and season with a touch of sea salt. Serve with tamari soy sauce.

MAKES 8 PIECES

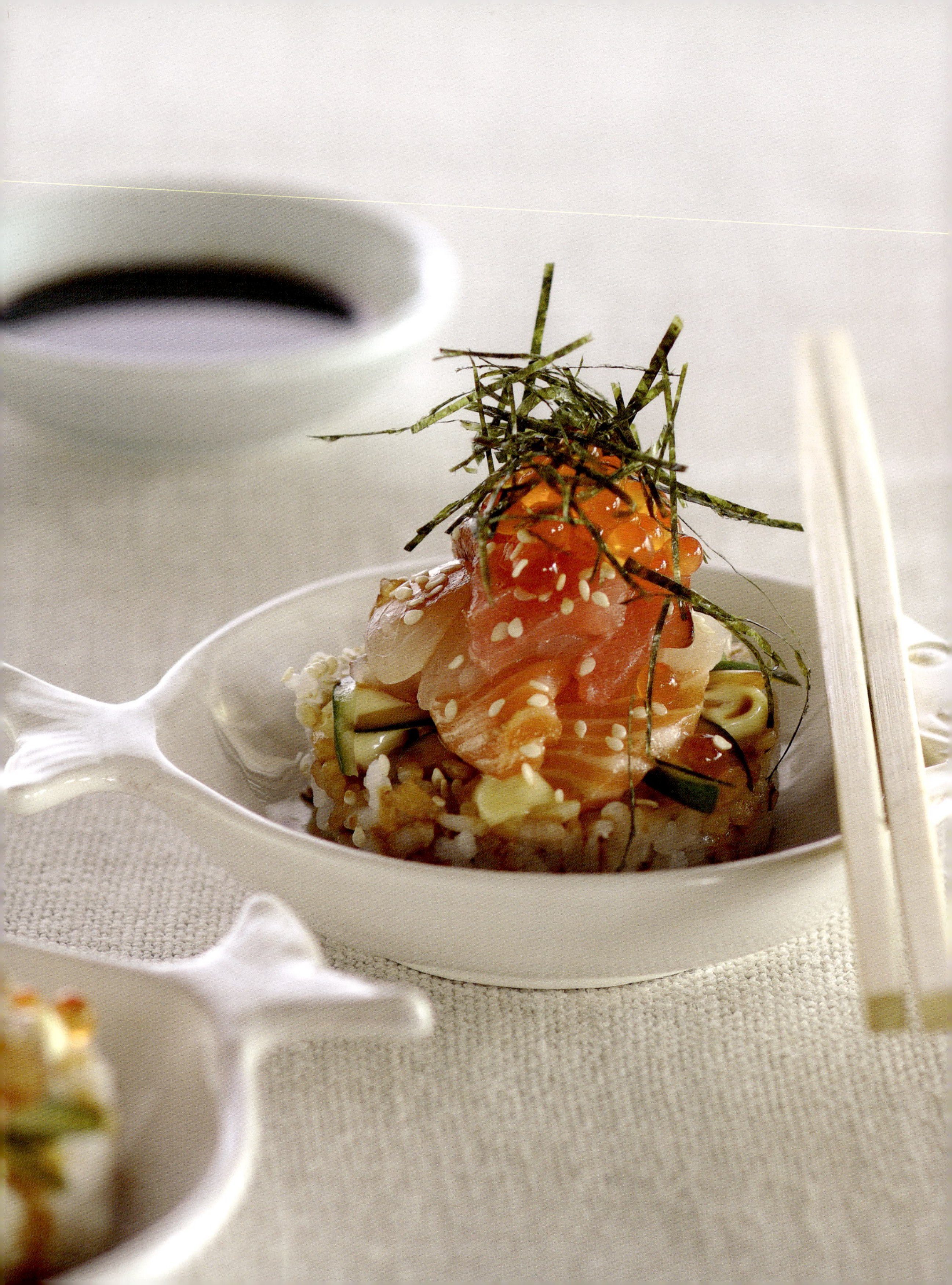

bimbimbap SUSHI

If I had one last dish to eat on earth, this would be it (well, it would be the starter anyway). It is a mixture of Japanese and Korean flavours and words cannot really do it justice.

You could also use any seafood that can be eaten raw (especially SEA URCHIN, CUTTLEFISH, SCAMPI, SCALLOP or PRAWN)

a handful of bean sprouts
3 tablespoons rice wine vinegar
1 tablespoon soy sauce
1 teaspoon salt
1 tablespoon sugar
a pinch of chilli powder
1 quantity sushi rice, page 230
4 quail eggs, separated (you won't be using the whites)
2 teaspoons toasted sesame seeds
2 tablespoons Japanese mayonnaise (from Asian supermarkets)
a handful of julienned cucumber
160 g (5¾ oz) Spanish mackerel or kingfish, thinly sliced
160 g (5¾ oz) bluefin, yellowfin or longtail tuna, thinly sliced
160 g (5¾ oz) trevally, ocean trout or Atlantic salmon, thinly sliced
tamari soy and wasabi
4 tablespoons salmon caviar
1 sheet toasted nori, julienned

Blanch the bean sprouts in boiling salted water for 30 seconds and then refresh under cold water. Mix together the rice wine vinegar, soy, salt, sugar and chilli powder and pour over the bean sprouts to make pickled bean sprouts. Leave to marinate for 20 minutes and then drain.

Place the rice in the bottom of four bowls or martini glasses. Make a small indentation in the rice and place the quail yolk into this. Top with half the sesame seeds and then dot the mayonnaise over the rice. Top with the bean sprouts, then the cucumber, then the fish. Drizzle the tamari soy sauce and wasabi over the fish, sprinkle with the rest of the sesame seeds, then top with the caviar and finally the nori. Serve with pickled ginger.

SERVES 4

soft-shell crab nori sushi rolls

My favourite sushi roll ever — this just can't be beaten.

2 soft-shell crabs
vegetable oil for deep-frying
60 g (2 oz/^{1}/$_3$ cup) rice flour
2 sheets toasted nori
1 quantity sushi rice, page 230
1 teaspoon wasabi paste
2 tablespoons Japanese mayonnaise
a pinch of chilli powder
1 teaspoon toasted sesame seeds
^{1}/$_2$ avocado, sliced
2 handfuls shredded iceberg lettuce
tamari soy sauce, to serve

Clean the crabs and cut into quarters. Heat the oil in a deep-fat fryer or large saucepan to 180°C (350°F) — either measure this with a thermometer or drop a cube of bread into the oil: it should brown in about 15 seconds. Dust the soft-shell crabs in rice flour and deep-fry until golden. Drain on kitchen paper.

Lay the nori sheets on your work surface with the long sides facing you. Spread the sushi rice evenly over the nori sheets. Turn the sheets over so the rice is facing down. Next, spread the mayonnaise and chilli powder halfway up the sheets. On top of this, place the sesame seeds, avocado and shredded lettuce. Finish with the quarters of crispy crab.

Tightly wrap up the nori rolls away from you. Cut each one into eight pieces and serve with tamari soy sauce.

SERVES 4

sushi of marinated mackerel

Marinated mackerel is a wonderful preparation — neither raw fish nor cooked fish, but something in between that just melts in your mouth.

50 ml (1^3/$_4$ fl oz) soy sauce
50 ml (1^3/$_4$ fl oz) mirin
a pinch of sugar
1 tablespoon lemon juice
2 tablespoons grapeseed oil
8 x 20 g (^{3}/$_4$ oz) mackerel fillets, no skin and bones
1 quantity sushi rice, page 230

Heat the soy sauce, mirin, sugar, lemon juice and oil in a small pan until the sugar dissolves. Pour over the mackerel and marinate for 2 hours. Squeeze the rice into 8 blocks, each about 5 cm (2 inches) long and 2 cm (^{3}/$_4$ inch) high. Drain the mackerel and place a piece on top of each block of sushi rice. Soy sauce isn't necessary with this sushi.

MAKES 8 PIECES

tuna tartare SUSHI

I have met quite a few commercial tuna fishermen in my time and they all have one thing in common... they're bloody mad.

There is little I can say about yellow-fin tuna that you don't already know, except in my mind it is an absolutely wonderful fish to eat and cook as long as it is fresh. Never buy dull-looking tuna: it must be pristine in colour and smell, otherwise don't waste your money.

1 quantity sushi rice, page 230
150 g (5$\frac{1}{2}$ oz) sashimi-grade yellowfin tuna, cut into small dice
1 teaspoon white and black toasted sesame seeds
1 teaspoon white sesame oil
1 teaspoon grapeseed oil
1 teaspoon finely grated fresh ginger
1 teaspoon tamari soy sauce
1 teaspoon mirin
1 teaspoon finely sliced spring onion, white part only
8 quail eggs, separated (you won't be using the whites)
1 tablespoon julienned toasted nori

Place a tablespoon or two of sushi rice into a 3–5 cm (1–2 inch) biscuit cutter and press down lightly. Mix the tuna with most of the sesame seeds, the oils, ginger, soy and mirin. Spoon the tuna mix on top of the sushi rice, place a quail yolk on top of the tuna and sprinkle with a few more sesame seeds. Carefully lift the biscuit cutter off, and top with some shredded nori.

MAKES 8 PIECES

SWORDFISH with spiced eggplant relish

This eggplant relish is so good that you can just eat it by itself with some crusty bread or steamed rice.

This relish works with just about any type of SEAFOOD except perhaps whiting and dory (their flesh is too delicate for its strong flavours).

SPICED EGGPLANT RELISH
vegetable oil, for deep-frying
1 small eggplant, diced
2 tablespoons olive oil
2 garlic cloves, finely diced
2 tablespoons chopped French shallots
2 tablespoons capers, rinsed
4 anchovies
2 tablespoons chilli jam, page 218
2 tablespoons red wine vinegar
4 tablespoons chopped flat-leaf (Italian) parsley

4 x 160 g (5¾ oz) swordfish steaks
⅓ cup chopped tomato confit, page 233
4 tablespoons extra virgin olive oil
1 tablespoon lemon juice
4 caperberries, sliced
1 cup chilli salt squid, page 172, definitely optional

To make the eggplant relish, heat the vegetable oil in a deep-fat fryer or saucepan to 185°C (365°F) — either measure this with a thermometer or drop a cube of bread into the oil: it should brown in about 10 seconds. Deep-fry the eggplant until golden, then drain on kitchen paper.

Heat the olive oil in a saucepan and fry the garlic and shallots until golden. Add the capers, anchovies, chilli jam, vinegar, parsley and eggplant and mix through. Cook for another 5 minutes over low heat until all the flavours are well blended. Season with salt and pepper.

Rub the swordfish with a touch of olive oil and salt and pepper and cook on a barbecue, chargrill or in a frying pan for 1–2 minutes on the first side, then 1 minute on the other side (this will be rare to medium-rare).

Mix the tomato with the olive oil, lemon juice and caperberries.

Spoon eggplant relish onto each plate and top with a piece of swordfish and some chilli squid if you're wanting to impress. Spoon a little of the tomato caperberry mix over the fish.

SERVES 4

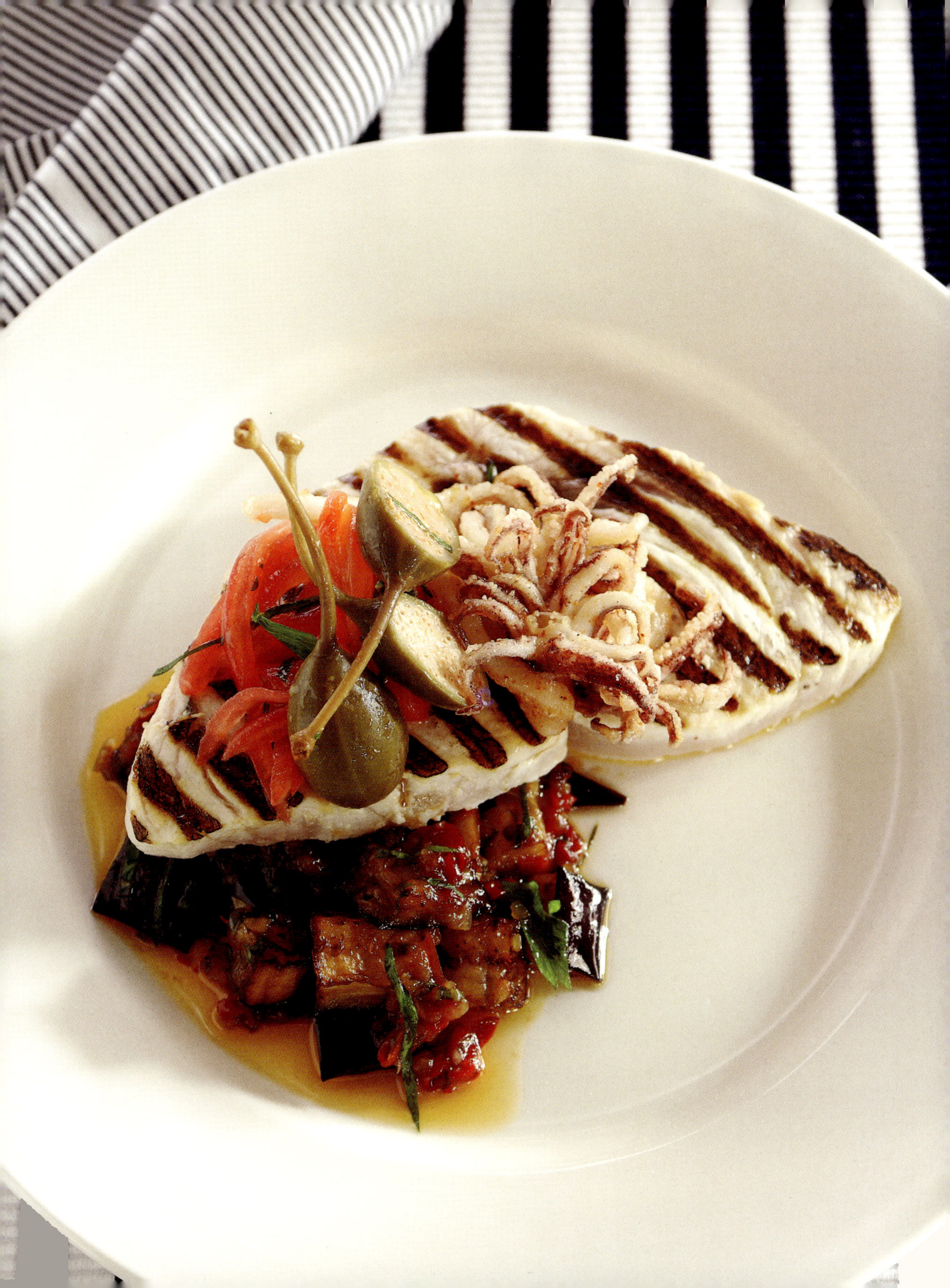

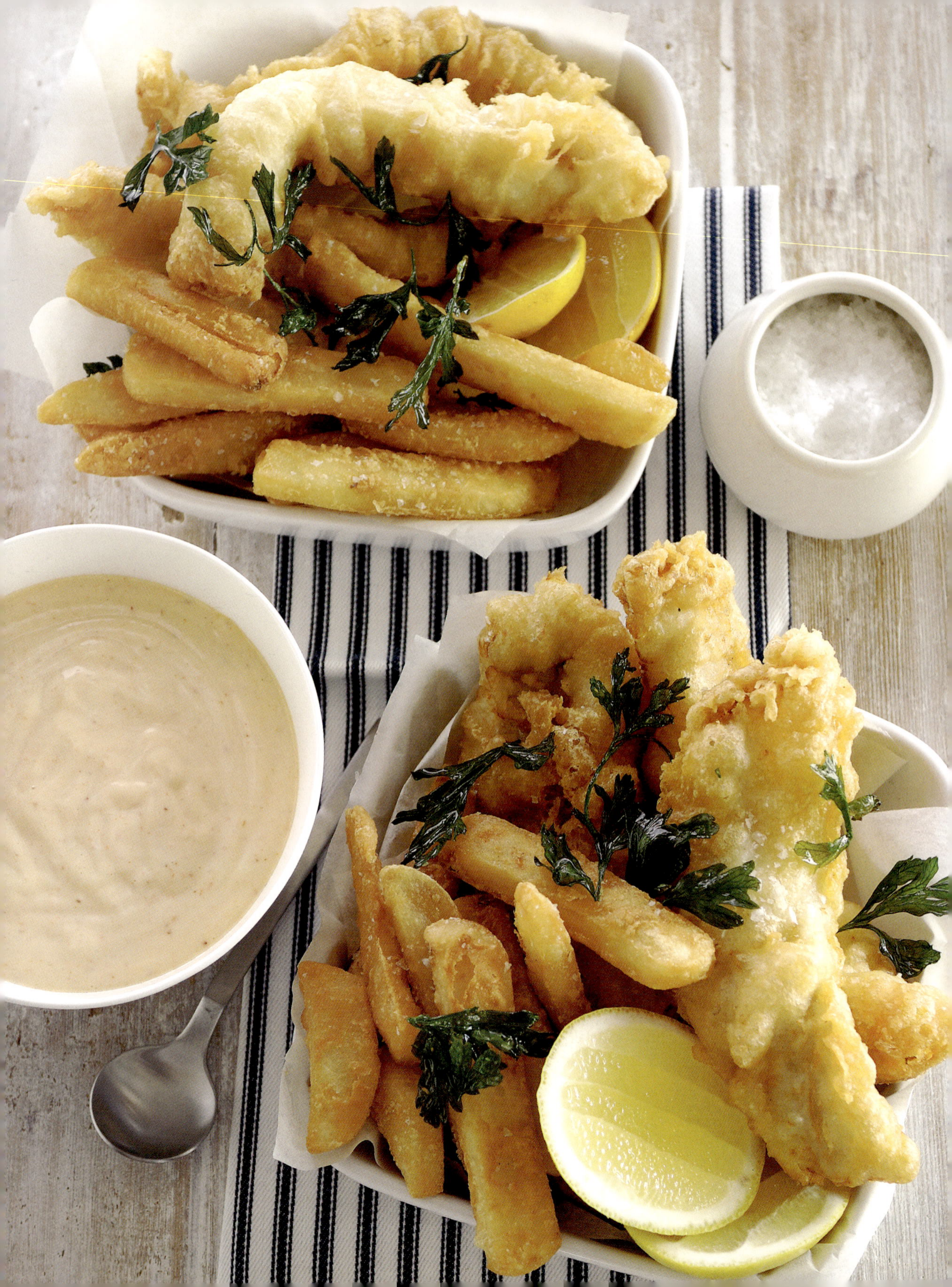

beer-battered THREADFIN SALMON with harissa mayonnaise

There are few things I enjoy more than eating fish and chips while I watch the sun set. The best fish and chips I've ever had was up in Darwin where the fish they used was a threadfin salmon. If you are ever up north and you get the opportunity to try some threadfin, do yourself a favour and tuck in.

You could also use GUMMY SHARK (FLAKE), FLATHEAD, OCEAN PERCH, BARRAMUNDI or WHITING

olive oil, for deep-frying
4 x 150 g (5$\frac{1}{2}$ oz) threadfin salmon fillets, skin and bones removed
plain flour, seasoned with salt and pepper, for dusting
1 quantity beer batter, page 213
1$\frac{1}{2}$ teaspoons harissa (a Middle Eastern chilli condiment available from delis)
4 tablespoons mayonnaise
lemon wedges, to serve

Heat the oil in a deep-fat fryer or large pan to 180°C (350°F) — either measure this with a thermometer or drop a cube of bread into the oil: it should brown in about 15 seconds. Season the fish with sea salt and cracked pepper. Dust the fish in seasoned flour and shake off the excess. Dip the fish in the batter and drain off the excess. Deep-fry the fish until golden. Drain on kitchen paper and season with salt.

Stir the harissa into the mayonnaise. Serve the fish with harissa mayonnaise and lemon wedges.

SERVES 4

Kids from the Ngamakoon community, WA.

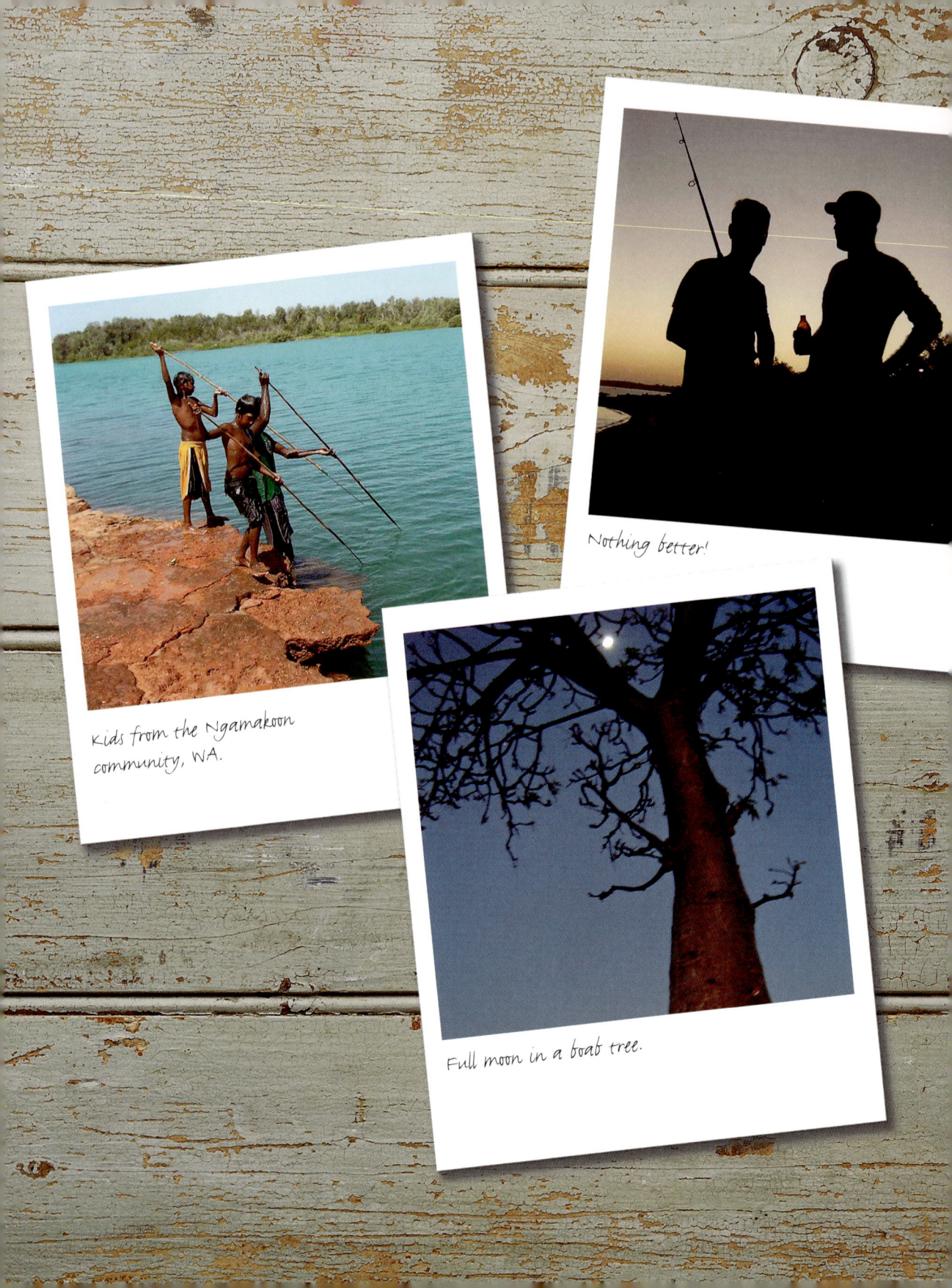

Nothing better!

Full moon in a boab tree.

Flying the flag — serious game fishing.

A beautiful sight.

tommy ruff
trout tuna vongole whitebait whiting
yabby

escabeche of **TOMMY RUFF** (australian herring) with saffron and toasted almonds

This recipe from Spain is a unique celebration of seafood. It is a perfect summer lunch dish for sharing — the best thing about it is you can prepare it a day or two in advance and it just gets better the longer it is marinated.

You could also use MULLET, SARDINES, TROUT or SALMON

300 ml (10½ fl oz) red wine vinegar
3 bay leaves
3 garlic cloves
10 black peppercorns
½ teaspoon coriander seeds
½ teaspoon fennel seeds
pinch of chilli flakes
a good pinch of saffron threads, infused in a little boiling water
½ teaspoon caster sugar
grated zest of 1 orange
a few sprigs of rosemary or thyme
3 tablespoons olive oil
4 whole tommy ruff, scaled and gutted
plain flour, seasoned with salt and pepper, for dusting
½ red onion, cut into thin rings
50 g (1¾ oz) toasted chopped almonds

Bring the vinegar, bay leaves, garlic, peppercorns, coriander seeds, fennel seeds, chilli flakes, saffron, sugar, orange zest, rosemary, a pinch of sea salt and 250 ml (9 fl oz/1 cup) water to the boil for 5 minutes to make a marinade.

Heat the olive oil in a frying pan. Coat the tommy ruff in seasoned flour and fry for 3–4 minutes on each side until golden. Transfer to a dish and scatter with the onion and almonds. Pour the marinade over the top, cover and leave in the fridge for at least a day or up to 4 days.

Serve cold or at room temperature with crusty bread and a salad of rocket or watercress.

SERVES 4 AS A STARTER

italian smoked **TROUT** dip

This is a very simple recipe that is great with some crusty bread when you have friends over. It's also lovely spread on warm toast.

You could also use SMOKED EEL or CRAB meat

1 whole smoked trout
juice of 1 lemon
1 tablespoon chopped flat-leaf (Italian) parsley
4 tablespoons olive oil
1 bird's eye chilli, finely chopped
sourdough bread or brioche, to serve

Take all the meat off the trout and remove all the bones. Mix the fish with the lemon juice, parsley, olive oil, chilli and some sea salt and cracked black pepper in a mortar and pestle. Serve on slices of toasted sourdough or brioche.

SERVES 4 AS A STARTER

scrambled eggs with smoked **TROUT**, tarragon and horseradish

The jury is out (well, mine is anyway!) on what tastes better: brown or rainbow trout. Rainbow trout is much easier to find in the marketplace, but I think a smoked, freshly caught, brown trout is a magical thing. When I'm trout fishing in the mountains I like to have a hearty breakfast and the unique combination of tarragon, horseradish and smoked trout is like cheese and crackers — it just works.

You could also use SMOKED SALMON, CRAB meat or SEA URCHIN

8 eggs
250 ml (9 fl oz/1 cup) cream
40 g (1 1/2 oz) butter
2 tablespoons extra virgin olive oil
1 1/2 cups flaked smoked trout flesh (you will need 1–2 trout for this amount)
30 tarragon leaves, torn
4 pieces of toast
grated horseradish, to taste
4 tablespoons caviar (salmon or sturgeon)
lemon wedges, to serve

Whisk the eggs and cream together and season with a pinch of sea salt and pepper. Heat the butter and olive oil in a non-stick frying pan over medium heat until hot but not coloured. Pour in the eggs and cook, stirring with a wooden spoon until they are just starting to firm up but are still really moist. Add the trout and tarragon and serve immediately on toast, topped with grated horseradish, caviar and a lemon wedge.

SERVES 4

smoked **TROUT** and green mango salad

When I was in Thailand many years ago I visited a market stall and tried the local version of this salad. Approximately one minute later I was running around the market crying (much to Astrid's amusement). I have never stolen anything in my life, but I pinched a cucumber from the nextdoor stall and wolfed it down to try to quench the intense heat in my mouth. My only real salvation came in the form of a couple of icy long-neck beers (although I suspect they numbed all the senses rather than cooled my mouth). This recipe isn't as punishing, but increase the amount of chilli if you like — just have a couple of beers ready.

You could also use CRAB meat, PRAWNS, BUGS, SMOKED TROUT or EEL

1 tablespoon dried shrimp
2 garlic cloves, chopped
1 banana chilli, chopped
1 ripe tomato, chopped
1 tablespoon palm sugar
1 tablespoon fish sauce
1 tablespoon tamarind pulp concentrate
2 snake beans, cut into 2 cm (3/4 inch) pieces
2 tablespoons crushed peanuts
1 green mango, julienned
1 tablespoon lime juice
a large handful of bean sprouts
6 Thai basil leaves
3 Vietnamese mint leaves
3 mint leaves
3 red Asian shallots, very thinly sliced
200 g (7 oz) smoked trout, flaked
1 tablespoon crushed peanuts, extra, to garnish

Soak the dried shrimp in water for 10 minutes, then drain. Pound the garlic and chilli to a paste with a large mortar and pestle. Add the tomato and shrimp and keep pounding. Add the palm sugar, fish sauce and tamarind pulp. Add the snake beans and crushed peanuts (the flavour should be quite sweet, hot and sour).

Add the mango and mix well, then add the lime juice and mix again. Transfer to a serving bowl and add the bean sprouts, Thai basil, mint leaves, shallots and smoked trout. Mix well and serve with the extra peanuts sprinkled over the top.

SERVES 4 AS A STARTER

mountain-style rainbow TROUT

Rainbow trout are my favourite fish to catch: all that clean mountain air, the walking, the flora and fauna, and then to catch a fish... that's a bonus. But the real treat is to cook it simply over a campfire — all the meals you've ever eaten pale in comparison. I recommend catching your own trout as I often find the farmed variety don't have the same unique taste (and then cook it over your own campfire, even if it's in the backyard).

You could also use BROWN TROUT, BARRAMUNDI, SNAPPER, BREAM, MULLOWAY or PRAWNS

4 tablespoons olive oil
4 whole rainbow trout, cleaned and gutted
plain flour, seasoned with salt and pepper, for dusting
4 tablespoons butter
juice of 2 lemons, plus 2 more lemons, halved
4 garlic cloves, thinly sliced
2 banana chillies, seeded and thinly sliced
16 sage leaves
2 kipfler potatoes, boiled and thickly sliced
16 cherry tomatoes, cut in half
12 caperberries
16 olives

Heat the oil in a large frying pan. Dust the fish with seasoned flour and add to the hot oil. Cook the trout until golden and crisp on one side, then turn over, add the butter and cook until it turns nut brown.

Add the lemon juice, garlic, chilli and sage leaves and cook for a minute, then add the potatoes, tomatoes, caperberries, olives and lemon halves, cut side down, and cook for a further minute until the fish is cooked through.

SERVES 4

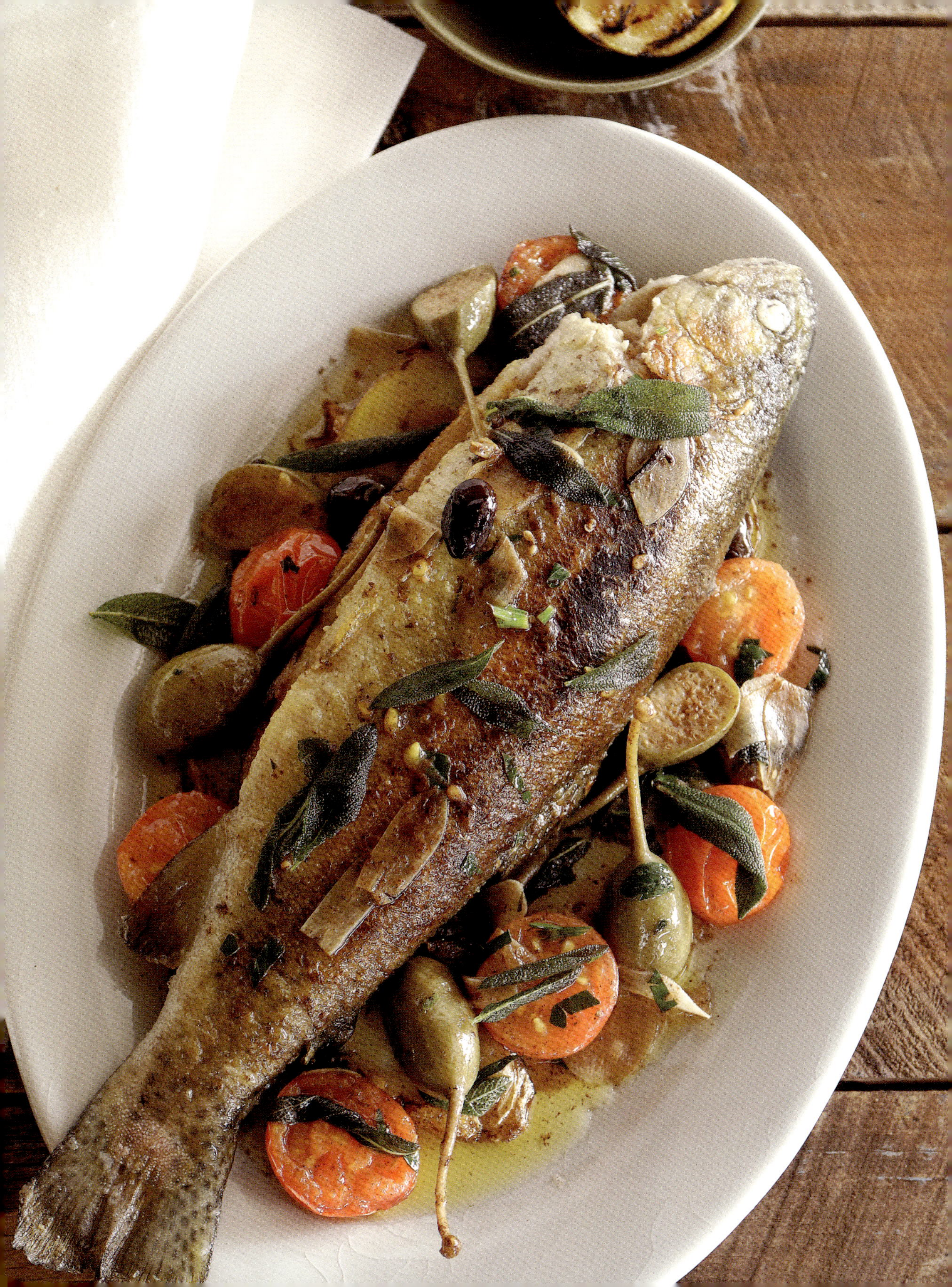

steamed TROUT with chillies, lime and roasted cashews

What a wonderful way to enjoy some spanking fresh trout. This recipe will take no more than ten minutes to prepare and is packed full of flavour — it will probably become a weekly regular in your house.

You could also use any TROUT variety, GARFISH, WHITING, SCALLOPS, OYSTERS or SCAMPI

4 x 160 g (5¾ oz) brown trout fillets, with skin on, bones removed
2 hot green chillies (or red bird's eye chillies)
2 garlic cloves
1 tablespoon finely chopped coriander
2 tablespoons fish sauce
2 tablespoons lime juice
2 tablespoons roasted cashew nuts, roughly chopped

Steam the trout, skin side down, for 4–5 minutes or until it is just cooked through. Pound together the chillies and garlic with a mortar and pestle. Stir in the coriander, fish sauce and lime juice, then pour the dressing over the fish and sprinkle with the cashew nuts.

SERVES 4

rainbow TROUT with green pea risotto

I am very proud of this recipe — it is something I created for my first series of 'home' with the Lifestyle Channel back in 2000. I really wanted to come up with a dish that shows off just how good rainbow trout fillets can be. They are so cheap and delicious, and I think the pairing of the fish with the stunning risotto and simple dressing does the job perfectly. Fresh peas are best for the risotto, but frozen are fine if there aren't any fresh around.

You could also use BROWN TROUT, FLAKED SMOKED TROUT, SALMON or OCEAN TROUT

30 g (1 oz/¼ cup) chopped semi-dried tomatoes
2 teaspoons chopped dill
1 tablespoon aged balsamic vinegar
3 tablespoons extra virgin olive oil
450 g (1 lb/3 cups) peas
2 tablespoons cream
2 tablespoons olive oil
2 tablespoons butter
½ onion, finely chopped
1 garlic clove, minced
300 g (10½ oz/1½ cups) arborio rice
125 ml (4 fl oz/½ cup) dry white wine
400 ml (14 fl oz) hot chicken stock
2 tablespoons grated parmesan
1 tablespoon chopped mint
1 tablespoon chopped dill, extra
juice of ½ lemon
4 x 150 g (5½ oz) pieces rainbow trout fillet
salmon roe, to garnish

Mix the tomatoes, dill, balsamic vinegar and extra virgin olive oil together to make a dressing.

Cook the peas in lots of salted boiling water for 1–2 minutes until soft but not overcooked, then refresh in cold water and drain thoroughly. Blend half the peas with the cream and season with a bit of salt and pepper.

Heat the oil and 1 tablespoon of the butter in a wide heavy-based saucepan and gently fry the onion and garlic until soft but not coloured. Add the rice and cook for a minute, stirring well to coat all the grains with the oil and butter. Add the wine and stir for about 2 minutes until it has almost evaporated. Add the hot stock and stir well. Put the lid on the pan, turn down the heat to its lowest setting and leave for 12–15 minutes, or until the rice is cooked. Fold in the whole peas, the blended peas, the parmesan, the rest of the butter, the herbs and lemon juice and season with salt and pepper.

A few minutes before the risotto is ready, heat a touch of oil in a frying pan. Season the fish and cook, skin side down, until crisp. Turn over and cook for 15–20 seconds on the other side (the trout should be rare to medium-rare and melt in your mouth; if you cook it for longer it will become dry).

Serve the fish on a small mound of risotto. Spoon a little of the balsamic dressing around the plate and garnish with some salmon roe.

Great with a glass of chardonnay.

SERVES 4

spaghetti with ocean TROUT and capers

I like to toss raw fish into the pasta at the last minute just to warm it through. That way the fish is served very rare.

You could also use SALMON, TUNA or SWORDFISH

500 g (1 lb 2 oz) spaghetti
125 ml (4 fl oz/½ cup) extra virgin olive oil
4 tablespoons finely chopped garlic
2 tablespoons finely chopped banana chilli
6 anchovies, roughly torn
60 g (2 oz/⅓ cup) chopped green olives
2 tablespoons baby capers
a large handful of chopped flat-leaf (Italian) parsley
juice of 2 lemons
400 g (14 oz) ocean trout, skin and bones removed, cut into small cubes
3 handfuls of rocket
4 tablespoons salmon roe

Cook the pasta in a large pan of boiling salted water until al dente. Meanwhile, heat the oil, garlic and chilli in a saucepan until the garlic starts to turn golden. Add the anchovies, olives, capers and parsley.

Drain the pasta, add to the saucepan and toss well. Add the lemon juice and ocean trout and season with sea salt and cracked pepper, then stir through for 30 seconds. (You want the fish to be served rare, so just warm it slightly around the edges and it will continue cooking on the plate from the heat of the pasta.)

Add the rocket and mix through until lightly wilted. Garnish with salmon roe.

SERVES 4

orecchiette with broccolini, smoked **TROUT** and anchovies

I am not a huge fan of commercially packaged smoked trout — usually it has lost all its moisture by the time it's been packed, just so that it will last longer on the shelf. If you get the chance, try smoking your own fish and experience what all the fuss used to be about. The best way to eat it is warm and succulent from the smoker but, if you can wait for the trout to cool down, this is one of my all-time favourite pasta recipes. I know it looks like a lot of anchovies, but trust me and cook them down slowly. This could well become your favourite pasta, too.

You could also use SMOKED EEL, CRAB meat, PRAWNS, SALMON or MUSSELS

500 g (1 lb 2 oz) dried orecchiette
200 g (7 oz) broccolini
125 ml (4 fl oz/$1/2$ cup) olive oil
4 French shallots, finely sliced
6 garlic cloves, crushed
12 anchovies
2 tablespoons pine nuts, toasted
1 teaspoon hot chilli flakes
6 tablespoons chopped flat-leaf (Italian) parsley
$1 1/2$ cups flaked smoked trout flesh (you will need 1–2 trout for this amount)
1 lemon

Cook the pasta in a large pan of boiling salted water until al dente. Cut the broccolini into small pieces, blanch in boiling water and then refresh in cold water and drain.

Heat the olive oil in a frying pan, add the shallots, garlic and anchovies and cook gently until softened and broken down to a paste. Add the broccolini, pine nuts, chilli, parsley and plenty of pepper and toss until heated through. Drain the pasta and toss with the sauce. Add the trout and a squeeze of lemon juice before serving.

SERVES 4

orecchiette with broccolini,
smoked trout and anchovies

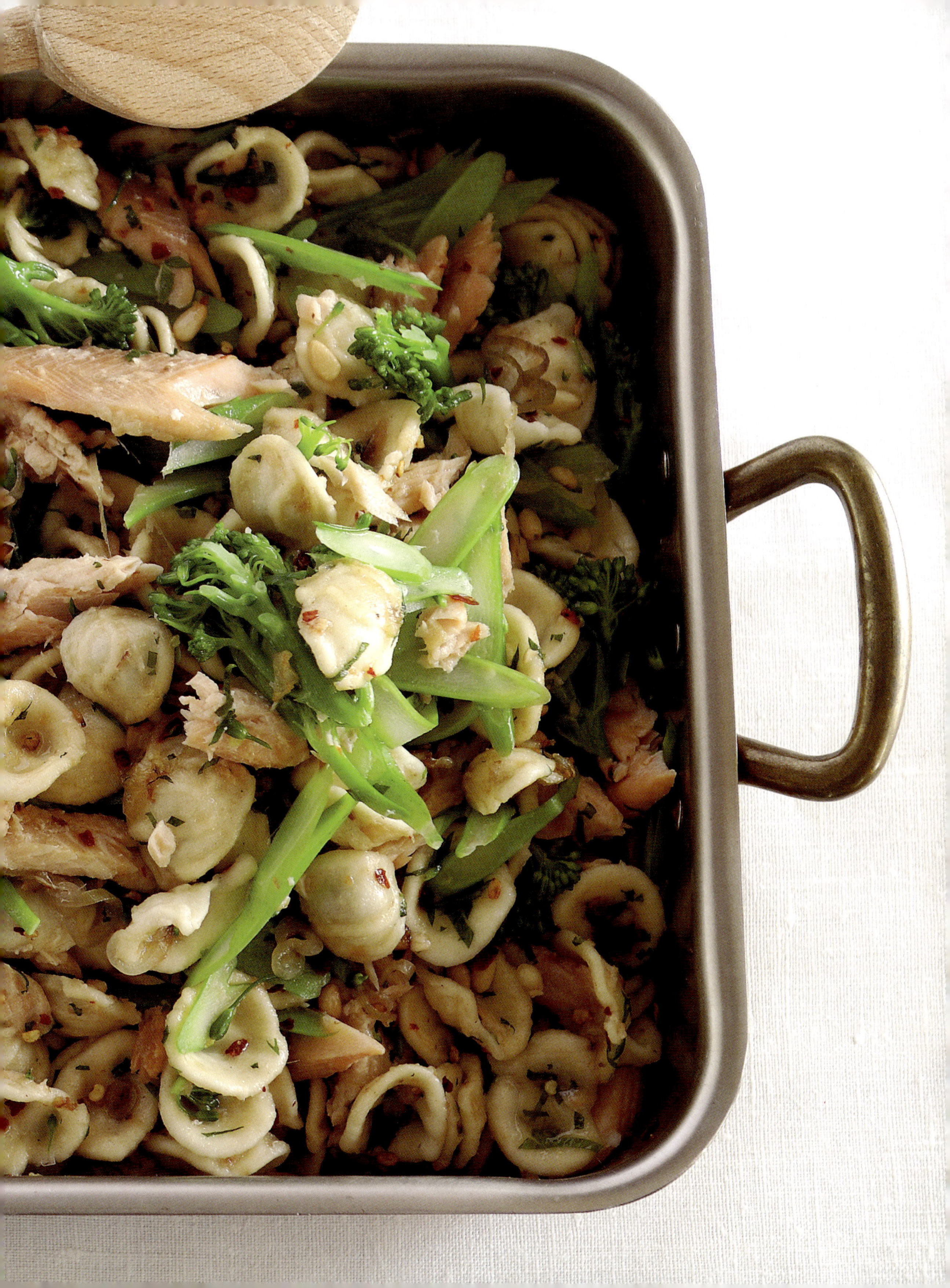

wild brown TROUT with tarragon beurre blanc

If you are ever fortunate enough to hook a wild brown trout out of a river or lake, please try this simple campfire recipe that is as old as the hills you've caught the trout from. Cooking doesn't get any better than this.

You could also use rainbow TROUT or any firm white-fleshed FISH

4 whole brown trout, cleaned and gutted
1 lemon, roughly chopped
4 bay leaves
butter
a handful of tarragon leaves
1 quantity beurre blanc, page 214

Preheat your barbecue or oven to 160°C (315°F/Gas 2–3).
Fill the cavity of each fish with lemon and a bay leaf. Take four squares of foil (each one large enough to wrap up a fish) and rub them with butter. Put the trout on the foil and wrap up into parcels.
Cook on the hot coals or in the oven for 7–8 minutes, or until the fish is just cooked through. Stir the tarragon leaves into the beurre blanc and serve with the fish.

SERVES 4

TUNA with a warm potato salad

The flavours in this dish really speak volumes about what is possible with just a few simple ingredients cooked correctly. You can try potato mash instead of boiled kipflers for a bit of variety occasionally.

You could also use any FISH fillet

oil, for deep-frying
2 eggplants, cut into 2 cm ($3/4$ inch) dice
extra virgin olive oil
2 anchovies
2 teaspoons ground cumin
2 punnets cherry tomatoes, cut in half
2 teaspoons baby capers
a handful of flat-leaf (Italian) parsley leaves
4 kipfler potatoes, boiled and cut in half lengthways
4 x 160 g ($5^{3}/4$ oz) tuna steaks
4 lime cheeks

Heat the oil in a deep-fat fryer or large pan to 180°C (350°F) — either measure this with a thermometer or drop a cube of bread into the oil: it should brown in about 15 seconds. Deep-fry the eggplant until golden.

Heat a little olive oil in a saucepan and add the anchovies. Cook gently, stirring until they become a paste, then add the cumin, tomatoes and capers and cook for 5 minutes until soft. Add the eggplant, parsley and potatoes and season with sea salt and pepper.

Heat a touch of oil in a frying pan and cook the fish for 2 minutes. Season with salt and pepper, then flip over and cook for a further 2 minutes on the other side (this will be rare to medium-rare). Add the lime cheeks to the pan, flesh side down.

Arrange the potato salad on plates, top with the fish and serve with the caramelised lime cheeks.

SERVES 4

vitello TONNATO

This means 'veal and tuna' in Italian (more 'surf and turf'!). Traditionally, the veal was slow roasted and served with cooked tuna folded through an aioli or mayonnaise. I like to step it up a notch and team the veal with some very quickly seared tuna. This gives a great textural contrast, from the slow-roasted veal to the melt-in-your-mouth tuna, to the creamy tuna aioli. (Then I really send it off the Richter scale with some crispy garlic chips.)

You can't make this with anything other than tuna

olive oil
125 g (4^1/$_2$ oz) veal fillet
120 g (4 oz) sashimi-grade tuna fillet
100 g (3^1/$_2$ oz) tinned tuna
^{2}/$_3$ cup aioli, page 212
3 teaspoons capers
3 anchovies, chopped
1 tablespoon chopped flat-leaf (Italian) parsley
grated zest of 1 lemon (or 1 tablespoon julienned preserved lemon) and a squeeze of lemon juice
2 handfuls watercress or rocket leaves, dressed in lemon juice
20 crispy garlic chips, page 220

Preheat the oven to 140°C (275°F/Gas 1). Heat a touch of olive oil in an ovenproof frying pan and sear the veal fillet on all sides until golden. Transfer to the oven and cook for about 10 minutes, or until rare to medium-rare, then leave to rest for 20 minutes. Thinly slice the veal.

Heat a touch of olive oil in a frying pan and sear the tuna fillet for about 2 minutes on each side until rare to medium-rare. Cut the tuna into slices of the same thickness as the veal.

Mix together the tinned tuna, aioli, capers, anchovies, parsley, lemon zest and juice and season with salt and pepper.

Place one slice of veal on a plate, then one slice of tuna slightly overlapping, then veal, then tuna down the centre of the plate. Spoon the sauce down the centre and top with the watercress leaves dressed in lemon juice and some crispy garlic chips.

SERVES 4

TUNA penne puttanesca

As you are probably aware, puttanesca translates from Italian as 'in the style of the whore'. There are a few explanations as to how the dish came about its sordid name: the first being that the sauce is quick and easy to make, so the prostitutes could keep the interruption of their business to a minimum; the second is that it was made for the men waiting their turn at the brothel; and there are a couple more that I won't go into here. All I will say is that it is a wonderful dish that has stood the test of time.

You could also use any firm white-fleshed FISH

500 g (1 lb 2 oz) penne
2 tablespoons olive oil
4 garlic cloves, finely chopped
1 bird's eye chilli, finely chopped
6 anchovies, torn into pieces
1 tablespoon baby capers
16 kalamata olives, pitted
200 g (7 oz) tuna fillet, cut into 2 cm (3/4 inch) cubes
1 quantity Italian tomato sauce, page 223
4 tablespoons chopped flat-leaf (Italian) parsley
grated zest of 1 lemon

Cook the pasta in a large pan of boiling salted water until al dente.
    Meanwhile, heat the oil in a frying pan and fry the garlic and chilli for 20 seconds. Add the anchovies, capers and olives and fry for another 20 seconds. Add the tuna and cook for 10 seconds before adding the tomato sauce. Heat through, drain the penne and add to the sauce. Stir in the parsley, lemon zest and some black pepper.

SERVES 4

spaghetti VONGOLE with bottarga

Spaghetti vongole is a classic Italian dish and there are two main methods for preparing it: one using a tomato base, the other with a white wine base. I don't have a favourite, but if I'm adding bottarga (the dried pressed roe of the tuna or mullet) I like to use this white wine version.

You could also use PIPIS

500 g (1 lb 2 oz) spaghetti
4 tablespoons olive oil
2 garlic cloves, finely chopped
2 tablespoons chopped flat-leaf (Italian) parsley
a pinch of dried chilli flakes
800 g (1 lb 12 oz) fresh vongole (Italian clams)
4 tablespoons white wine
1 tablespoon butter
1 tablespoon grated bottarga

Cook the pasta in a large pan of boiling salted water until al dente. Meanwhile, heat the oil and garlic in a saucepan until the garlic starts to turn golden. Add the parsley and chilli flakes and cook for 10 seconds. Add the vongole and cook for about 30 seconds. Add the wine and cover the pan for about a minute until the vongole open. Add the drained pasta and butter and toss well.
    Serve in hot bowls and sprinkle the bottarga over the top.

SERVES 4

fried WHITEBAIT with szechuan pepper and lemon dipping sauce

Szechuan peppers are actually the berries of the prickly ash tree, which is why some spice blends are called prickly ash. They have a tantalising flavour and are a wonderful accompaniment to most seafood. Here the peppercorns are dry-roasted to release their flavour and then ground to a fine powder and stirred into fresh lemon juice to make a dipping sauce. Szechuan pepper can make your mouth tingle, which is a fun side effect.

You could also use SQUID, CUTTLEFISH, PRAWNS, OYSTERS or pieces of firm white-fleshed FISH

1 tablespoon Szechuan peppercorns
juice of 1 lemon
vegetable oil, for deep-frying
200 g (7 oz) large whitebait
125 g (4 1/2 oz/1 cup) plain flour, seasoned with salt and pepper

Put the Szechuan peppercorns in a frying pan over medium heat and dry-roast for a few minutes until fragrant. Tip into a mortar and crush well with the pestle. Mix with the lemon juice to make a dipping sauce.

Heat the oil in a deep-fat fryer or large pan to 185°C (365°F) — either measure this with a thermometer or drop a cube of bread into the oil: it should brown in about 10 seconds. Lightly dust the whitebait with flour and deep-fry until golden. Drain on kitchen paper and sprinkle with sea salt. Serve with the dipping sauce.

SERVES 4 AS A STARTER

WHITEBAIT fritters

These fantastic little fish are just singing out to be dipped in flour and fried, but they also make the most amazing fritters with just a touch of egg and seasoning. Serve them with a really thick, creamy tartare sauce.

You could also use CRAB meat, PRAWNS or SALT COD

150 g (5 1/2 oz) whitebait
1 egg, lightly beaten
30 g (1 oz/ 1/4 cup) plain flour
2 tablespoons finely chopped flat-leaf (Italian) parsley
2 cloves garlic confit, chopped, page 222
olive oil, for frying
4 handfuls of rocket, dressed in lemon juice and extra virgin olive oil
1 quantity tartare sauce, page 231

Mix the whitebait with the egg, flour, parsley and garlic and season with sea salt and cracked black pepper. Form into fritters, using about 2 tablespoons of mixture for each.

Heat the oil in a frying pan and shallow-fry the fritters until golden and crisp on both sides. Drain on kitchen paper.

Arrange the rocket on serving plates and serve the fritters on a bed of rocket with the tartare sauce.

SERVES 4 AS A STARTER

grilled king george WHITING with limoncello and oregano

This is a very simple dish but with beautiful subtle flavours. It is particularly lovely with a side dish of roasted fennel.

You could also use MARRON, LOBSTER, PRAWNS, BUGS, SCALLOPS or any white-fleshed FISH

250 ml (9 fl oz/1 cup) extra virgin olive oil
grated zest and juice of 2 lemons, plus 2 lemons to serve
1 bunch oregano
90 ml (3 fl oz) limoncello or other lemon liqueur
4 whole King George whiting

Stir together the olive oil, lemon zest and juice in a saucepan and place over medium heat until nearly boiling. Pour into a large flat bowl, immediately add the oregano and limoncello and leave for 30 minutes. Add the whiting to the marinade and leave for 10 minutes.

Heat your barbecue grill and cook the whiting until cooked through, basting with the marinade several times. Pour a little more marinade over the fish and serve with lemon quarters.

SERVES 4

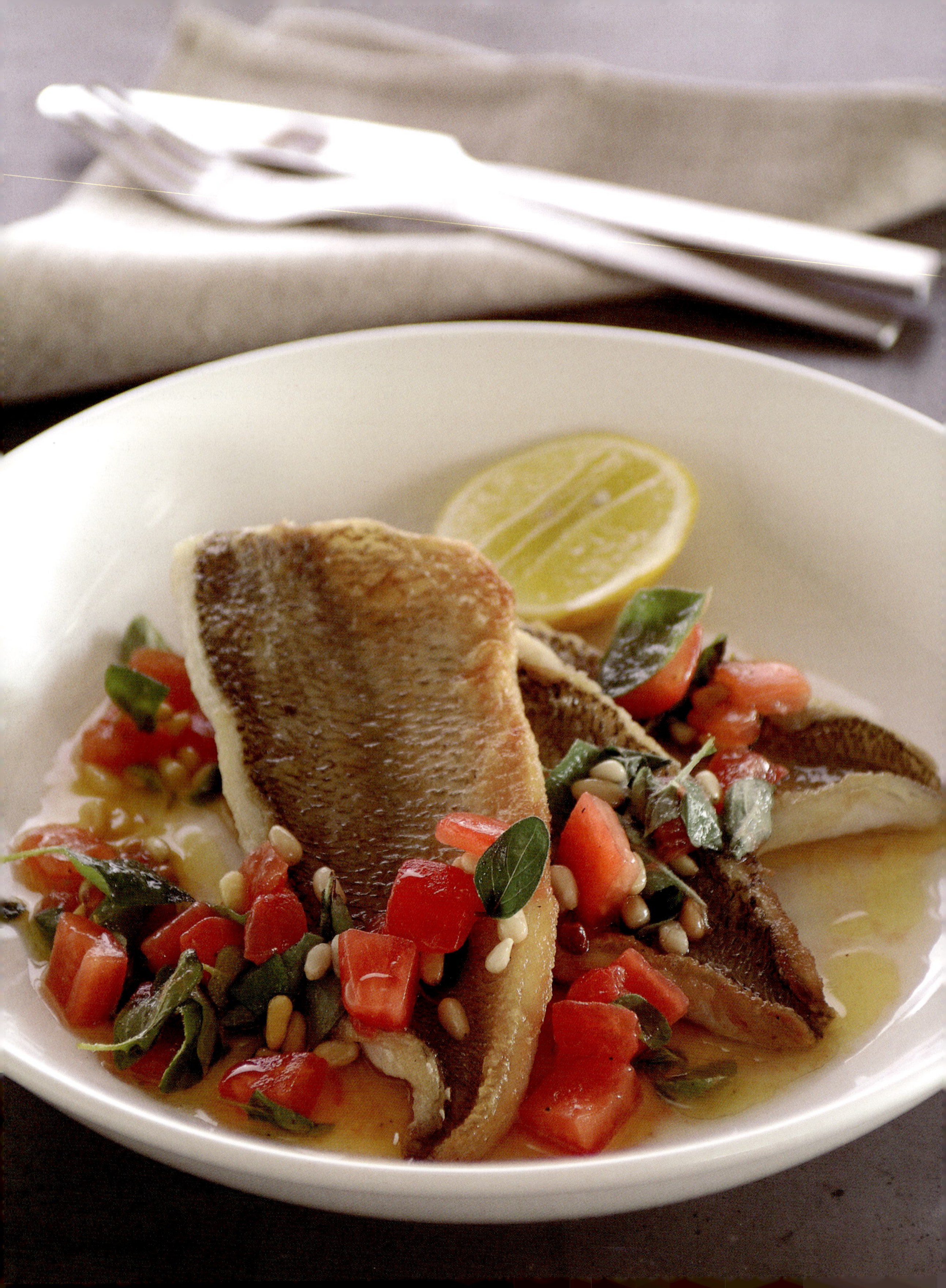

sand WHITING with a warm dressing of tomato, oregano and pine nuts

I fish for whiting most summer afternoons out at Bondi. They have a habit of weaving between swimmers' legs, which makes the fishing sometimes hilarious, or downright scary if you hook the wrong person. My brother-in-law and I have a technique where we snorkel out from the beach to find the school of whiting, then race back and get the rods and worms and start fishing where we spotted them (it's a bit like using a fish finder on a boat, but a lot more fun). We generally do very well, however, sometimes just standing there with the fishing rod in your hand, watching the sun go down is all you need to be happy.

You could also use GARFISH, SNAPPER, SARDINES, BREAM, SCALLOPS, PRAWNS or LOBSTER

- 125 ml (4 fl oz/½ cup) extra virgin olive oil
- 3 tablespoons chopped tomato confit, page 233, or peeled, diced tomato
- 1 tablespoon toasted pine nuts
- 2 teaspoons oregano leaves
- juice of 1 lemon
- 4 x 160 g (5¾ oz) whiting fillets, with skin on, bones removed
- lemon wedges, to serve

Put the olive oil in a saucepan and heat until warm. Add the tomato, pine nuts, oregano and lemon juice and season with salt and pepper.

Heat a touch of oil in a frying pan or on a barbecue plate and cook the whiting, skin side down, until golden, then flip over and cook for another minute (be careful not to overcook).

Lift the fish onto plates and spoon the warm dressing over the top. Serve with lemon wedges.

SERVES 4

barry's snowy mountain YABBIES

Yabbies are funny creatures. They aren't generally something that calls out to be cooked when you're at the fish markets — I suppose because of their size they look as if they might be a lot of hard work for not much gain. Don't let that put you off: give them a try next time and you'll discover they are very sweet and have a wonderful ability to soak up the other flavours in the pan. This recipe is from Barry (who is the fire ranger down on the Monaro Plains in the Snowy Mountains, and also a good mate of mine). He cooked this the last time I visited and it is the best damned plate of yabbies I have ever tasted. Thanks Barry, you're a legend.

You could also use PRAWNS, SCAMPI, LOBSTER or MARRON

40 yabbies
2 tablespoons finely chopped garlic
4 tablespoons sweet chilli sauce
olive oil
2 pearl onions, thinly sliced
4 spring onions, green part only, sliced

If you're using live yabbies, put them in the freezer for 45 minutes or until they're inactive, then put them in a large pan of boiling water until they change colour. Drain and refresh them immediately in iced water and, when they're cool, remove the shells, keeping the claws whole. Devein the yabbies. Mix together the garlic and sweet chilli sauce, add the yabbies and marinate for at least 30 minutes.

Heat a little olive oil in a heavy-based frying pan and fry the pearl onions for 20 seconds. Add the yabbies and let them heat through (you want them to go a bit crusty on the outside). Add the spring onions and serve.

SERVES 4 AS A SHARED PLATE

red-claw YABBIES with tomato gazpacho

Gazpacho is a refreshingly cold soup from southern Spain. It is generally made in the summer, when tomatoes are at their sweetest and most flavoursome, and it's a perfect way to start a meal. Gazpacho is one of the simplest recipes as it requires no cooking — everything is puréed and then chilled. To turn it into a meal, just serve with some cooked and chilled seafood such as red-claw yabbies.

You could also use CRAB meat, PRAWNS, BUGS, FLAKED WHITING, MUSSELS or raw OYSTERS

6–12 red-claw yabbies (depending on their size)
500 g (1 lb 2 oz) vine-ripened tomatoes
1 Lebanese cucumber, halved lengthways and deseeded
½ garlic clove
1 bird's eye chilli
1 red capsicum, halved and deseeded
½ red onion
50 ml (1¾ fl oz) extra virgin olive oil, plus a little extra to serve
30 ml (1 fl oz) sherry vinegar or red wine vinegar
15 basil leaves, thinly sliced

If you're using live yabbies, put them in the freezer for 45 minutes or until they're inactive, then put them in a large pan of boiling water until they change colour. Drain and refresh them immdediately in iced water and, when they're cool, remove the flesh from the shell and claws and keep refrigerated until ready to use.

Roughly chop the tomatoes, cucumber, garlic, chilli, capsicum and onion and put in a blender with the oil. Purée and then pass through a sieve if you like a refined soup, or leave a bit chunky if you prefer that texture. Add the vinegar and salt and pepper to taste and refrigerate until cold. Pour into cold bowls and top with the yabbie meat, a touch of olive oil and the basil leaves when serving.

SERVES 4

A unique fish: "the frying pan snapper".

Tokyo fish markets — check out his knife.

One of the best sights: a red emperor in tropical waters. Nothing better.

The long walk, Snowy Mountains, NSW.

A big Darwin jewfish.

basic
recipes

aioli chilli oil sashimi dressing and more

aioli

4 egg yolks
2 teaspoons dijon mustard
2 tablespoons white wine vinegar
2 tablespoons lemon juice
6 cloves garlic confit, finely chopped, page 222
200 ml (7 fl oz) olive oil
200 ml (7 fl oz) vegetable oil

Blend the yolks, mustard, vinegar, lemon juice, garlic and some sea salt with a hand blender. As you blend, slowly pour in the oil until the aioli is creamy. Season with salt and pepper.

Makes about 500 ml (17 fl oz/2 cups)

baccala (salt cod) sauce

75 g (2¾ oz) salt cod (baccala), soaked in cold water for 48 hours (change the water every 24 hours)
2 tablespoons olive oil
4 cloves garlic confit, page 222
2 teaspoons chilli confit, page 217
2 teaspoons onion confit, page 226
2 anchovies
1 tablespoon capers, rinsed
1 tablespoon chopped green pitted olives
175 g (6 oz) tinned tomatoes
a handful of finely chopped flat-leaf (Italian) parsley
50 ml (1¾ fl oz) fish stock

Break the soaked salt cod into flakes. Heat the oil in a saucepan and sauté the garlic, chilli, onion, anchovies, capers, green olives and salt cod until fragrant. Drain the tinned tomatoes and crush them in your hand. Add to the pan with the parsley and stock and cook over low to medium heat until the sauce has a consistency you like. Season with sea salt and pepper.

Makes about 300 ml (11 fl oz/1¼ cups)

balsamic truffle dressing

60 g (2¼ oz) unsalted butter
25 ml (1 fl oz) aged balsamic vinegar
1–2 teaspoons truffle salsa (available at good delis)
2 teaspoons chopped flat-leaf (Italian) parsley

Put the butter in a saucepan over medium heat until it turns nut brown (you will be able to smell it). Remove from the heat and add the vinegar (stand back as it will bubble and spit at you). Leave to cool and add the truffle salsa and parsley and season with sea salt and cracked pepper.

Makes about 125 ml (4 fl oz/½ cup)

basil oil

4 handfuls of basil leaves
250 ml (9 fl oz/1 cup) olive oil
1 tablespoon lemon juice

Blanch the basil in boiling water and then refresh in iced water. Drain well and wring out in a clean tea towel to remove all the moisture. Put in a blender with the oil and lemon juice and mix until smooth. Season to taste. Keep in a clean screw-top jar.

Makes about 500 ml (17 fl oz/2 cups)

beer batter

375 ml (13 fl oz/1½ cups) ice-cold beer
plain flour
10 ice cubes

Pour the beer into a mixing bowl and gradually stir in the flour until the batter has the consistency of thick cream. Then add the ice cubes to keep it cool. Use within 5 minutes.

Makes about 500 ml (17 fl oz/2 cups)

beurre blanc (white wine butter sauce)

1 teaspoon butter
2 French shallots, finely diced
1 tarragon stalk with leaves
3 tablespoons white wine vinegar
250 ml (9 fl oz/1 cup) white wine
250 g (9 oz) cold butter, cubed
1 tablespoon cream

Heat the butter in a pan and sauté the shallots and tarragon. Add the vinegar and cook until it has almost disappeared. Add the wine and cook until it has reduced to a quarter of the amount.

Strain into another pan, off the heat, and whisk in the butter a few cubes at a time until it is thoroughly mixed in. Stir in the cream. Season with sea salt and cracked pepper and serve immediately.

Makes about 250 ml (9 fl oz/1 cup)

beurre rouge (red wine butter sauce)

1 teaspoon butter
1 French shallot, finely diced
1 thyme stalk
1 garlic clove, chopped
3 tablespoons red wine vinegar
250 ml (9 fl oz/1 cup) red wine (preferably a pinot, so it isn't too heavy)
250 g (9 oz) cold butter, cubed
1 tablespoon cream (optional)

Heat the butter in a pan and sauté the shallot with the thyme and garlic. Add the vinegar and cook until it has almost disappeared. Add the wine and cook until it has reduced to a quarter of the amount.

Strain into another pan, off the heat, and whisk in the butter a few cubes at a time until it is thoroughly mixed in. Stir in the cream. Season with sea salt and cracked pepper and serve immediately.

Makes about 250 ml (9 fl oz/1 cup)

candied ginger

115 g (4 oz/^{1}/$_2$ cup) sugar
4 tablespoons julienned fresh ginger

Put the sugar in a pan with 125 ml (4 fl oz/^{1}/$_2$ cup) of water and stir over heat until the sugar has dissolved. Bring to the boil and simmer for 5 minutes without stirring. Remove from the heat.

Put 1 litre (35 fl oz/4 cups) of water in a saucepan and bring to the boil. Drop the ginger into the water for 10 seconds and then refresh under cold water. Repeat this process twice more.

Reheat the sugar syrup, blanch the ginger in the sugar syrup and then leave to cool down on a wire rack.

Makes about 4 tablespoons of candied ginger

candied lime

115 g (4 oz/^{1}/$_2$ cup) sugar
4 tablespoons julienned lime peel

Put the sugar in a pan with 125 ml (4 fl oz/^{1}/$_2$ cup) of water and stir over heat until the sugar has dissolved. Bring to the boil and simmer for 5 minutes without stirring. Remove from the heat.

Put 1 litre (35 fl oz/4 cups) of water in a saucepan and bring to the boil. Drop the lime into the water for 10 seconds and then refresh under cold water. Repeat this process twice more.

Reheat the sugar syrup, blanch the lime in the sugar syrup and then leave to cool down on a wire rack.

Makes about 4 tablespoons of candied lime

capsicum sauce

4 large red capsicums
100 g (3 1/2 oz) cold unsalted butter, cubed
juice of 1/2 lime

Put the capsicums through a juicer or blend them and strain the juice, discarding the solids. Put the juice in a pan and simmer until thick and syrupy. Remove from the heat, whisk in the butter a cube at a time, and season with salt and pepper and lime juice.
 Keep in a warm spot before serving.

Makes about 185 ml (6 fl oz/3/4 cup)

cauliflower purée

350 g (12 oz) cauliflower, finely chopped
250 ml (9 fl oz/1 cup) milk
250 ml (9 fl oz/1 cup) cream
1 tablespoon butter

Put the cauliflower in a saucepan, cover with the milk and cream and cook gently until tender. Strain off the liquid and keep it on one side, then purée the cauliflower with the butter. Pour in the liquid until you have a lovely smooth purée and then season to taste with sea salt and white pepper.

Makes about 375 ml (13 fl oz/1 1/2 cups)

chilli caramel dipping sauce

3 tablespoons grated palm sugar
3 tablespoons deseeded and finely chopped banana chillies
2–3 tablespoons white vinegar

Put the palm sugar in a cold pan and cook until it melts and then starts to caramelise. Take the pan off the heat and carefully add the chilli, vinegar and 2 tablespoons of water (be careful as it may spit at you). Stir to combine, put back on the heat and cook for a few minutes until the caramel breaks down.

Makes about 80 ml (2½ fl oz/⅓ cup)

chilli confit

120 g (4 oz/1 cup) deseeded and chopped banana chillies
250 ml (9 fl oz/1 cup) olive oil

Put the chilli and olive oil in a saucepan, place over the lowest heat possible on your stove and cook for 2 hours until the chilli is soft (you don't want the oil boiling, you want it just past warm). This makes the chilli beautifully soft.

    I like to make this with a whole 1 kg (2 lb 4 oz) chopped chillies and 1 litre (35 fl oz/4 cups) of olive oil. I keep the chillies in the oil in a screw-top jar in the fridge and use the flavoured oil to dress pasta, salads and all sorts of seafoods.

chilli jam

1 tablespoon olive oil
1 red onion, diced
1 red capsicum, chopped
1 punnet cherry tomatoes
10 banana chillies, deseeded and chopped
2 tablespoons chopped coriander root and stem
115 g (4 oz/½ cup) brown sugar
2 tablespoons sambal oelek
1–2 tablespoons fish sauce
1 lemon, peeled and chopped, pips removed

Heat the oil and fry the onion and capsicum until soft. Add the remaining ingredients and simmer for 30 minutes. Blend until smooth and then season with sea salt and cracked pepper.

Makes about 1 litre (35 fl oz/4 cups)

chilli oil

2 bird's eye chillies, roughly chopped
1 red capsicum, roughly chopped
300 ml (10 1/2 fl oz) olive oil

Put the chilli, capsicum and oil in a blender and mix together. Pass through a fine strainer and season with salt and pepper.

Makes about 375 ml (13 fl oz/1 1/2 cups)

chilli salt spice

20 small dried red chillies
3 tablespoons sea salt
2 tablespoons black peppercorns
2 tablespoons Szechuan peppercorns

Dry-roast all the ingredients in a pan over low heat until the salt is turning from white to blonde and the spices are fragrant. Tip into a mortar and leave to cool, then finely grind with the pestle.

Makes about 125 g (4 1/2 oz/ 1/2 cup)

coconut dressing

150 ml (5 fl oz) coconut cream
2 tablespoons lime juice
1 tablespoon fish sauce

Mix together all the ingredients.

Makes about 185 ml (6 fl oz/$^3/_4$ cup)

crispy garlic chips

4 garlic cloves, finely sliced
250 ml (9 fl oz/1 cup) vegetable oil

Put the garlic and oil in a saucepan and heat until the garlic starts to turn golden. Lift out the garlic with a slotted spoon and drain on kitchen paper before serving.

Makes about 4 tablespoons of garlic chips

crispy leek

85 g (3 oz/½ cup) julienned leek
500 ml (17 fl oz/2 cups) vegetable oil

Put the leek and oil in a saucepan and heat until the leek starts to turn golden. Lift out the leek with a slotted spoon and drain on kitchen paper.

Makes about 85 g (3 oz/½ cup)

crispy shallots

4 French shallots, thinly sliced
500 ml (17 fl oz/2 cups) vegetable oil

Put the shallots and oil in a saucepan and heat until the shallots start to turn golden. Lift out the shallots with a slotted spoon and drain on kitchen paper.

Makes about 4 tablespoons of crispy shallots

fennel seed and pepper spice mix

100 g (3 1/2 oz) fennel seeds
30 g (1 oz) black peppercorns
15 g (1/2 oz) sea salt

Put everything in a pan over medium heat and cook until the spices are fragrant and the salt is just starting to turn golden. Cool and then grind with a mortar and pestle or spice grinder.

Makes about 150 g (5 1/2 oz / 1/2 cup)

garlic confit

200 g (7 oz/1 cup) peeled garlic cloves
250 ml (9 fl oz/1 cup) olive oil

Put the garlic cloves and olive oil in a saucepan, place over the lowest heat possible on your stove and cook for 2 hours until the garlic is soft (you don't want the oil boiling, you want it just past warm).
    This makes the garlic beautifully soft. I like to make this with a whole 1 kg (2 lb 4 oz) peeled garlic and 1 litre (35 fl oz/4 cups) of olive oil. I keep the garlic in the oil in a screw-top jar in the fridge and use the flavoured oil to dress pasta, salads and seafoods.

ginger oil

2 tablespoons finely chopped fresh ginger
3 tablespoons olive oil

Put the ginger and olive oil in a saucepan, place over the lowest heat possible on your stove and cook for 2 hours until the ginger is soft (you don't want the oil boiling, you want it just past warm).

Makes about 80 ml (2$^{1}/_{2}$ fl oz/$^{1}/_{3}$ cup)

italian tomato sauce

2 tablespoons olive oil
3 garlic cloves, thinly sliced
500 g (1 lb 2 oz) tinned crushed tomatoes
8 basil leaves, chopped

Heat the oil in a saucepan and cook the garlic until it's starting to colour. Add the tomatoes and 250 ml (9 fl oz/1 cup) of water and simmer for 20–25 minutes. Add the basil and cook for another 5 minutes. Season to taste and blend until smooth.

Makes about 500 ml (17 fl oz/2 cups)

japanese salad dressing

3 tablespoons grapeseed oil
2 tablespoons rice wine vinegar
1 teaspoon sliced spring onion, white part only
1 teaspoon English mustard
1 teaspoon light soy sauce
1 teaspoon mirin
a few drops of fish sauce
a pinch of chilli powder

Either whisk or blend together all the ingredients and season with sea salt and cracked pepper.

Makes about 125 ml (4 fl oz/$1/2$ cup)

mayonnaise (and seeded mustard mayonnaise)

4 egg yolks
3 teaspoons dijon mustard
2 teaspoons sugar
2 tablespoons white wine vinegar
2 tablespoons lemon juice
200 ml (7 fl oz) olive oil
200 ml (7 fl oz) vegetable oil

Blend the yolks, mustard, sugar, vinegar, lemon juice and some sea salt with a hand blender. Drizzle in the oil slowly and continue blending until creamy.
　　To make a seeded mustard mayonnaise, mix 125 ml (4 fl oz/$1/2$ cup) of mayonnaise with 2 tablespoons of seeded mustard and 1 teaspoon of lemon juice.

Makes about 500 ml (17 fl oz/2 cups)

miso broth

250 ml (9 fl oz/1 cup) chicken or fish stock
4 tablespoons orange juice
1 teaspoon finely chopped fresh ginger
2 kaffir lime leaves, torn in half (or a squeeze of lime juice)
1 teaspoon Szechuan peppercorns
1 tablespoon kecap manis (sweet soy sauce from Indonesia)
2 teaspoons miso paste

Put all the ingredients in a saucepan and bring almost to the boil. Reduce the heat and simmer for 20 minutes, then strain.

Makes about 185 ml (6 fl oz/$^3/_4$ cup)

nam jim dressing

4 red Asian shallots
2 red bird's eye chillies
2 garlic cloves
1 teaspoon chopped coriander root
100 ml (3$^1/_2$ fl oz) lime juice
75 g (2$^3/_4$ oz) grated palm sugar
50 ml (1$^3/_4$ fl oz) fish sauce

Pound the shallots, chillies, garlic and coriander root with a mortar and pestle and then add the lime juice. Season with palm sugar and fish sauce for a balance of hot, sour, salty and sweet.

Makes about 185 ml (6 fl oz/$^3/_4$ cup)

olive tapenade

125 g (4½ oz/1 cup) pitted black or green olives
juice of 1 lime (and a bit of grated zest is good)
8 basil leaves
2 garlic cloves
1 bird's eye chilli
2 anchovies
10 capers
about 3 tablespoons olive oil

Throw everything except the oil into a food processor and blend together. Drizzle in the oil until you get a nice consistency.

Makes about 185 g (6½ oz/¾ cup)

onion confit

155 g (5½ oz/1 cup) chopped onion
250 ml (9 fl oz/1 cup) olive oil

Put the onion and olive oil in a saucepan, place over the lowest heat possible on your stove and cook for 2 hours until the onion is soft (you don't want the oil boiling, you want it just past warm). This makes the onion beautiful and soft.

    I like to make this with a whole 1 kg (2 lb 4 oz) chopped onion and 1 litre (35 fl oz/4 cups) olive oil. I keep the onion in the oil in a screw-top jar in the fridge and use the flavoured oil to dress pasta, salads and seafoods.

pesto

80 g (2³/₄ oz) garlic confit, page 222
2 tablespoons toasted pine nuts
1 anchovy
100 g (3¹/₂ oz/2 cups) basil leaves
2 tablespoons grated parmesan cheese
grated zest and juice of 1 lemon
50 ml (1³/₄ fl oz) olive oil

Either using a mortar and pestle or a hand blender, pound the garlic to a paste with some sea salt, add the pine nuts and then the anchovy, pounding all the time. Next pound in the basil, and then the cheese (not as much as for normal pesto as we are matching this with seafood), then the lemon zest, lemon juice and the olive oil until you have a sauce consistency. Season with black pepper and more salt if needed.

Makes about 185 g (6¹/₂ oz/³/₄ cup)

pickled vegetables

¹/₂ red capsicum, finely sliced
2 tablespoons julienned fresh ginger
45 g (1¹/₂ oz/¹/₄ cup) deseeded, peeled and julienned cucumber
125 ml (4 fl oz/¹/₂ cup) rice wine vinegar

Put all the vegetables in a bowl or sterilised jar, add the vinegar and leave to sit for 10–30 minutes before using. Store in a sterilised screw-top jar in the fridge.

Makes about 150 g (5 oz/1¹/₂ cups)

pizza dough

3 teaspoons dried yeast
3 teaspoons sugar
3 teaspoons table salt
1 tablespoon olive oil
425 g (15 oz) 00 (bakers') flour

To make the dough, put the yeast, sugar, salt and olive oil in a mixing bowl with 250 ml (9 fl oz/1 cup) of warm water and stir gently. Leave for 15 minutes for the yeast to activate (it will look foamy). Add the flour slowly and knead for about 5 minutes until the dough is smooth.

Put in a lightly oiled boil and leave to sit in a warm place for about 30 minutes to an hour until doubled in size, then knock back with one good punch. Leave in a warm place until it has risen slightly.

Makes enough for four 30 cm (12 inch) pizza bases

salsa verde

1 slice of stale bread
250 ml (9 fl oz/1 cup) olive oil
100 g (3½ oz/2 cups) basil leaves
100 g (3½ oz/2 cups) flat-leaf (Italian) parsley leaves
4 anchovies
50 g (1¾ oz) capers
1 tablespoon finely chopped cornichons (optional)
1 tablespoon lemon juice
50 g (1¾ oz) pine nuts, toasted

Soak the bread in half the oil for 5 minutes. Mix all the ingredients in a blender and season with sea salt and pepper. Keep in a sterilised screw-top jar in the fridge.

Makes about 500 ml (17 fl oz/2 cups)

salt cod mash

200–250 g (7–9 oz) salt cod
500 g (1 lb 2 oz) mashing potatoes, peeled and cut into quarters
125 g (4½ oz) butter
250 ml (9 fl oz/1 cup) cream
500 ml (17 fl oz/2 cups) milk
3 cloves garlic confit, page 222
50 ml (1¾ fl oz) extra virgin olive oil
juice of ½ lemon

You need to soak the salt cod in cold water for 48 hours, changing the water after 24 hours.

Cook the potatoes in boiling salted water for about 30 minutes or until tender, then drain. Heat the butter and cream in a pan until warm and then mash with the potatoes. For a really fine purée pass the potatoes through a sieve first. Season with salt and white pepper.

Gently heat the milk in a pan, add the salt cod and poach until the flesh starts to come away from the bone. Strain and flake the pieces of salt cod with your hands. Blend with the garlic, olive oil and lemon juice. Fold in the warm potato purée and leave to cool.

Serves 4 (makes about 500 g/1 lb 2 oz)

sashimi dressing

2 tablespoons sake
3 tablespoons mirin
250 ml (9 fl oz/1 cup) dark soy sauce
3 tablespoons tamari soy sauce
10 g (¼ oz) dried bonito flakes

Mix the sake and mirin in a saucepan and bring to a simmer to 'burn off' the alcohol. Add the soy sauce, tamari and bonito flakes and transfer to a bowl. Leave overnight in a cool dark place.

Strain the dressing through a muslin or cheesecloth, and store in a sterilised screw-top jar in the fridge for up to a month. This works well with all preparations of sashimi, but I especially like it with bluefin tuna.

Makes about 375 ml (13 fl oz/1½ cups)

sushi rice

2 tablespoons sugar
1 teaspoon sea salt
2 tablespoons rice vinegar (or ponzu-flavoured vinegar)
225 g (8 oz/1 cup) short-grain rice, washed thoroughly

Put the sugar, salt and vinegar in a pan and heat gently until dissolved. Cook the rice with 330 ml (11 fl oz/1 1/3 cups) of water, following the instructions on the packet, in a saucepan, rice cooker or microwave. Spread the hot cooked rice in a large tray and pour the rice vinegar dressing over it. Stir with chopsticks or a fork to cool the rice down and distribute the dressing evenly. Place a damp cloth over the rice until you're ready to use it. This should be eaten the day it is made, and not refrigerated — I like it best when it's just above room temperature.

Makes enough for 8 pieces of sushi

szechuan spice mix

2 tablespoons Szechuan peppercorns
1 tablespoon black peppercorns
2 teaspoons sea salt

Dry-fry the spices in a pan over low heat until the salt starts to turn from white to blonde and becomes fragrant. Grind finely, while still warm, with a mortar and pestle or spice grinder.

Makes 2–3 tablespoons of spice mix

tamarind sauce

1 bird's eye chilli, finely chopped
1 garlic clove, finely chopped
1 tablespoon finely chopped coriander root
450 g (1 lb) jar tamarind pulp concentrate (from Asian grocers)
1 tablespoon fish sauce
1 tablespoon grated palm sugar

Heat a touch of oil in a pan and fry the chilli, garlic and coriander root until fragrant. Add the tamarind and 125 ml (4 fl oz/½ cup) of water. Simmer for 5 minutes, then add the fish sauce and palm sugar. Mix until the sugar has dissolved and then season with sea salt and cracked pepper to taste. Keep any leftover in an airtight container and warm gently before using.

Makes about 375 ml (13 fl oz/1½ cups)

tartare sauce

125 ml (4 fl oz/½ cup) mayonnaise, page 224
1 teaspoon baby capers
1 teaspoon finely chopped cornichons
1 teaspoon finely chopped green olives (optional)
1 teaspoon finely chopped French shallot
1 teaspoon finely chopped flat-leaf (Italian) parsley
1 teaspoon finely chopped anchovy
grated zest of 1 lemon

Mix together all the ingredients and season with sea salt and white pepper.

Makes about 125 ml (4 fl oz/½ cup)

tempura batter

150 g (5 1/2 oz/1 1/4 cups) tempura flour (available at Asian grocers)
350 ml (12 fl oz) cold sparkling mineral water

Put the flour in a mixing bowl and slowly pour in the mineral water while you whisk, until the batter has the consistency of cream.

Makes about 400 ml (14 fl oz)

thai salad dressing

1 tablespoon peanut oil
1 garlic clove, finely chopped
1 bird's eye chilli, finely chopped
2 coriander roots, finely chopped
2 tablespoons grated palm sugar
2 tablespoons rice wine vinegar
2 tablespoons fish sauce
1 tablespoon lime juice

Heat the peanut oil in a pan and fry the garlic, chilli and coriander roots until fragrant. Add the palm sugar and vinegar and heat until the sugar has dissolved. Stir in the fish sauce and lime juice.

Makes about 125 ml (4 fl oz/1/2 cup)

tomato confit

a handful of assorted herbs (parsley, rosemary, thyme or bay leaves)
1 head of garlic, broken into pieces
6 roma tomatoes, cut in half lengthways and deseeded
a drizzle of olive oil

Preheat your oven to 180°C (350°F/Gas 4). Lay the herbs and garlic in a baking tray and cover with a wire rack. Put the tomatoes on the rack, cut side down, and drizzle a bit of oil over the top. Cover with foil and bake for about 10 minutes or until the tomatoes are just becoming tender. Cool a little and then peel the skins off the tomatoes.

Makes 6 tomato pieces

yoghurt, coriander and mint sauce

20 coriander leaves, chopped
1 tablespoon chopped spearmint leaves
1 green bird's eye chilli, deseeded and finely chopped
1 teaspoon diced red onion
1 teaspoon fish sauce
1 teaspoon lime juice
100 ml (3^1/$_2$ fl oz) thick plain yoghurt

Gently stir together all the ingredients. Take care not to overwork or the yoghurt will split and make the sauce too thin.

Makes about 125 ml (4 fl oz/^{1}/$_2$ cup)

My daughter, Chilli, with a good catch.
Channel Point, Darwin.

My favourite fish to catch: the rainbow trout.

an A–Z of seafood

Whether you're chilling out with a rod and line after work, or 'catching' your seafood at the local fishmonger's, it's always a good idea to know a little bit about it.

abalone

Abalone (just the word sends a shiver up the spine) is surely one of the world's quintessential seafoods. Embodying luxury in every sense, it is rare, exotic, delicious and expensive. Elusive to find in the rock crevices and walls of Australia's east and southern coastlines, the abalone is harvested by the divers who are one of this ear-shaped shell's few predators.

The commercial value of Australian abalone has been driven by the demand from Japan and China, where it is one of the most prized 'occasion' seafoods. It is a fishery of such extreme value that abalone is rarely seen outside the Chinatowns of the larger Australian cities.

Available as either black lip or green lip, wild or farmed, live whole, frozen meat or cooked and tinned, abalone is universally expensive. For my money, I prefer wild-harvested live and I think the green-lipped variety from South Australia has the silkiest texture and most pronounced iodine flavour.

As 'supermarket' as it might initially appear, the tinned product is often very suitable, especially for Chinese-style recipes, where the liquor the abalone has been cooked in makes a delicious stock to add to any sauce or dressing.

Exquisite either cooked or raw, enjoy abalone for the special seafood it is: go to a Chinese fishmonger and order one live. Expect to find them most prevalent in late summer, autumn and winter (this is mainly a function of the fishing season, which commences on January 1) and at various Asian celebrations such as Chinese New Year. If you buy a live one, eat it on the same day and remove it from the shell as close as possible to the preparation or cooking time, so that the flavour and amazing perfume are retained and the flesh itself doesn't toughen.

bar cod

This superb eating fish is found in the deep ocean trenches off the east coast of Australia and the south west of Western Australia.

Caught commercially in small quantities, generally as a by-product of the blue-eye trevalla drop-line fishery, the bar cod is caught year round, but is in best condition in late winter. The fat-laden fillet is broad flaked, firm and cooks up moist. Very meaty in appearance, this fish has a beautiful sweet-yet-savoury flavour, making it extremely popular with Asian seafood buyers, especially the Vietnamese.

Usually weighing 3–20 kg, bar cod is an expensive fish but well worth the investment should you come across it.

barramundi

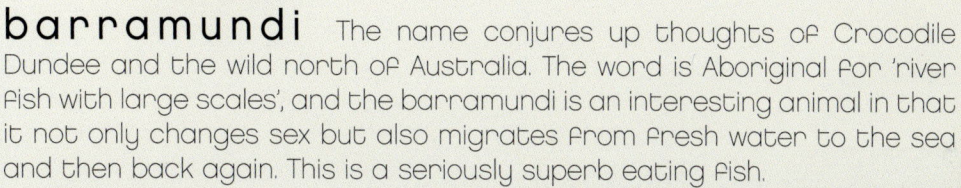

The name conjures up thoughts of Crocodile Dundee and the wild north of Australia. The word is Aboriginal for 'river fish with large scales', and the barramundi is an interesting animal in that it not only changes sex but also migrates from fresh water to the sea and then back again. This is a seriously superb eating fish.

Barra is widely farmed, with the farmed often proving better than the wild — not only because of its year-round availability (the wild is only available from February to November) but because of the consistency of size, flesh quality and flavour. However, if you can get your hands on a wild-caught, gill-bled, mature fish in season, it will probably be one of the best meals of your life.

Barramundi can be fried, grilled, steamed, baked and even barbecued, but its mild, sweet flesh is really quite delicate so take care not to overcook it.

blue-eye trevalla

If barramundi is everyman's hero, blue-eye is the rock star. With its firm, white and deliciously sweet flesh, chefs and gourmands regard the blue-eye as the absolute darling of the restaurant business.

Caught in the deep trenches off the continental shelves of Australia and New Zealand, its peak availability is in summer and autumn. But, for my money, the best eating fish are caught in the winter when they are carrying extra fat to protect them from the cold Antarctic currents of the Southern Ocean.

Commonly found in the 2–6 kg range, this broad-flaked fish is found at any decent fish market. Look for translucent flesh with no tears or seeping moisture and ensure it has a sweet, fresh aroma and is resilient to the touch.

bream

If only I had a dollar for every bream caught by the amateur angler. And the humble bream is as great a fish to eat as it is to catch.

Bream has a sweet distinctive taste, its iodine 'bite' making it versatile for a range of cuisines from Asian to Mediterranean. There are a number of species, the most common being the black bream, found predominantly in southern Australia and the yellowfin bream, fished off the east coast. Both are found mainly in the 500 g to 1 kg range, which can make them ideal for both pan-cooking whole or filleting. The peak time for bream is between February and June, when they are making their way along the coastline to put on weight before winter.

fish

bug The quirky name refers to two common species of sand or slipper lobsters: the Moreton Bay bug and the Balmain bug. The Moreton Bay is typically a larger, heavier creature with a long, flat head and grey/mustard shell. It is generally 10–20 cm long and can be up to 500 g in weight.

The Balmain bug is a smaller, more rounded animal, bright golden in colour with a wide, flat, frilly-edged head. At first glance, they seem hardly worth buying, with the giant armoured head taking up about two-thirds of the total body weight. But don't be fooled: these creatures are delicious. They are generally found in the cooler waters of southern Australia, especially along the New South Wales coastline, where they will often be landed live.

Like their close cousins, the rock lobsters, bugs are distinctly flavoursome with a rich, sweet taste and firm texture. The Balmain bug can sometimes have a distinctive 'garlic weed' or iodine aroma; this is a direct reflection of its feeding habitat and by no means indicates the quality or flavour.

If you see them live in a fish market, forget what you went for and buy them. They are most prevalent in late summer and autumn, although can be found year round, frozen whole or as cleaned meat.

coral trout Exotic, rare and mostly very expensive, the coral trout is not actually a trout at all but a member of the tropical rock-cod family.

Found throughout the north of Australia in the shallow to mid-depths of the coral-line and tropical reef habitats, the coral trout is exclusively caught by line.

Growing from 500 g to 3 kg, the moist, fine-flaked flesh is sweet with relatively few bones, making it ideal for a broad range of preparations, but particularly delicious steamed with Asian flavours.

Yes, the coral trout is expensive, but it is worth it — especially in late spring when it travels up the east coast of Australia and is in absolute peak condition.

crab In Australia we have an incredible variety of crabs, from the giant king crab, found in the deep cold waters off Tasmania, to the legendary mud crab from the tropics.

When choosing live crabs, look for those that are active, have hard shells and feel heavy for their size, and are not blowing bubbles or emitting any liquid. The shells should be evenly coloured and moist, not dry or flaky, and there shouldn't be any scaly white patches on the legs. Make sure that all limbs are intact

Balmain bug

an A-Z of seafood

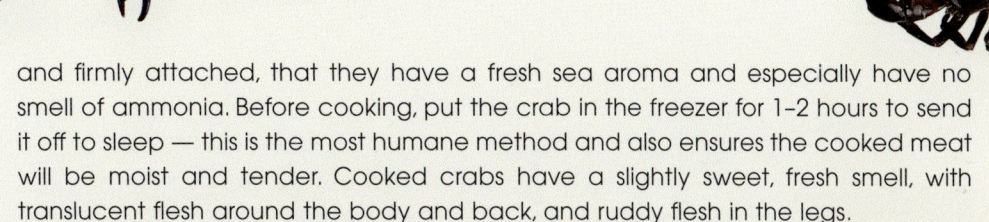

and firmly attached, that they have a fresh sea aroma and especially have no smell of ammonia. Before cooking, put the crab in the freezer for 1–2 hours to send it off to sleep — this is the most humane method and also ensures the cooked meat will be moist and tender. Cooked crabs have a slightly sweet, fresh smell, with translucent flesh around the body and back, and ruddy flesh in the legs.

Blue swimmer crabs (sand crabs) are Australia's most common crabs and are found year round with peak supply from November to April. They are usually sold cooked as they rarely live long out of water. With their sweet nutty flavour and firm, moist flesh, blue swimmers are excellent eating. They turn from bright blue to brilliant orange when cooked and the meat is easily extracted.

The **mud crab** of east and northern Australia is a genuine treat. Although the species (*scyalla serrata*) is found throughout South East Asia, the flavour and texture of the Australian mud crab is probably the sweetest in the world.

Found year round, peak supply in New South Wales and Queensland runs from January to April, and from May to August in the Northern Territory. Muddies are best bought live (they survive happily out of water). They will be tied tightly and should be handled with care as the powerful claws can give a painful pinch.

Spanner crabs are found throughout northern Australia but primarily along the coast of northern New South Wales and south eastern Queensland, from January to late October. These unique looking, orange-red crabs offer exceptional value for money and are best bought live. They are slow-moving and the ferocious looking claws are actually quite harmless, not needing tying like the muddie. Spanner crabs are especially popular in Asian restaurants, so search out an Asian fishmonger — he'll be sure to carry the tasty spanner.

cuttlefish

Cuttlefish are found everywhere around Australia and, unlike squid, all belong pretty much to the one family. They are found in warm seas and cold ones, in shallow waters and deep oceans, and are fished mainly by trawling.

The smaller ones are fat, almost circular, and the larger ones usually elongated, flattened ovals. They have ten arms, two of which are thinner than the others, with fat, paddle-like endings. The skin is softer and more slippery than that of the squid and often harder to remove. Cuttlefish are usually bought cleaned and, like squid, the dense, intensely white flesh actually freezes very well.

Cuttlefish has a slightly tougher bite than squid but its beautiful flavour and price (often less than half that of squid) make it worth seeking out.

fish

Flathead

flathead
If one fish has come to represent the changing face of Australian seafood, then it must be the previously humble flathead. Until as recently as a decade ago, the flathead was relegated to the fryers of suburban fish shops and cafes; today it is a star among the restaurant set.

With its distinctly sweet flavour and skinless, boneless form and its beautiful, broad-flaked, highly versatile flesh, it is no real wonder that the flathead has become a darling of the keen fish consumer. The cooked flesh is pearly white and capable of handling a broad range of flavours and cooking methods.

Although there are a number of species caught commercially year round, my favourite is the black river flathead, caught in late spring along the east coast. Its briny, iodine character makes for truly wonderful eating.

flounder
Although flounder are found year round off the entire coast of Australia, most that are sold commercially come from New Zealand.

Flounder are flat fish, ideally suited to serving whole. They can be distinguished from sole by the fact that their tail fins aren't fused with their dorsal fins. Flounder yield a high amount of flesh, making them popular with restaurants. They have a delicate to medium flavour and fine-textured flesh. The bay flounder from southern Australia is the most highly regarded as an eating fish.

Look for bright lustrous fish with firm flesh that springs back when touched, bright bulging eyes and a pleasant fresh sea smell. The best flounder come from the waters of southern Australia from April to August.

garfish

garfish
There is a broad range of garfish found throughout Australia but the most prolific are the southern and eastern sea garfish. These can be fished year round but are most easily caught from March to May.

Garfish must be really, really fresh — their unique flavour and texture can be lost if the fish are either poorly handled or old.

When catching or buying garfish whole, make sure to remove the guts as quickly as possible — the fish's constant diet of weed, which gives it its beautiful iodine flavour, can equally destroy the flesh if left to ferment.

The garfish has firm-grained, sweet flesh and a simple bone structure — after cooking, remove the backbone, and the rib bones can be eaten.

john dory

With the distinctive thumbprint of Saint Peter on its side, the john dory is one of eastern Australia's most prized table fish. Its thin, fine-grained flesh has a unique sweetness that more than justifies its premium price.

Caught year round in the waters off the continental shelf, john dory is often found hanging around the bays of eastern Australia. With low meat recovery (around a third of the fish) the boneless fillet is as versatile as it is easy to use. If you have an opportunity, cook it on the bone — and notice how moist it stays.

The john dory is sometimes mistaken for its poor relations, the silver or mirror dory. While these make excellent substitutes, just one forkful will confirm what fantastic eating the real thing is.

kingfish

Found throughout the southern states of Australia and now farmed in South Australia, yellowtail kingfish is available year round in both forms. The farmed fish is known as Hiramasa, the Japanese name for the species, and tends to have a slightly higher fat content than the wild fish.

With a flesh to whole weight yield of about two-thirds, kingfish cuts a great fillet or cutlet. Although the skin appears quite thick, if it is scaled it cooks up crisply. The layer of fat under the skin forms a delicious, almost crackling-like outer. The clean, white flesh has a rich flavour and firm texture, ideally suited to a range of preparations and flavourings. This is a favoured sashimi fish.

Both the wild and farmed fish have a great shelf life and, while they look to be quite high in price, represent excellent value for quality. Seek fish in the 3–4 kg range — typically mature and carrying loads of delicious, healthy fat.

leatherjacket

There are a number of different species of leatherjacket found throughout the waters of southern Australia. The most prevalent of those sold in the commercial market is the ocean jacket, caught in the Great Australian Bight region.

With its mild, delicate sweet flavour and firm texture, the leatherjacket is highly versatile. Its firm flesh is suitable for braising, sautéing, grilling or baking, and ideally suited to preparing nutritious and delicious meals for children.

Usually sold with head and skin removed, 'jackets' yield about thirty per cent flesh. The fillets are pearly white and boneless. Available year round, this is one of the great bargains of the sea, being inexpensive, plentiful and delicious.

fish

lobster

Surely nothing says celebration like the lobster (sometimes referred to as crayfish in Victoria and South Australia). The lobster is truly one of life's great eating experiences, its sweet, rich flavour and firm texture reflecting its regal position as culinary king of the crustaceans. In Australia we have four main varieties of rock lobster:

The **eastern rock lobster** is endemic to the coastline of New South Wales. This lobster (sometimes referred to as the 'local' by the trade in Sydney) is as distinctive in appearance (a smooth, dark green shell, with red highlights on the extremities of its legs and feelers) as it is in its scarcity. It is a tiny commercial fishery but if you come across it, buy it and enjoy it. I think it is the best eating rock lobster in the world. Found throughout the year, it is most plentiful from September to March.

The **southern rock lobster** is found throughout the southern states of Australia and primarily fished commercially in Tasmania, Victoria and South Australia. This variety is also often referred to as the **Tassie cray**. There are a number of area closures throughout the year, with the southern rock being at its most plentiful from October to June.

An initiative by the industry's managing body has achieved sustainable certification for this fishery — look for the 'clean and green' tag on the lobster horn. Ranging in size from 600 g to 3 kg, consider the large lobsters as an option — often less expensive than the 'single serve' sizes, a 2.5 kg lobster can be used to prepare nine or ten servings and, with some careful planning, used across a range of dishes. The meat is exceptionally sweet and delicious.

The **western rock lobster**, which comes from Australia's largest lobster fishery on the coast of Western Australia, is one of our most prized seafood exports. Highly regarded in Japan for sashimi preparations, the western rock lobster is typically smaller than the other species, averaging just 400–900 g. It has a slightly firmer texture and more savoury character than either the southern or eastern rock lobsters but is still a delicious, exotic treat.

Available from November to June, supply peaks at Christmas and the western rock is often found ready-cooked at the major retailers.

The **tropical rock lobster**, with its distinctive light green, spotted shell, is sometimes referred to as the **'painted cray'**. Caught by hand in the wilds of the tropical north of Australia, the tropical lobster is mainly available from March to October and is typically sold as frozen, green (uncooked) tails.

Softer and milder in flavour than the other rock lobsters, the tropical is a great carrier of flavours and is especially good in Asian recipes.

rock lobster

an A-Z of seafood

With all varieties, it's best not to buy uncooked, chilled rock lobsters as it is hard to tell how long they've been dead. Instead, buy whole, live lobsters — look for those that are active, not sluggish, in their tanks. If the lobsters are displayed in a holding tank, the water should be clear and smell clean, not fishy. When the lobsters are picked up, their tails should curl tightly under their bodies, and they should wave their feelers vigorously. Before cooking, put them in the freezer for an hour or so until they become unconscious — this is more humane, and also renders the meat more tender.

You can also buy rock lobsters pre-cooked. These have typically been boiled in seawater on the catching boat or a processing facility on the wharf. Look for lobsters that have all of their legs and feelers intact and a tail that has a firm 'spring' when extended. Ensure the smell is clean and sweet, with no trace of ammonia or brackish water.

mackerel

The Spanish/narrow-banded mackerel is found across the north of Australia from northern New South Wales to Geraldton in Western Australia. This is one of the great-eating game fish of Australia.

Caught year round, the **Spanish mackerel** is most prevalent during September and October, especially in the north west of Western Australia, where it can be seen leaping high out of the water in a spectacular mating ritual.

Its high oil content and medium to firm texture make this fish ideally suited to high-heat cooking such as barbecuing, stir-frying and pan-frying. Its natural moistness will ensure the flesh remains soft. The high fat content and rich flavour also make it ideal for use with strong and acidic accompaniments or marinades, especially Asian salty-sour type dishes.

Even more than most other fish, Spanish mackerel is best eaten super fresh — it doesn't freeze well and, if poorly handled, can deteriorate quickly.

The **blue mackerel** sometimes goes by the less than glamorous name of 'slimy mackerel' but when it is really fresh this is one of the tastiest, inexpensive fish you can buy. Found year round throughout Australia, this dark-fleshed fish cooks up white and is absolutely delicious marinated and barbecued or soused and pickled. The English prefer smoking blue mackerel; while for the Japanese it is one of the sushi standards.

Blue mackerel are commonly found in the 500 g to 1 kg range and are generally sold whole, which may sound daunting but their high fat content and simple bone structure make these easy fish to fillet. Like other mackerel, the blue doesn't keep or freeze well.

mahi mahi

mahi mahi Sometimes this beautiful tropical fish is called 'dolphin fish', which is quite confusing — it has nothing whatsoever to do with Flipper.

This large (3–20 kg), brightly coloured fish is prized by sports fishermen and found along Australia's east, north and west coasts, but caught commercially by the tuna long liners operating along the east coast from Sydney to Cairns. Caught throughout the year, it is most prevalent in autumn when high volume landings can see prices drop to 'everyday use' prices.

With its sweet, mild flavour, broad-scalloped flesh and clean, fresh aftertaste, mahi can be used in many of the same dishes as tuna or swordfish. The fillet is reddish pink, but turns pearl white when cooked. When buying, look for a bright, consistent colour and no signs of greyness or browning bloodline.

mangrove jack This guy sounds like he should be a Hollywood star, but this member of the Sea Perch family is more familiar with the north of Australia than the north of Los Angeles.

Found year round, from northern New South Wales, right across the north to Shark Bay in the west, the mangrove jack is mostly caught in the estuaries and near ocean reefs.

The mild, moist and delicate white flesh makes this one of the finest eating fish from our northern waters. Weighing from 2–5 kg, the mangrove jack is moderately priced — especially the smaller fish that are ideal for cooking whole, keeping the delicate flesh soft and moist. Popular in Asian cuisines, the flesh is especially delicious steamed, fried and grilled.

marron The French chef, Paul Bocusse, once described the marron as 'one of the five great tastes of the world'. Indeed, the moist, sweet and light-flavoured flesh is a direct reflection of the unique, pristine environment these animals inhabit.

A native of the freshwater streams of the south west of Western Australia, marron are now farmed in a number of regions: notably, their native Western Australia but also Kangaroo Island and the Limestone Coast of South Australia.

The marron is one of the world's largest freshwater crayfish, and one of the most expensive crustaceans available, and you will probably have to find a good fishmonger to order some in for you — it's rare to find them hanging around with the other lobsters and prawns in your average fish shop.

Buy them live and store them carefully, preferably under a moist cloth in a coolish, but not cold, dark area (a laundry is ideal). The translucent raw flesh turns pearly white when cooked, sometimes with a slight orange tinge.

monkfish

More correctly known as stargazer, this strange-looking, deep-water fish is NOT the famed monkfish of northern Europe, although the boneless fillet provides good eating — comparable to flathead.

Caught mainly as a by-catch by fishermen working the south east trawl area of the Great Australian Bight and the south eastern marine slopes surrounding Tasmania, monkfish is more often found in winter.

The light pink flesh has a soft, sweet flavour and firm texture that is ideal for classic fried fish and chips. Expect to pay less than for flathead, but, if it is good fresh fish, expect to enjoy it just as much.

moonfish

This big, slow-moving, almost cartoon character of a fish is more often caught by accident than design.

Found throughout eastern Australia, moonfish tends to be by-catch of the east coast tuna fishery and so is not available with much consistency. The fillet, which is orange-red with a bright lustre, weighs 2–5 kg — ask for it to be sliced into steaks like tuna or swordfish.

Moonfish fillet is ideal for grilling, pan-frying and roasting, and the sweet, mild flavour is highly regarded by chefs. Fresh fillet, well wrapped, will keep happily in the fridge for up to four days.

morwong

Sometimes known as jackass, rubber lip and deep sea bream, the morwong is caught all year round along the south east and southern coastlines.

Morwong have sweet, moist, creamy white flesh with a distinctive iodine 'zing' and are popular with adults and children. They are generally caught in the 800 g to 1.25 kg range, making them perfect for fillet or whole cooking.

At the lower end of the price scale, the morwong is a great-value, high-quality, everyday fish that won't disappoint.

mullet

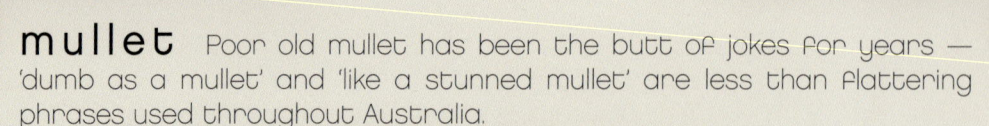

Poor old mullet has been the butt of jokes for years — 'dumb as a mullet' and 'like a stunned mullet' are less than flattering phrases used throughout Australia.

However, not all mullet are the same. In particular, the yellow eye mullet of southern Australia and the sea or bully mullet of south eastern Australia can proudly stand in the company of much more exotic species of high-oil-content, dark-fleshed fish, including tuna and mackerel.

Available year round, on the east coast, mullet is in best condition in winter and spring, and on the southern coast of Victoria and South Australia, it is best in late autumn and winter.

Mullet is probably some of the best value fish we catch in Australia — its soft, dark flesh cooks up white and, when very fresh (which is fortunately the only way you can buy it), it grills, bakes, stir-fries and (especially) barbecues brilliantly. It is a good idea to get your fishmonger to fillet and 'deep skin' the flesh, removing a large amount of the oil sacks and dark surface meat — this will result in a flavoursome, consistent and delicious flesh.

mulloway

This member of the jewfish family is much softer fleshed and sweeter flavoured than either the east coast or northern (black) jewfish.

Found along the eastern and southern coastlines of Australia in the coastal embankments, estuaries and river mouths, the mulloway is great to catch and even better to eat. The smaller fish (say under 1.5 kg) can be soft fleshed and are sometimes referred to as 'soapies'. The best, in my opinion, are winter fish of around 3–5 kg from southern Australia.

Its readily identifiable iodine flavour and pearly white, broad-flaked flesh make mulloway a popular pan-frying, baking or steaming fish, and it remains hugely popular in the fish and chip shops of South Australia.

Mulloway is now farmed in South Australia under its Japanese name, Suzuki. Suzuki mulloway is one of Japan's most highly sought-after sashimi fish.

Murray cod

Regarded as the finest eating, giant freshwater perch in the world, the Murray cod is a legendary fish — part of Australian folklore along the Murray, Darling and Murrumbidgee rivers. This is a very, very special fish that is worthy of an occasion in its own right.

The advent of fish farming has caused a renaissance for this amazingly tasty fish, providing year-round availability even though it is no longer commercially caught from the wild, Murray cod are typically brought to market at 800 g to 1 kg. The moderately deep, short fillet is chock-full of fat and the creamy flesh is soft, sweet and unctuous.

Expensive and tricky to find, you are most likely to come across these fish, often live, in the Chinatowns of larger Australian towns.

mussel Mussels are fast food for the seafood lover, and recent production levels around the country have responded to the rapid increase in demand. Even the most modest cook can prepare a delicious feast with these simple bivalves.

Superb extra lean meat, low in sodium, cholesterol free, high in protein and higher in omega 3 than any other shellfish, mussels represent great value in many ways.

Here in Australia we grow the **black mussel** (sometimes known as the **blue mussel**), a similar species to those grown in Europe and North America. Black mussels are produced on farms throughout southern Australia, primarily in Tasmania, Victoria and South Australia, with several smaller farms in southern New South Wales.

Historically, the mussel industry in Australia has been somewhat provincial, with many smaller operations unable to offer the consistency and quality control sought by the market. A new breed of grower is now taking the industry to a level that can guarantee great-quality mussels year round.

Regional and seasonal variation occurs with mussels and, just as you may determine a favourite area or time of year for oysters, so you can with mussels.

When buying mussels, pick up a few and make sure that they feel heavy in their shells, that the shells aren't cracked or broken and that they shut firmly when you tap them. If they don't, discard them. The black mussel should be soft and sweet eating, with a rich buttery flavour.

Several growers are now processing their mussels before sending them to market — scrubbing and cleaning them and even removing their beards.

The **New Zealand green shell mussel** is also commonly available here in Australia, although, due to quarantine reasons, it can only be purchased frozen or cooked. It is a very large, green-shelled variety with an enormous amount of flesh. It is much stronger in taste and tougher in texture than the local black mussel and is therefore better suited to recipes with stronger flavours.

black mussel and New Zealand green shell mussel (right)

ocean perch

ocean perch
Sometimes known as red rock cod or coral cod, the ocean perch is caught year round throughout Australia, but predominantly on the inner continental shelf from Noosa in south east Queensland to Jervis Bay in New South Wales.

This spiny, prehistoric looking fish is similar to the famous European rascasse — a standard ingredient in any quality bouillabaisse. The ocean perch displays many of the characteristics sought by the bouillabaisse cook: it has mild, white, delicate flesh, which imbues a sweet, clean flavour, and the gelatinous bones, spikes and skin provide a natural thickening agent for the classic soup.

Although it is a difficult and unfriendly fish to fillet, the flesh is delicious. The ocean perch is also especially good when fried whole, Asian-style.

octopus
Octopus is found throughout Australia and is generalised as the 'large' — which tends to be a by-product of the lobster fishery (octopus being a major predator of lobster); and the 'small' — a by-product of the eastern prawn trawl fishery.

It is common these days to find both small and large octopus cleaned and tenderised. You will recognise if your octopus has been tenderised (a process often completed by the fishmonger in an adapted concrete mixer), as it presents as a firm, tight ball. If it hasn't been tenderised, put it in a bowl with some grated daikon radish for a few hours. Clean the octopus as soon as you can, discarding the gut and beak, then store tightly wrapped. Like squid and calamari, octopus freezes well (some claim it even improves the tenderness).

Like squid and cuttlefish, avoid octopus that is limp and colouring more pink/purple than steely grey/green. It should have a fresh sea aroma and no obvious ammonia smell. If you find local product you will notice the firm texture and incredible sweetness, sadly not often found in much imported octopus.

octopus

oyster
Is this not the quintessential seafood? Luxurious, sweet, salty, rich, delicious... Exotic yet simple, the oyster reflects the mood of its environment at any given time — its flavour is physically responsive to the weather, water and hour of the day. Oysters have been more written about than any other seafood, and deservedly so.

Oysters are hermaphrodites, starting off as males and changing into females at least once in their lifetime. They are at their best just before spawning, which can vary depending on the species, location and time of the year.

an A-Z of seafood

rock oyster

angassi oyster

Most oysters are usually sold shucked on the half shell, but try opening them yourself and enjoy the difference. Although it can be a little tricky at first, shucking is a social skill somewhat akin to being able to open a bottle of champagne well; and the reward is equally pleasurable. Make the investment in a sturdy, short-handled and heavy-bladed oyster knife, buy a few dozen oysters and a strong glove and practise — you will soon be able to crack open a dozen in the time it takes to drink a glass of chardonnay.

Experiment with the varieties, regions and seasons of the oysters we have in Australia. It is fascinating to experience the flavour and texture differences even between two neighbouring estuaries. You will find yourself approaching oyster eating rather like wine tasting, searching for that one elusive flavour.

Pacific oysters were originally introduced into Australia from Japan and are now our most prolifically grown oysters. Primarily grown in Tasmania and on the west coast of South Australia, but in more recent times in New South Wales, these are large with spiky shells and clean white interiors. The Pacific oyster can be characterised by its fresh, clean and salty flavour — just like being rolled in the surf. As it spends its entire life underwater, this is a relatively easy oyster to open and makes good shucking practice for the novice. The Pacific oyster is popular as a cooking oyster, particularly with Japanese and Chinese chefs, who regard its simple flavour and texture as a great vehicle for flavours. The Pacific oyster prefers the cooler months, spawning in summer. Depending on the region, it is available from March to early December.

The **Sydney rock oyster** is without a doubt one of the great eating oysters of the world and we have it here right on our doorstep. It is a strange name for an oyster that grows inter-tidally among the estuaries, lakes and inlets along some 1500 km of Australia's east coast, from Morton Bay in south east Queensland to Malacoota on the Victorian/New South Wales border. The rock oyster has a lasting, deep, rich, sweet flavour that is truly unique.

In general, the north coast of New South Wales has its best rock oysters in the summer months, while the south coast has them in winter. However, it's always best to check with your local supplier on any given day.

Angassi — flat or native oysters as they are sometimes called — are hard to find, expensive and very special indeed. Although one of the first seafoods farmed in Australia (by the Aborigines some 6000 years ago), the angassi is difficult to grow and has only recently become fashionable with farmers. If the Pacific is the sauvignon blanc of oysters, and the rock oyster is the chardonnay, the angassi has to be the shiraz. Full flavoured and textured, the angassi is big, rich and almost meaty. This oyster is often sought out by chefs.

parrot fish Also known as tusk fish, the parrot fish is a colourful wrasse found in Australia's north, from southern New South Wales, across the 'top end' to Geraldton in Western Australia.

Caught mostly at 500 g to 2 kg, the parrot fish has gained cult status as a live fish in the Asian restaurant community. Eating mainly coral and algae, parrot fish rarely take baits and are commercially caught by net. The firm white flesh is very mild in flavour and moist in texture; it is a great carrier of flavours.

pearl meat Arguably the rarest seafood in Australia, pearl meat is hardly ever seen in restaurants (especially those south east of Broome), let alone in shops. It is very special and well worth the effort of seeking out.

Pearl meat is the adductor mussel of the gold-lipped pearl oyster. The pearl oyster is one of Australia's most valuable aquaculture industries, primarily for the world-famous pearls and mother-of-pearl shell. Hand harvested by divers in the northern waters of north west Australia, the pearl oysters are seeded to produce pearls, once a year for about four years. After this time they become unproductive and are shucked, with the shells being used in the jewellery trade and the meat, usually frozen or dried, sent to market, mostly in South East Asia.

If you are really keen, contact one of the large pearl companies (who seem to have glamorous stores in every major city these days) — they will probably be more able to help you find pearl meat than your local fish shop.

With a texture not dissimilar to abalone and a flavour somewhere between scallop, lobster and prawn, pearl meat should be savoured as simply as possible. Its natural sweetness and amazing texture are best sampled raw.

pearl perch — Western Australian dhufish These two cousins, one from the east coast of northern New South Wales and south east Queensland, the other found off south west Western Australia, are among the finest eating fish in Australia. Although similar in shape, size and colour, they are readily distinguished by the pearl perch's unique 'pearly' bone extending from its lower gill plate.

The dhufish of Western Australia (not to be confused with the jewfish) prefers colder, deeper water than the pearl perch and is slightly fuller flavoured. Both have a magnificent deep, rich, sweet flavour and firm, moist texture.

an A–Z of seafood   251

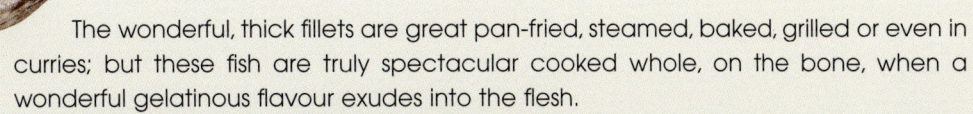

The wonderful, thick fillets are great pan-fried, steamed, baked, grilled or even in curries; but these fish are truly spectacular cooked whole, on the bone, when a wonderful gelatinous flavour exudes into the flesh.

The dhufish is one of the most highly sought after table fish in Western Australia, as is the pearl perch in the east. Both are almost exclusively found in the hands of chefs and restaurants, as their price makes them almost prohibitive to retailers. If you do happen across one in the fish market, buy it quick!

pipis

The problem with pipis, like vongole, is their habitat. These molluscs live along the shoreline in the sand, gathering food as the waves wash through their open shells. To them, sand is no problem — part of their digestive system almost — but to any fussy creature that likes its food 'sandless', this poses certain difficulties.

The process of harvesting is known as 'cockling' and for the amateur involves a quirky jig around the shoreline, using the wriggling toes to bring the pipis to the surface. So, if you get to the beach and see crowds of people swaying and dancing in the wet sand, get your bucket and join in.

Commercially, pipis are hand-raked by blokes with some of the biggest shoulders around. The pipis from the east coast tend to be slightly bigger than their southern cousins and are typically more plentiful in the warmer months — although this might have something to do with the harvesting requirements of standing chest deep in water in mid-winter.

Like all molluscs, try to buy pipis live, discarding any that don't snap shut when tapped. In order to eliminate the grittiness of the sand that has been swilling through them, pipis from the fishmonger are purged in seawater for about 24 hours, leaving them pot ready. If you've harvested your own, when you get your pipis home, run them under a very slow tap for a few hours if you are cooking them that night. Alternatively, and this is a preferable option in times of water shortage, put them in a bucket of salted water overnight and cook them the next day.

Particularly popular in the Chinese restaurants of the east coast, pipis have a delicious rich flavour and firm texture, making them great for strong-flavoured preparations.

The pipi is excellent value — often half the price of vongole or other clams and with a much higher meat to shell ratio,

Be careful not to overcook pipis as they can toughen quickly, but if all else fails they make excellent bait for whiting, garfish and jewfish.

king prawns

prawn If there is an iconic Australian seafood, then surely it must be the prawn — thanks to the work of Paul Hogan and the thousands of holidaymakers every summer who grab a cold beer and a kilo of prawns and spend the afternoon listening to the cricket.

There are literally hundreds of species of prawns, some found throughout large areas of water and others confined to specific locations. Generally, they start life in the open sea where they hatch out in their millions, then move into the coastal areas, estuaries, lakes and inlets. There they find plentiful food on the muddy and sandy seabed, and grow quickly before moving back out to sea. Prawns are the scavengers of the seas, eating pretty much anything they come across; this gives them their amazing flavour and texture, but is also, in part, the reason why they are so fragile. The onset of prawn farming has seen vast quantities of high-quality prawns become available at very reasonable prices.

As a general rule, if you are going to use prawns for a hot dish, buy them 'green' (the term used in the trade for uncooked) and cook them only once. If you are going to use them for a salad or eat them as they are, buy them pre-cooked. A prawn cooked live, then refreshed in brine ice, will always be firmer, crisper and sweeter than a dead green prawn put through the same process. In fact, in the case of green prawns, frozen should be your preference — the integrity and quality of a green prawn packed and frozen from live will always be superior to a 'fresh' one that has endured days of variable handling.

Either way, your prawns' tails should glow with bright colours, and the flesh should show translucent through firm shells with no discolouration at the base of the heads or legs. They should neither look nor feel soggy — always avoid buying any that are displayed floating in a pool of water in a plastic tray.

With a cooked prawn, ask the fishmonger if you can taste one. Inspect it first: see that it has all its legs, feelers and eyes and that the tail has a firm spring in it. It should have a crisp, clean iodine aroma, with no scent of ammonia, old fish or brackish water. When you peel and taste it, it should be firm in texture and immediately sweet, with a long, clean finish and no strong aftertaste.

Store prawns in a plastic container with a drip insert, cover with a moist cloth and put a few pieces of ice on the cloth. Seal the container tightly and put on the coldest shelf of your fridge. Ideally, use within the next day or two.

Because there are so many varieties, the best way to classify prawns is by size. Following are some of the more common varieties found in Australia:

Small (school) prawns are netted inshore in shallow bays, lagoons and rivers, but the larger species are usually caught in the deeper waters above the continental shelf, where they return to spawn.

Tiger prawns are pale brown to bluey green with distinct grey, blue or black stripes. These are the most commonly farmed prawns in Australia and have a distinct clean, light flavour and firmish texture. Tiger prawns can also be wild-harvested all year round, with peak supply in February to May — these are characterised by a meaty, sweet flavour and firm texture and are particularly sought after by the Japanese.

King prawns have cream to light brown bodies and are generally larger than tiger Prawns. The legs and tailfins are a distinctive bright blue in the southern and western varieties, and cream in the eastern. This is a delicious eating prawn, regarded by many as the true 'king of prawns'.

Redspot prawns are closely related to king prawns, though often smaller. They have a distinctive red spot on each side of the body shell and are typically lighter in flavour and softer in texture than the kings.

Banana prawns are caught by trawlers off northern Australia. Translucent to yellow in colour, with tiny dark spots, these are very sweet, firm prawns, which although quite fragile, are generally excellent value.

Royal red prawns are trawled mostly off the south coast of New South Wales. These are pink/red even when raw, with thick hard shells. Usually sold as frozen meat (they spoil quickly), this is an inexpensive alternative when a recipe calls for chopped or minced prawns.

Vannamei prawns are small, cheap aquaculture prawns, imported frozen from South East Asia. While light in flavour and often soft in texture, they are perfectly suitable for a range of preparations.

Endeavour prawns are similar in appearance to kings but lack spines, making them much more fragile. These blue prawns have a generally softer texture and more savoury flavour but are great value, wild-harvest prawns.

red emperor

This is possibly one of the greatest eating reef fishes, along with coral trout, in the world. The firm, flaky, delicate flesh is amazing, with the line-caught, gill-bled fish among the finest eating proteins available.

Found across the north of Australia, often in the vicinity of the coral reefs and sandy bottoms of the relatively shallow waters, the red emperor is caught year round, with the best eating fish found in late autumn off the Queensland north coast.

The pearly white flesh typically comes from a fish in the 2–3 kg range and is equally delicious cooked on or off the bone.

fish

red mullet

Red mullet is one of the most prized fish available in Europe, where it is known by a variety of names, such as rouget, barbounia or triglia.

Completely unrelated to the humble sea or bully mullet, the red mullet is typically small (400–600 g) and bright crimson, with several distinctive whiskers hanging off its bottom lip. Caught by the line and net fishermen working the sandy-bottom, inshore areas around southern and eastern Australia, these are an inconsistent catch, making them quite rare and very special. You will probably have to ask your fishmonger to keep an eye out for them at his local fish market or auction.

This fish is usually cooked whole and, because of its high oil and fat content, is ideally suited to high heat and high flavour preparations.

salmon, Atlantic

It seems that Atlantic salmon really has become the 'chicken of the sea'. Available just about everywhere, it is as versatile as it is uniform. Introduced in the 1960s, most of the Atlantic salmon available in Australia is farmed in Tasmania. Despite its not being a natural inhabitant of this country, it suits the cold clear waters of the south.

Through good farm management practices and a commitment to quality, Australia produces some of the finest Atlantic salmon in the world, renowned for its clean flavour and firm texture. These days, farmed salmon is available year round, although I still prefer it in the summer months when it carries a high volume of delicious fat just under the skin.

Atlantic salmon has an excellent shelf life and, if well handled, a fresh fish will keep for 8–10 days, allowing you to create a number of meals from one fish.

salmon, Australian

Completely unrelated to the mighty Atlantic, the Australian salmon is known in New Zealand as the kahawai and is a well-regarded sport fish for the amateur angler. It must be absolutely fresh, so catching your own is a good option.

With strong-flavoured, dark flesh, these guys are often accused of being poor eating, but well handled (bled and rapidly chilled) they cook up white, from their raw pink-red and are delicious.

The Australian salmon's reasonably high oil content offers maximum versatility, handling both strong flavours and high heat well.

salt cod

Known variously around the world as baccala, bacalhua, morue salée and saltfisk, salt cod is a fish responsible for changing the course of history. In the Middle Ages the great sea-faring nations of Portugal, Spain and Holland would preserve cod by salting and then wind-drying it to remove the moisture. This could then be used as a staple ration to allow merchant, war and fishing vessels to travel further afield from their native European ports, leading to a golden age for those countries. In the sixteenth and seventeenth centuries, the grand banks off the east coast of the USA became so popular with European fishermen that a need to salt the fish heavily to preserve it for the long homeward journey resulted in the product often still seen today.

Anyone who has been into a delicatessen in Europe may recall having seen a vast selection of salt cod — the most expensive, and arguably the best, often a small, soft, moist fillet, packed in a traditional wooden box.

The majority of the salt cod we see in Australia is imported from North Africa (generally via Europe) and tends to be at the drier/saltier end of the scale of available product. Most is sold as whole, butterfly-flattened and very dry fish, often suspended from the ceiling of a traditional Italian, Portuguese or Greek grocery store. Try to find a fish that is not completely stiff and that, while strong smelling, has no sign of rancidity or 'yeastiness'.

You can also produce your own: buy a piece of good, fresh ling fillet, completely cover it in coarse rock salt and leave it in the fridge for a few days. The salt will turn to brine and the fish will be firm to touch. Remove the cod from the brine and brush off any excess salt. Before cooking, soak it in cold water for 24–48 hours, changing the water every 6–8 hours. It seems like an awful lot of bother, but this is a truly great and versatile fish.

sardine

What a bad rap the humble sardine has had over the years — mashed on toast and force fed to children, relegated to the cat bowl or the end of an angler's hook. The sardine can thank thousands of enthusiastic Italian cooks for its rise to a deservedly respected status on the restaurant menus of our larger cities.

The frog-mouthed pilchard, as it was formally known, is caught year round throughout southern Australia, predominantly in South and Western Australia, where several processors now even produce natty, boneless fillets.

Like all oily, dark-fleshed fish, sardines should be purchased very fresh, handled with care and eaten as quickly as possible. The flavoursome, moist flesh is soft and giving, but can take high heat and strong accompaniments.

scallop

If there is a seafood that deserves to be regarded as the princess of the sea, it is the scallop. The clean sweet flavour and rich texture of this simple bivalve make it delicious raw and even richer cooked. The meat of a fresh scallop should be plump, have a distinct seaweed aroma and possess a near-firm texture, never wet or flaccid.

The scallop can indeed be a bit of a princess in the kitchen. It is delicate and requires very little cooking — overcooking detracts badly from the flavour and texture. Even for the fussy eater who prefers their seafood cooked through, take the scallop off the heat quickly and let it rest in a warm place to finish cooking.

If you don't have access to fresh scallops in season, feel confident buying good-quality frozen ones — much of the catch is processed for the French and Japanese export markets, where quality is a must. Buy frozen scallops that have not been dipped in water or additives; defrost slowly in the fridge overnight.

When storing fresh scallops, keep them cold and dry, well away from any other foods (and especially water). Scallops, like crabs, are sponge-like and will take on flavour and moisture quickly.

There are two main varieties caught in Australia: both are exceptional by world standards and should be treasured if you find them in season.

Bay or **Tassie scallops** are caught by trawler across southern Australia, particularly in the Bass Strait, from May to December. Their distinctive shells feature as the logo of a famous petrol company! Their flesh is firm and round, usually presented with its bright roe (sometimes known as coral) still attached.

Saucer or **sea scallops** are caught year round (with some local closures) in the north west of Western Australia and north of Queensland. These are often sold on their smooth, clean half shells. The meat is almost translucent white — the better the quality, the more translucent the meat. The sea scallop can be easily distinguished from the bay scallop as it is usually sold without its roe — in this species the roe is part of the gut and is removed at processing. This is regarded as one of the finest scallops in the world; its characteristic sweetness and silky texture are highly regarded, especially by the gourmands of Japan and China.

scampi

Strangely, we use the Italian name 'scampo' (scampi is the plural) for this spectacular crayfish, found in the cold, deep waters off the top of Western Australia.

This is very similar to other species found around the world, particularly the lobster known as langoustine in many parts of Europe. Like their northern hemisphere cousins, scampi have two long feelers and are usually about the size of a large prawn or yabby. They have pale pink, thin, fragile shells and their sweet flesh is delicious raw. If cooking, be gentle as they can easily toughen.

Coming from very deep water, and such a long way from market, scampi are typically frozen on the catching boats and packed with their tails folded under and their feelers laid back against their bodies. They are often displayed on ice in fish shops, slowly defrosting — they should be cooked as soon as possible and never refrozen.

sea urchin

The sea urchin is indeed an enigma, creating strong differences of opinion between those who love them and those who don't. Often the 'don'ts' are prejudiced by having stepped on one in a rock pool and suffered the memorably dreadful pain inflicted by the sharp spines.

However, sea urchins are a true delicacy, regarded by real seafood lovers around the world as one of the great flavour and texture rewards for a little effort in extracting the soft, juicy roe.

Found throughout southern Australia in relatively shallow waters close to shore, sea urchins are hand collected by divers and often sent to market live. They are also processed; the five fingers of roe are removed from the spiny shell and placed in small wooden packs, ready for sashimi.

Although available almost all year round, the sweet, musk-flavoured roe is at its absolute peak from September to December.

skate

There are actually several types of skate, but they tend to be generically marketed as one variety. All have much in common with sharks: tough, inedible skin, a propensity to ammoniate if poorly handled and firm, mild flesh that sits on cartilage.

Available pretty much year round in southern Australia, the most consistent quality skate come from southern New South Wales and Tasmania.

Look for wings that are 800 g to 1.2 kg, which will be medium textured, sweet and mild (if there is the slightest whiff of ammonia, don't buy). Each of the skate's two flat wings contains two layers of meat separated by the cartilage. Although some people take the flesh off the cartilage to cook, I find it retains both moisture and flavour when cooked as a wing.

Skate is a delicate flesh: keep it well wrapped and sealed and away from other flavours on the coldest shelf of your fridge. Use it as quickly as possible.

fish

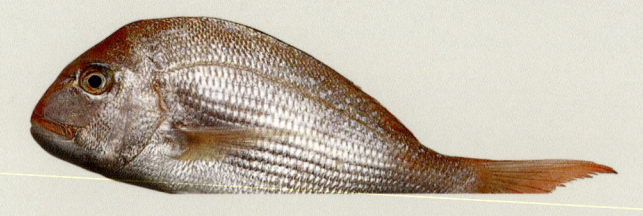

snapper
If there is one truly iconic, firm, white-fleshed, all-purpose, delicious fish then the snapper is it. The tender, white-pink flesh and sweet mild flavour make this incredibly popular fish suitable for everything from sashimi to deep-frying.

Snapper are caught right across the southern coastline year round, with some local commercial closures in South Australia (November) and Western Australia (September). Their absolute peak for flavour and fat content is in winter.

I would always advise buying snapper whole and asking your fishmonger to prepare it for you, either dressing it whole or scaling and filleting it. Look to buy a fish that is firm with clear bright eyes and a fresh cover of sweet-smelling sea slime. Snapper comes in a range of sizes, from plate sized (750 g) to large 5 kg-plus fish best suited to baking whole, or cutlets to pan-fry or barbecue.

sole
Although found throughout Australia, the majority of sole are small and a by-catch of the northern prawn fishery.

In Asia the fine-grained flesh is well regarded, in particular for frying whole, but again, due to the smaller size of the fish found in Australia, it is rarely seen in fillets. Generally inexpensive, sole is most often found in Queensland in summer.

spangled emperor
The spangled emperor is a supreme-eating, medium-priced reef fish, found abundantly, year round, in the north of Australia.

This is probably one of Australia's most important commercial species of reef fish. The flesh is moist, firm and flavoursome, with large, scalloping, pearly white flakes when cooked. Spangled emperor is found predominantly in the 1–3 kg range, making it ideal for cooking whole on the bone or as skinless fillets.

squid
One man's squid is another man's calamari... Although calamari is the name of particular varieties of squid, the term is widely used to describe the ubiquitous rings found battered and fried in fish shops around the country.

Squid range in size from transparent creatures almost too tiny to see, to real Jules Verne-type monsters of the deep. A common catch throughout the commercial fisheries around Australia, squid of one variety or another are always available at the fish markets. Most of the inshore squid are members of the

snapper

Loliginidae family, of which the main commercial catches are the arrow or flying squid, with long slender mantles and short fins set to the rear, and the southern calamari, with their rounder bodies and fins that stretch the full distance of the mantle. These are two of the best eating, with a sweeter, more subtle flavour than the deep sea trawled variety.

Squid can be purchased fresh and whole, ready cleaned and skinned, or cleaned and frozen. They are incredibly fragile and can start to oxidise quickly and turn sour — freshness and temperature are vital to the quality of fresh squid. Luckily, the dense white flesh freezes well, so if that's the only way they are available, don't consider you're missing out.

If the ink sacks are needed, you will be restricted, however, to either fresh whole or frozen whole (again, the ink freezes incredibly well, retaining both flavour and colour).

When buying fresh squid, look for those that are as transparent as possible, with minimal broken skin. Avoid any whose flesh is turning pink/purple (a sure sign of temperature or fresh water abuse). Like any other whole seafood, they should have clear eyes and a fresh-smelling covering of sea slime.

When cleaning, prepare the squid as close as possible to the cooking time and avoid the use of excess water (which can be tricky as they are innately messy). This will vastly improve the flavour and aroma.

stripey trumpeter

Found almost exclusively in southern Victoria, Tasmania and south east South Australia, the striped trumpeter, or 'stripey' as it is more commonly known, is without question one of the finest eating fish found in Australia.

Although the stripey has quite a high oil content, it is the delicious fat deposits along the belly and shoulder that keep the flesh moist while retaining a firm texture when cooked.

Caught year round, this fish is in absolute peak condition in late winter and spring, when the flesh takes on a marked iodine-seaweed character, which is absolutely delicious, especially for sashimi. Most are 1–3 kg in size, yielding about fifty per cent flesh to total weight.

Stripeys are best prepared using one of the drier methods of cooking, such as grilling, pan-frying or baking; the delicate flesh requires hardly any additional flavouring or condiments. Expect to pay handsomely for this fish, as it is rare and special, but enjoy the experience of eating one of the world's best.

swordfish

Swordfish, with its meaty texture and full, rich flavour, is the perfect fish for the committed omnivore. Although not as versatile as some of the other large ocean fish such as tuna, swordfish is the ideal barbecue fish, its fat content and structure preventing it from falling apart on the grill.

Caught predominantly off the east coast of Australia, swordfish is generally available year round, although the best quality and price is during its peak summer season. These are large fish and are usually offered in fillet or steak form — look for bright white flesh with a thin, cherry-red bloodline running through the centre of the fillet.

Quality swordfish should smell sweet. Wrapped tightly and stored in the coldest part of the fridge, it should hold for 4–5 days.

threadfin salmon

Absolutely no relation to the Atlantic or Australian salmon, this quite ugly looking fellow is sometimes known as the poor man's barra.

Found in the same waters as the mighty barramundi, namely the estuaries and coastal waters of northern Australia, the threadfin is greatly underrated.

High yielding, in terms of flesh to total weight, with a moist, medium-flavoured flesh with broad flakes and a clean white appearance; the threadfin is highly versatile and suits a broad range of cooking styles, from barbecuing, grilling and baking, to pan-fries, stir-fries and curries.

Inexpensive, readily available and good eating — it sure beats plenty of the inferior-quality imported, skinless, boneless fillets we see in our supermarkets.

tommy ruff

The Australian herring, tommy ruff is a small, dark-fleshed and very flavoursome fish, hugely popular in its predominant catching area, South Australia.

With the fish generally found at 300–600 g, the butterflied, boneless fillet is a staple of every fish shop in Adelaide.

Its high oil content makes tommy ruff ideal for barbecuing, grilling, pickling and smoking — smoked tommy is commonly sold in front bars of the pubs along the coast of South Australia.

A low-priced fish, the humble tommy is not only most Adelaide kids' first seafood eating experience, but also often their first catch.

So, when in Adelaide…

an A–Z of seafood **261**

trevally

There are more than sixty species of trevally in Australia (not to be confused with the trevalla, or blue-eye). The main two are the golden (or giant) trevally of northern Australia and the silver trevally found along the coasts of New South Wales and South Australia.

Both are caught year round, with the silver being better eating in late autumn/winter and the golden in spring.

The trevallies have superb eating qualities, something to which any Japanese cook or amateur angler will testify, with a characteristic full-but-not-overpowering flavour and medium to firm texture.

Typically, they are low priced and although dark-red in their raw state, when cooked they turn brilliant white. The high oil content makes them suitable for a range of preparations, even, surprisingly, for fish and chips.

Like other high-oil fish, choose the freshest trevally, handle with care, keep cold and eat as soon as you can.

trout — rainbow, brown and ocean

Like their famous cousins the salmon, trout were introduced to Australia from Europe over 150 years ago.

Being geographically 'upside down' as it were, trout have not been especially good at breeding in the wild and Australia's lakes, streams and rivers are generally restocked from hatchery-raised fingerlings. These fingerlings are also the supply for the fish farms of south eastern Australia, in particular Tasmania, where ocean trout is the second most prolifically farmed finfish.

The rainbow and ocean trouts are the same fellow — one spending its entire life in fresh water, where it is generally harvested at plate size (around 500 g); the other being introduced to the sea, where it is cage-farmed in the open ocean.

The trouts, all of them, tend to reflect the environment in which they are raised and the food they are fed, with the flavour varying from earthy to clean. The basic characteristic of all the varieties is a rich texture, with a mouth-filling flavour that lends itself to any number of cooking preparations from baking to steaming.

All trout carry a layer of fat just below the skin, which makes superb eating when it is rendered crisp and shouldn't be discarded.

Trout, being farm-raised and managed, have an excellent shelf life and can be confidently stored in the fridge at home, well wrapped, for several days.

tuna

yellowfin tuna

Tuna are among the most beautiful and impressive of all the sea's creatures. These fish, with their delicate colours and wonderfully streamlined bodies, have evolved to the limit of hydrodynamic refinement. When tuna are swimming rapidly, their fins are retracted into grooves and their eyes form a smooth surface against the head.

Tuna live in the open sea rather than near the shore and stay for the most part in the upper layer of water called the 'mixed layer'. The mixed layer is warmed by the sun and air, stirred by the wind and waves, and is a rich environment for tuna. Where the currents are warm, the tuna can be found.

The constant physical action also creates an enormous demand for energy and a need to eat large quantities of food. A typical tuna may eat one-quarter of his own bodyweight each day. The general diet of the tuna includes fish, crustaceans and molluscs. This is one of the reasons they make such incredible eating. Here in Australia we are fortunate to have a number of different species available. The fisheries are tightly controlled, which means we have some of the highest quality, sustainable tuna anywhere on the planet.

Albacore is sometimes known as 'white tuna' or 'chicken of the sea'. It is much maligned in Australia but, as our fleet, especially on the east coast where most albacore is found, handle their catch for the Japanese market, the quality is outstanding. Much less expensive than yellowfin or bluefin, good-quality albacore is readily available just about all year round and ideal for most uses.

Yellowfin is the world's most valuable tuna catch and is found throughout the tropical and sub-tropical waters of both the east and west coasts of Australia. The fish are typically caught by specialist long-line fishing boats and are handled with absolute care by the fishermen. They are graded according to fat content, freshness and colour of the flesh. This is a highly prized sashimi fish but over the past ten or so years has also gained popularity for grilling. Because of the delicate flesh structure, yellowfin is best quickly seared and left rare in the middle, allowing the sweet flesh to retain its natural moisture and flavour.

The mighty **bluefin**, once the staple of the tuna canning industries of South Australia and New South Wales, is now the most prized of all Australia's tunas. These days, bluefin are mostly caught by large net boats and whole schools are slowly towed back to Port Lincoln in South Australia, where the fish are fattened before being prepared for the sashimi markets of Japan. The meat is a rich, dark burgundy and the flesh typically soft, due to the incredible fat content that makes it so prized for sashimi. If you can get your hands on fresh bluefin you'll experience a rare and special treat that deserves only the simplest of condiments.

Longtail is one of the great bargains of the sea. This is sometimes known as **northern bluefin** and is found mainly in Queensland and the Northern Territory, where the savvy fish-lover seeks it out as the barbecue fish of choice. It has a high oil content, keeping it moist during high-heat preparations and giving it the power to handle highly flavoured condiments.

vongole

Known in Italy as the vongole and in America as the littleneck clam, the katalaysia clam is found in the cool southern waters off Tasmania and South Australia.

The vongole, a relatively small commercial fishery, is found mainly in the shallow bays and inlets where there is a strong ocean current feeding into an estuary.

The two main varieties are the larger yellow vongole, which spends its life submerged underwater, and the smaller purple/grey, which is mostly found on intertidal sand banks. Like pipis, vongole are hand harvested by rakers using nets attached to the heads of long-handled rakes.

After purging in seawater for 24–36 hours, the flavour of the vongole, especially those from Coffin Bay in South Australia, is truly wonderful — deep, rich and intensely flavoured. Don't expect a lot of meat from them, and make sure to capture the absolutely delicious liquor they exude during cooking.

Try to buy live vongole as, like all molluscs, they quickly lose their natural sweetness. Store them in a cool, damp container with a moist cloth covering — they should live happily for 3–4 days in the bottom of the fridge. If you can't get live, believe it or not, the tinned meat in liquor is actually a pretty good substitute — cooked from live, they manage to retain a fair amount of sweetness and are rarely ever tough.

warehou

Sometimes mistakenly called trevally, the warehou is a member of the trevalla family and, while not nearly as well known as its famous cousin the blue-eye, this is a superb tasting fish and excellent value for everyday eating.

Caught in the deep, cold waters of south eastern Australia, particularly around Tasmania, the warehou is available year round, but in peak quantities from June to September. The medium-flavoured, thick fillet, with its broad scalloping flesh and good moisture content, is highly versatile for a range of preparations from frying to smoking.

Warehou are mainly found as whole fish in the 1–2 kg range.

whitebait

whitebait Whitebait are the baby, or very small, fish of almost any species. They are often confused with 'silverfish' or baby elvers, popular in New Zealand and China, where the imported product is also known as whitebait.

The local whitebait in Australia varies from the tiny, almost translucent 'nanata', caught in the bays, lakes and estuaries of the east coast, to a wide variety of fish less than 60 mm long that are caught almost everywhere — these may be sand whiting, bream, tailor, Australian salmon or herring.

It's pretty hard to generalise about the qualities of whitebait, except the most fundamental aspects of appearance and aroma. They should be whole, even sized with no blown bellies or heads, and have a sweet, sea aroma. Do not buy if there is the slightest brackish or ammonia scent.

Buying frozen is a viable option, especially if you're anticipating the special treat that is New Zealand whitebait.

As whitebait are always eaten whole, don't be surprised by the rich, gamey flavour that belies the size of the fish.

whiting

whiting There are about ten different species of whiting caught around Australia. All of them are delicious in their own right and no relation to that staple of the fast-food trade, the very pedestrian southern blue whiting.

The three main varieties are the mighty King George whiting, found in south eastern Victoria, South Australia and south west Western Australia (in, not surprisingly, King George Sound); the sand whiting, found throughout south eastern Australia; and the school whiting, which is found along the east and west coasts.

The **King George whiting**, long prized by Victorian and South Australian gourmands, is regarded for its delicate, sweet flavour and firm, tight texture. The King George has an amazing iodine 'zing' and requires careful preparation to avoid over-flavouring and over-cooking. Available all year round, supply peaks over summer and the prized winter whiting is as special as it is rare. Expensive but delicious, King George whiting is generally of consistently excellent quality as it is all hand-line caught.

The **sand whiting** is caught predominantly in the estuaries and inshore waterways of New South Wales and is highly prized by Japanese chefs — both in Japan and Australia — for its firm texture and clean sweet flavour and aroma. Caught throughout the year, it is at its best in late autumn.

The much smaller **school whiting** comprises one of the more prolific inshore fisheries in Australia. The small fish are filleted into butterfly fillets that are especially popular with Japanese chefs.

All whiting are delicate, with a distinctive sweetness and mild flavour. Their thin fillets can be prepared by a broad range of cooking methods, from steaming to frying. Whiting, with the rib out and pin bones removed, is an absolute star fish for children, the natural sweetness and very little oil making it enjoyably easy to eat.

yabbies

The collective marketing term 'yabby' is applied to the two main species of freshwater crayfish found in Australia.

Wild caught in waterholes, streams and creeks, and farmed in specially designed ponds and farm dams throughout south eastern and south western Australia, the yabby takes on the conditions of the water in which it grows. Although still commercially fished in New South Wales, Victoria and South Australia, the majority of the commercial supply comes from yabby farms.

These are hardy creatures, which can last for up to a week out of water, and are best purchased live. Store them in a lidded basket, covering them with a moist towel that is, ideally, covered with ice to slow them down and keep them cool. Make sure that the lid is closed, however — the yabby has a propensity to wander and can quickly find its way to the biscuits in your pantry.

Available from farms year round, yabbies tend to be in their best condition in winter, when they are carrying extra fat.

yabbies, red-claw

The tropical cousin of the yabby, the red-claw is found in the north of Australia, in the north-flowing rivers and streams of Queensland and the Northern Territory.

Although a wild capture fishery still exists in some parts of Queensland, the majority of red-claw is farmed and available year round.

About the size of a medium-sized prawn, each red-claw yields approximately 25 per cent of its weight in flesh. The light-flavoured, moist meat typically has a firm texture. Try to purchase red-claws live, like yabbies. If stored carefully they will be happy for up to a week in your laundry or garage.

fish

a
abalone 236
   abalone schnitzels 16
aioli 212
albacore tuna 262
angassi oysters 249
   with ginger and shallot dressing 97
Atlantic salmon 254
   slow-poached with cauliflower purée 132
Australian herring *see* tommy ruff
Australian salmon 254
avocado salsa 121

b
baccala (salt cod) sauce 212
   blue-eye trevalla with baccala sauce on soft polenta 23
Balmain bug 238
balsamic truffle dressing 213
banana prawns 253
bar cod 236
   black pepper-crusted with lime and ginger 17
barramundi 237
   barra burgers from the top end 21
   barramundi with porcini risotto 22
   steamed barramundi with lime coconut sauce 18
basil oil 213
bay scallop 256
beer batter 213
   beer-battered threadfin salmon with harissa mayonnaise 183
beurre blanc 214
   wild brown trout with tarragon beurre blanc 198
beurre rouge 214
   pan-fried coral trout with mud crab ravioli and beurre rouge 34
bimbimbap sushi 177
black mussel 247
blue mackerel 243
blue swimmer crab 239
   blue swimmer crab linguine 35
   deep-fried blue swimmer crab with lemon aioli 39
blue-eye trevalla 237
   blue-eye trevalla with baccala sauce on soft polenta 23
bluefin tuna 262
bouillabaisse 24
bream 237
   pan-fried bream with potatoes and tamarind sauce 26
brown trout 261
   wild brown trout with tarragon beurre blanc 198
bugs 238
bug meat fu yung with Chinese sausage 28
bug tails with cucumber and roasted peanut salad 29
bug tails with sweetcorn broth 31

c
candied ginger 215
candied lime 215
capsicum sauce 216
carrot and cardamom sauce 79
cauliflower purée 216
champagne creamed leek 150
chermoula-rubbed pearl perch 108
chawan-mushi 152
chilli caramel dipping sauce 217
chilli confit 217
chilli jam 218
chilli oil 219
chilli salt spice 219
coconut dressing 220
confits
   chilli 217
   garlic 222
   onion 226
   tomato 233
coral trout 238
   deep-fried coral trout salad with Japanese dressing 32
   pan-fried coral trout with mud crab ravioli and beurre rouge 34
corn fritters, prawn and 118
crab 238–9
   blue swimmer crab linguine 35
   chilli mud crab 43
   chilli salt soft-shell crab 40
   deep-fried blue swimmer crab with lemon aioli 39
   hot and sour soup with crab meat and tofu 44
   linguine with mud crab aglio e olio 45
   mud crab and Chinese roast pork in rice paper rolls 38
   soft-shell crab nori sushi rolls 178
crayfish *see* lobster; marron; scampi; yabbies
crispy garlic chips 220
crispy leek 221
crispy shallots 221
curry
   chu chee curry of monkfish 84
   laksa 54
   light prawn curry with bok choy and shiitakes 123

index

steamed fish curry 56
cuttlefish 239
  cuttlefish in squid ink with risotto 48
  cuttlefish sushi with lemon, sesame and shiso 174

d

dhufish 250-1
dolphin fish 244
  mahi mahi Szechuan noodles 78
dressings
  balsamic truffle dressing 213
  coconut dressing 220
  Japanese salad dressing 224
  mayonnaise 224
  nam jim dressing 225
  sashimi dressing 229
  seeded mustard mayonnaise 224
  tomato, oregano and pine nuts 207
  Thai salad dressing 232

e

eggplant relish 180

f

fennel seed and pepper spice mix 222

fish
  baked, with organic lemon jam 59
  barbecued whole, with green mango relish 58
  steamed whole, with shaoxing wine and soy 51
fish cakes, old-school 49
fish in crazy water 159
fish curry, steamed 56
fish laksa 54
fish tortillas, Mexican, with guacamole 50
flathead 240
  crumbed flathead with chilli sauce 61
  Tetsuya's warm flathead carpaccio with black bean dressing 62
flounder 240
  deep-fried flounder with Chinese shiitake mushroom sauce 65
  salt and pepper flounder 66
fritters
  prawn and corn 118
  salt cod 139
  whitebait 204

g

garfish 240
  pan-fried garfish with sea urchin butter 67

garlic chips, crispy 220
garlic confit 222
garlic prawns 116
gazpacho 209
ginger, candied 215
ginger oil 223
gnocchi, potato, with red mullet 131
granita, blood orange bellini 96
guacamole 50

h

herring, Australian 260
Hiramasa kingfish 241
ho mok pla 56
horseradish-baked oysters, Parmesan and 99

i

Italian tomato sauce 223

j

Japanese salad dressing 224
john dory 241

k

kahawai 254
King George whiting 264
  grilled with limoncello and oregano 205

king prawns 253
kingfish 241
  kingfish sashimi with pineapple, crispy shallots and nam jim 70
  salad of fennel-crusted kingfish with grapefruit and mint 68

l

laksa 54
leatherjacket 241
leek, crispy 221
leek and potato soup 143
lemon jam 59
lime, candied 215
lobster 242-3
  lobster martini 73
  rock lobster with drunken noodles 76
  san choy bau of slipper lobster and water chestnuts 74
  stir-fried rock lobster with chilli jam 71

m

mackerel 243
  carpaccio with capers and lemon 77
  sushi of marinated mackerel 178

fish

mahi mahi 244
   mahi mahi Szechuan noodles 78
mangrove jack 244
   with spiced spinach and cardamom carrot sauce 79
mango relish, green 58
marron 244–5
   grilled marron with chilli, rosemary and lemon butter 83
mayonnaise 224
   seeded mustard mayonnaise 224
Mexican fish tortillas with guacamole 50
miso broth 225
monkfish 245
   chu chee curry of monkfish 84
moonfish 245
   Thai moonfish cakes 85
Moreton Bay bug 238
morwong 245
mud crab 239
   chilli mud crab 43
   linguine with mud crab aglio e olio 45
   mud crab and Chinese roast pork in rice paper rolls 38
mullet 246
mulloway 246
   olive-crusted 86
Murray cod 246–7
   salt-baked Murray cod with lime 87
mussels 247
   mussels with tomato, white wine and basil 92
   orecchiette with mussels and Italian sausage ragu 91
   Thai-style mussels 90

n

nam jim dressing 225

o

ocean perch 248
   with roasted tomato and fennel sauce 94
ocean trout 261
   spaghetti with trout and capers 194
octopus 248
   braised in tomato and garlic 95
olive tapenade 226
omelette, scallop and Szechuan duck 144
onion confit 226
oysters 248–9
   with blood orange bellini granita 96
   with ginger and shallot dressing 97
   with guanciale, balsamic and goat's cheese 102
   with Merguez sausage and fennel 100
   parmesan and horseradish-baked oysters 99
   tempura oysters with wasabi tartare 103

p

Pacific oysters 249
   with guanciale, balsamic, goat's cheese 102
paella 105
parrot fish 250
   parrot fish with three-flavoured sauce 106
pearl meat 250
   with ginger and soy 107
   with lemon and parsley 107
pearl perch 250–1
   chermoula-rubbed pearl perch with yoghurt, coriander, mint sauce 108
peppers, Basque 129
pesto 227
pickled vegetables 227
pipis 251
   with black beans 113
pizza, chilli prawn with salsa verde 124
pizza dough 228
pizza pie, snapper 163
potato gnocchi with red mullet 131
prawns 252–3
   chilli prawn pizzas 124
   Chinese vermicelli noodles with prawns and pork 119
   garlic prawns 116
   light prawn curry with bok choy and shiitakes 123
   prawn and corn fritters 118
   prawn, radicchio and red wine risotto 126
   prawn won tons with hot English mustard 115
   prawns on avocado salsa 121
   tandoori prawns 114
   tom yum soup with prawn dumplings 122

r

rainbow trout 261
   mountain-style rainbow trout 190
   rainbow trout with green pea risotto 193
ravioli, mud crab 34
red emperor 253
   red emperor with Basque peppers 129
   sweet and sour red emperor 127
red mullet 254
   gnocchi with red mullet 131

index

pan-fried red mullet
   with lentils **130**
red wine butter
   sauce **214**
red-claw yabbies **265**
   with tomato
   gazpacho **209**
risotto
   cuttlefish in squid ink
     with risotto **48**
   green pea **193**
   porcini **22**
   prawn, radicchio and
     red wine **126**
   scampi and
     saffron **149**
rock lobsters **242-3**
   with drunken
     noodles **76**
   stir-fried with chilli
     jam **71**
romesco sauce **173**

S

salad dressing
   Japanese **224**
   Thai **232**
salmon **9**
   Atlantic **254**
   Australian **254**
   crisp-skinned with
     celery sauce and
     salt cod mash **133**
   eggs benedict with
     smoked **134**
   slow-poached
     with cauliflower
     purée **132**
   sushi, seared **175**

salsa verde **228**
salt and pepper
   flounder **66**
salt cod **255**
   baccala sauce **212**
   salt cod fritters with
     lemon aioli **139**
   salt cod mash **229**
san choy bau of slipper
   lobster and water
   chestnuts **74**
sand crab **239**
sand whiting **264**
   with warm dressing,
     tomato, oregano
     and pine nuts **207**
sardine **255**
   barbecued panata-
     crumbed **141**
   grilled with
     saffron dressing **140**
sashimi dressing **229**
saucer scallop **256**
sauces
   baccala
     (salt cod) **212**
   capsicum **216**
   chilli caramel
     dipping **217**
   Italian tomato **223**
   red wine butter **214**
   tamarind **231**
   tartare **231**
   white wine butter **214**
   yoghurt, coriander
     and mint **233**
scallops **256**
   fettucine with
     scallops and
     tomato pesto **148**

scallop and
   Szechuan duck
   omelette **144**
scallops with
   cauliflower purée
   and pine nuts **147**
scallops with leek
   and potato
   soup **143**
seared scallops with
   angel hair pasta
   and truffle
   dressing **142**
scampi **256-7**
   Japanese steamed
     egg custard with
     scampi **152**
   scampi and saffron
     risotto **149**
   steamed scampi
     sandwiches **150**
   sushi of scampi **174**
school prawns **252**
school whiting **264-5**
sea scallop **256**
sea urchin **257**
   with angel hair pasta
     and lemon **155**
   sea urchin
     sandwiches **153**
shallots, crispy **221**
skate **257**
   with brown butter,
     lime and
     capers **156**
slipper lobster **238**
   san choy bau **74**
smoked trout dip **187**
snapper **258**
   aqua pazza **159**

carpaccio with
   blood orange
   and lemon
   thyme **157**
ceviche with
   coconut, mint
   and
   cucumber **158**
pizza pie **163**
whole on the
   barbie **162**
sole **258**
   pan-fried with
     salmoriglio **166**
soups
   gazpacho **209**
   laksa **54**
   leek and potato **143**
   sweetcorn broth **31**
   tom yum **122**
spaghetti vongole **202**
spangled emperor
   258
Spanish mackerel **243**
spanner crab **239**
spice mixes
   chilli salt spice **219**
   fennel seed and
     pepper **222**
   Szechuan **230**
squid **258-9**
   barbecued Thai
     squid salad **167**
   chilli salt squid **172**
   sautéed squid with
     Malaysian water
     spinach **170**
   squid, chorizo, white
     bean and fennel
     salad **169**

fish

tagliatelle with squid and pesto 168
stargazer 245
stripey trumpeter 259
   pan-roasted with romesco sauce 173
sushi
   bimbimbap sushi 177
   cuttlefish sushi with lemon, sesame and shiso 174
   soft-shell crab nori sushi rolls 178
   sushi of marinated mackerel 178
   sushi of scampi 174
   sushi of seared salmon belly 175
   sushi of toro (tuna belly) 175
   tuna tartare sushi 179
sushi rice 230
sweet and sour red emperor 127
sweetcorn broth 31
swordfish 260
   with spiced eggplant relish 180
Sydney rock oysters 249
   with blood orange bellini granita 96
Szechuan spice mix 230

t

tamarind sauce 231
tartare sauce 231
Tassie cray 242
Tassie scallop 256

tempura batter 232
Thai salad dressing 232
threadfin salmon 260
   beer-battered with harissa mayonnaise 183
tiger prawns 253
tom yum soup with prawn dumplings 122
tomato confit 233
tomato gazpacho 209
tomato sauce, Italian 223
tommy ruff 260
   escabeche of tommy ruff with saffron and toasted almonds 186
tortillas, Mexican, fish with guacamole 50
trevally 261
trout 261
   Italian smoked trout dip 187
   mountain-style rainbow trout 190
   orecchiette with broccolini, smoked trout and anchovies 195
   rainbow trout with pea risotto 193
   scrambled eggs with smoked trout, tarragon and horseradish 188
   smoked trout and mango salad 189

spaghetti with ocean trout and capers 194
steamed trout with chillies, lime and roasted cashews 192
wild brown trout with tarragon buerre blanc 198
tuna 262-3
   sushi of toro (tuna belly) 175
   tuna penne puttanesca 201
   tuna tartare sushi 179
   tuna with a warm potato salad 199
   vitello tonnato 200

v

vegetables, pickled 227
vitello tonnato 200
vongole 263
   spaghetti vongole with bottarga 202

w

warehou 263
white wine butter sauce 214
whitebait 264
   fried with Szechuan pepper and lemon dipping sauce 203
   fritters 204

whiting 264-5
   grilled King George whiting with limoncello and oregano 205
   sand whiting with a warm dressing of tomato, oregano and pine nuts 207

y

yabbies 265
   Barry's Snowy Mountain 208
yabbies, red-claw 265
   with tomato gazpacho 209
yellowfin tuna 262
yoghurt, coriander and mint sauce 233
   chermoula-rubbed pearl perch with yoghurt, coriander, mint sauce 108

thanks

Dedicated to my two beautiful daughters, Chilli and Indii. May there be plenty of fish in the sea for you both.

Thanks go to Kay Scarlett for giving a young bloke a go, when others might not have done. To Jane Price, for her skill at making what I say sound much better and, of course, her sense of humour. Sarah Odgers, you have created a wonderful book — I look forward to working on many more with you. To Alan Benson, for the beautiful photography — it was great to work with such a professional. Yael Grinham is the best bloody stylist! Thank you, Yael, for making my food look amazing.

Thanks to my business partners, Dave Evans, Dave Corsi, Daniel Vaughan, Guy Mainwaring and Dad, for the support and encouragement to pursue my dreams. To John Susman for his incredible input into the species information — you are a wealth of knowledge. To John Lanzafame for being an amazing chef to work with over the past few years — I couldn't do what I do without you, mate. To Phil Matthews for being the most organised bloke I know, and for making everything so perfect for this book — love your work. To all my loyal staff, past and present, who have helped shape the way I cook today, and given me the time to achieve my goals, with special mentions to: Simon Fawcett, Tristian Hope, Hamish Lindsay, Phil Davenport, Madeline Hayes, John Pye, Richard 'Gee' Massey, Kevin O'Connor and Gerard D'ombrille.

A big thanks has to go to my mum, Joy, and my parents-in-law, Walter and Poldi, for helping to look after my girls when I'm off on another adventure. Udo, my brother-in-law, you are a legend. Without you I never would've plunged into the world of fishing and had all the great times that have come from it — I owe you one!

And finally, Astrid. I love that you let me live my life to the fullest, and this book wouldn't have come about without your love and support. You're the best, chuck out the rest.

Published in 2007 by Murdoch Books Pty Limited
www.murdochbooks.com.au

Murdoch Books Australia
Pier 8/9
23 Hickson Road
Millers Point NSW 2000
Phone: +61 (0) 2 8220 2000
Fax: +61 (0) 2 8220 2558

Murdoch Books UK Limited
Erico House
6th Floor
93-99 Upper Richmond Road
Putney, London SW15 2TG
Phone: +44 (0) 20 8785 5995
Fax: +44 (0) 20 8785 5985

www.murdochbooks.co.uk

Chief Executive: Juliet Rogers
Publishing Director: Kay Scarlett

Editor: Jane Price
Design Concept: Sarah Odgers
Designer: Annette Fitzgerald
Production: Monique Layt
Food and cover photography: Alan Benson
Stylist: Yael Grinham
Additional text: John Susman

© Text copyright 2007 Pete Evans
© Design and photography copyright 2007 Murdoch Books

All rights reserved. No part of this publication may be reproduced, stored in a retrieval system or transmitted in any form or by any means, electronic, mechanical, photocopying, recording or otherwise, without the prior written permission of the publisher.
Tuna photograph, page 262, from photolibrary.com

National Library of Australia Cataloguing-in-Publication Data
Evans, Peter Daryl, 1973–. Fish. Includes index. ISBN 9781 921 208584
1. Cookery (Fish). 2. Cookery (Seafood). 3. Seafood – Australia. 4. Australia – Description and travel.
I. Title. 641.692

Printed by 1010 Printing International Ltd in 2007. PRINTED IN CHINA.
Reprinted 2007.

CONVERSION GUIDE: You may find cooking times vary depending on the oven you are using.
For fan-forced ovens, as a general rule, set the oven temperature to 20°C (35°F) lower than indicated in the recipe. We have used 20 ml (4 teaspoon) tablespoon measures.